OPTICAL ILLUSIONS

LES
ILLUSIONS
D'OPTIQUE
LA MAGIE
DU GRAPHISME

ILUSIONES
ÓPTICAS
LA MAGIA
DEL DISEÑO
GRÁFICO

promopress

Optical Illusions

Les illusions d'optique, la magie du graphisme
Ilusiones ópticas, la magia del diseño gráfico

Editor: Wang Shaoqiang
English preface revised by: Tom Corkett
Translators of the preface:
Leïla Bendifallah, French translation
Jesús de Cos Pinto, Spanish translation

PROMOPRESS is a brand of:
Promotora de Prensa Internacional S.A.
C/ Ausiàs March, 124
08013 Barcelona, Spain
Phone: 0034 93 245 14 64
Fax: 0034 93 265 48 83
info@promopress.es
www.promopresseditions.com
Facebook: Promopress Editions
Twitter: Promopress Editions @PromopressEd
Sponsored by Design 360°
– Concept and Design Magazine
Edited and produced by
Sandu Publishing Co., Ltd.
Book design, concepts & art direction by
Sandu Publishing Co., Ltd.
info@sandupublishing.com

Cover design:
spread: David Lorente

Cover project by David Massara

ISBN 978-84-16504-50-3

Printed in China

CONTENTS

Down the Rabbit Hole

By Marta Cutler / Creative Director, Blok Design

"There are things known and there are things unknown, and in between are the doors of perception." Aldous Huxley

What is it about optical illusions that fascinates and delights us, and that leaves us feeling a little like Alice peering down the rabbit hole? Perhaps it's the fact that illusions are in violent disagreement with how we perceive the world around us. That something can be so completely different from what we believe to be real is nothing short of astonishing.

The question of how and why perception can be so radically different from reality has puzzled philosophers, scientists, and artists since the fifth century BC. Back then, a Greek philosopher named Epicharmus first attempted to explain why our eyes could be so easily fooled. He laid the blame squarely on our sensory organs, saying that while the mind knows and understands everything clearly, it was these that could deceive us and cause an optical illusion. Others attributed our altered views to environmental causes.

A few hundred years later, Aristotle weighed in on the subject. He believed that we could trust our senses to help us to determine what's real, but he added that the senses could also be fooled. His famous example was the waterfall. If one looked at the moving water long enough then looked at the rocks beside it, these too would appear to be moving, but in the opposite direction.

It wasn't until the nineteenth century that Hermann von Helmholtz, a German physicist, introduced the idea of cognitive illusion. His theory was that illusions arise from assumptions that a person holds about his environment or the world as a whole. His views, and those of other psychologists of the time, sparked an interest in the study of the subject, and a series of illusions was created to test how the brain perceives patterns and shapes. These included the Kanizsa Triangle, which tricks your brain into seeing a shape that isn't visibly present, and the Titchener Circles, which trick you into thinking that an object is a different size than what it actually is. Each is proof that our brains can easily be fooled into seeing something that's not there.

Thanks to the research of brilliant neuroscientists around the world, we now know why. Our brain takes the trillions of pieces of raw data bombarding us every day through our retinas and organizes them into information using memory to make sense of it all. You can imagine how daunting that is. So the brain, in its infinite, deeply mysterious wisdom, takes short cuts. It fills in or amplifies the fragments of reality that it's given, simplifying everything and choosing the most likely interpretation.

To compound the situation, individual context matters. "For what you see and hear depends a good deal on where you are standing: it also depends on what sort of person you are," as C. S. Lewis wrote in *The Magician's Nephew*. Each brain decodes what it sees differently according to the experiences of the person and the knowledge and impressions that are stored in memory.

With so many factors at play, it's not surprising that the subject of perception and reality has enthralled and inspired artists and designers throughout time, from early trompe l'oeil painters to the op art movement of the 1960s. M.C. Escher, Salvador Dali, and Duchamp were old hands at the art of visual manipulation, as was Victor Vasarely, widely considered the father of the movement.

What fascinates us about illusions is that because they're a fixed point between what's real and what's not real, they are spaces in between and therefore full of ambiguity. Ambiguity requires us to embrace uncertainty and the possibility that there may be multiple answers to a given problem, each of which is as valid as the next. This can be disconcerting, but it can also be exhilarating. Think of the delight we take in going back and forth between the two interpretations of the famous black-and-white line drawing of the woman as we ask ourselves: Is she young? Is she old?

Illusions, then, are marvelous tools to manipulate emotion, from engendering a sense of childlike delight and wonder to making us feel uncomfortable and tense. Who can forget Saul Bass's stunning use of spiraling lines and patterns for his poster series promoting Hitchcock's *Vertigo*?

As designers, we have a magician's chest of effects at our disposal, as evidenced in the work contained within these pages. Geometry, the action of light on a surface, the play of lines and angles, and the beautiful clarity of abstraction: all can be used with stunning results to alter how we perceive space, form, information, and even brands.

We also have access to a plethora of increasingly sophisticated production techniques, from architecture to digital technology and printing processes. Legendary American graphic designer Bradbury Thompson was the first to experiment with overprinting during the forties and fifties. He created extraordinary magazine spreads that had startling depth and complexity, inspiring generations of designers to come.

No matter what form they take, illusions beckon the eye to enter and to question what we see. In the face of such provocative imagery, we cannot remain passive bystanders; we're catapulted into a state of engagement and interaction.

This, then, is illusion's power and draw.

M. C. Escher wrote that "he who wonders discovers that this in itself is wonder." We've always believed that design is at its best when it challenges our assumptions about what we believe to be true and shifts how we see society and ourselves. In *Optical Illusions*, we have a potent tool that can help us do just that—one that with its captivating, magical qualities can also instill in us a profound sense of wonder at the world around us.

Dans le terrier du lapin

Par Marta Cutler / Directrice créative, Blok Design

« Il y a le connu et il y a l'inconnu. Entre les deux, il y a les portes de la perception. » Aldous Huxley

Quelle est cette chose qui nous fascine et nous enchante dans les illusions d'optique, et qui nous fait nous sentir comme Alice regardant dans le terrier du lapin ? C'est peut-être le fait que les illusions sont en désaccord violent avec la manière dont nous percevons le monde qui nous entoure. Le fait que quelque chose puisse être si différent de ce que nous croyons être réel est tout à fait stupéfiant.

La question de savoir comment et pourquoi la perception peut être si radicalement différente de la réalité intrigue les philosophes, les scientifiques et les artistes depuis le Vème siècle av. J.C.. À cette époque, un philosophe grec du nom d'Épicharme est le premier à tenter d'expliquer pourquoi nos yeux peuvent être trompés si facilement. Il jette directement la faute sur nos organes sensoriels, affirmant que si notre esprit connaît et comprend tout clairement, ce sont eux qui peuvent nous tromper et provoquer une illusion d'optique. D'autres attribuent nos visions altérées à des causes environnementales.

Quelques centaines d'années plus tard, Aristote se penche sur le sujet. Il croit que nous pouvons nous fier à nos sens pour nous aider à déterminer ce qui est réel, mais il ajoute qu'ils peuvent également être dupés. Son exemple le plus connu est celui de la chute d'eau. Si l'on regardait l'eau en mouvement suffisamment longtemps avant de regarder les rochers à côté, ces derniers sembleraient être en mouvement également, mais dans le sens opposé.

Ce n'est qu'au XIXème siècle que le physicien allemand Herman von Helmholtz introduit l'idée de l'illusion cognitive. Selon lui, les illusions proviennent d'hypothèses qu'une personne fait à propos de son environnement ou du monde. Sa théorie et celles d'autres psychologues de l'époque suscitent un intérêt dans l'étude de ce sujet et une série d'illusions sont créées pour tester la manière dont le cerveau perçoit les structures et les formes. Parmi elles, on trouve le motif de Kanizsa, qui pousse le cerveau à voir une forme qui n'est pas visiblement présente, et l'illusion de Titchener, qui nous fait croire que la taille d'un objet est autre qu'elle ne l'est en réalité. Chacune de ces illusions est une preuve que nos cerveaux peuvent être facilement dupés et qu'ils sont capables de voir quelque chose qui n'existe pas.

Grâce aux recherches de neuroscientifiques brillants du monde entier, nous en connaissons aujourd'hui l'explication. Le cerveau absorbe les milliers de milliards de données brutes dont nous sommes bombardés chaque jour à travers la rétine et les organise en informations en utilisant la mémoire pour leur donner un sens. Il s'agit d'un travail considérable. Alors, dans sa sagesse infinie et profondément mystérieuse, le cerveau prend des raccourcis. Il remplit ou amplifie les fragments de réalité qu'il reçoit en simplifiant tout et en choisissant l'interprétation la plus probable.

Pour composer la situation, il faut tenir compte du contexte de l'individu. « Ce que vous voyez et entendez dépend non seulement de l'endroit où vous êtes, mais également de qui vous êtes, » comme l'écrit C. S. Lewis dans *Le neveu du magicien*. Chaque cerveau déchiffre ce qu'il voit différemment en fonction des expériences de chacun et des connaissances et impressions conservées dans la mémoire.

Avec autant de facteurs en jeu, il n'est pas surprenant que le sujet de la perception et de la réalité ait captivé et inspiré les artistes et les créateurs de tout temps, des peintres en trompe l'œil au mouvement Op art des années 1960. M. C. Escher, Salvador Dali et Duchamp sont des pionniers de l'art de la manipulation visuelle, tout comme Victor Vasarely qui est généralement considéré comme le père de ce mouvement.

Ce qui nous fascine à propos des illusions, c'est le fait que, du fait d'être des points fixes entre le réel et l'irréel, elles sont des espaces entre les deux et elles sont donc pleines d'ambigüité. L'ambigüité nécessite que nous acceptions l'incertitude et la possibilité qu'il peut exister de multiples réponses à un même problème, toutes aussi valables que les autres. Cela peut être déroutant, mais stimulant à la fois. Pensez au plaisir que nous prenons à nous balancer entre les deux interprétations du fameux dessin d'une femme en noir et blanc en nous posant la question suivante : est-elle jeune ou âgée ?

Les illusions sont donc de merveilleux outils pour manipuler les émotions, allant de la sensation de plaisir et d'émerveillement enfantin au malaise et à la tension. Qui peut oublier la manière sensationnelle dont Saul Bass utilisait les lignes et formes en spirale dans sa série de posters pour la promotion de *Sueurs froides* d'Hitchcock ?

En tant que créateurs, nous avons une boîte à effets de magicien à notre disposition, comme le montre le travail exposé dans cet ouvrage. La géométrie, l'action de la lumière sur une surface, le jeu des lignes et des angles et la magnifique clarté de l'abstraction : tous peuvent servir et donner des résultats époustouflants pour modifier notre perception de l'espace, des formes, des informations et même des marques.

Nous avons également accès à pléthore de techniques de production de plus en plus sophistiquées, allant de l'architecture à la technologie numérique et aux processus d'impression. Le graphiste américain légendaire Bradbury Thompson est le premier à expérimenter avec la surimpression dans les années 1940 et 1950. Il crée d'extraordinaires dossiers de magazines dotés d'une incroyable profondeur et complexité, inspirant des générations d'artistes à venir.

Sous toutes les formes, les illusions attirent l'œil et pénètrent ce que nous voyons pour le remettre en cause. Face à cette provocation de l'image, il est impossible de demeurer de simples spectateurs passifs. Nous sommes catapultés dans un état d'implication et d'interaction.

Voilà le pouvoir de l'illusion.

M. C. Escher écrit que « celui qui se demande découvre que c'est dans cela que repose la merveille. » Nous avons toujours considéré que le design de qualité défie nos suppositions sur ce que nous croyons être vrai et change notre façon de voir la société et nous-mêmes. C'est ce qu'*Optical Illusions* peut nous aider à faire ; il s'agit d'un outil puissant qui, avec ses qualités captivantes et magiques, peut également nous inculquer un sens profond de l'émerveillement pour le monde qui nous entoure.

En la madriguera del conejo

De Marta Cutler / Director Creativo, Blok Design

«Hay cosas conocidas y cosas desconocidas, y entre ambas están las puertas de la percepción.» Aldous Huxley

¿Qué tienen las ilusiones ópticas que nos fascinan y nos deleitan y hacen que nos sintamos un poco como Alicia espiando en la madriguera del conejo? Tal vez sea que las ilusiones están en violenta discordia con nuestra percepción del mundo que nos rodea. Que algo pueda ser tan completamente diferente de lo que creemos que es real resulta, como mínimo, asombroso.

La cuestión de cómo y por qué la percepción puede ser tan radicalmente distinta de la realidad ha desconcertado a filósofos, científicos y artistas desde el siglo v a. de C. Ya entonces, un filósofo griego llamado Epicarmo realizó un primer intento de explicar por qué es tan fácil engañar a nuestros ojos. Acusó de ello a los órganos sensoriales y afirmó que mientras que la mente conoce y entiende todo con claridad, los sentidos pueden engañarnos y causar ilusiones ópticas. Otros atribuyeron nuestras visiones alteradas a causas ambientales.

Pocos siglos después, Aristóteles meditó sobre el tema. Creía que podemos confiar en nuestros sentidos para ayudarnos a determinar lo que es real, pero admitía que los sentidos pueden ser engañados y ofreció el famoso ejemplo de la catarata: si miramos el agua en movimiento durante un buen rato y después fijamos la vista en las rocas que hay a su lado, parecerá que las rocas se mueven en dirección opuesta.

No fue hasta el siglo XIX que el médico y físico alemán Hermann von Helmholtz introdujo la idea de *ilusión cognitiva*. Su teoría era que las ilusiones proceden de las suposiciones que hace la persona sobre su entorno o sobre el mundo en general. Sus ideas y las de otros psicólogos de la época despertaron el interés por el estudio del tema, y se crearon diversas ilusiones para estudiar el modo en que el cerebro percibe patrones y formas. Entre estas ilusiones se encuentra el triángulo Kanizsa, que engaña al cerebro y le hace ver una forma que no está presente en realidad, y los círculos Titchener, que inducen a creer que un objeto tiene un tamaño diferente al verdadero. Ambas son pruebas de que es fácil engañar a nuestro cerebro para hacerle ver algo que no existe.

Gracias a las investigaciones de brillantes neurocientíficos de todo el mundo, ahora sabemos el por qué. Nuestro cerebro toma los billones de trozos de datos en bruto que nos bombardean a diario a través de la retina y los organiza como información empleando la memoria para darles sentido. Cuesta imaginar lo abrumador que resulta este trabajo. Por ello, el cerebro, en su infinita y profundamente misteriosa sabiduría, toma atajos y rellena o amplía los fragmentos de realidad que recibe, lo simplifica todo y escoge la interpretación más probable.

Para complicar aún más las cosas, el contexto individual influye: «Lo que ves y lo que escuchas depende en gran medida de dónde estás y también de la clase de persona que eres» como escribió C. S. Lewis en *El sobrino del mago*. Cada cerebro decodifica lo que ve de un modo distinto según las experiencias de la persona y el conocimiento y las impresiones almacenados en la memoria.

Con tantos factores en juego, no es sorprendente que el tema de la percepción y la realidad haya cautivado e inspirado a artistas y diseñadores a lo largo del tiempo, desde los primitivos pintores de trampantojos hasta el movimiento op art de la década de 1960. M.C. Escher, Salvador Dalí y Duchamp fueron maestros en el arte de la manipulación visual, lo mismo que Victor Vasarely, ampliamente considerado como el padre del movimiento.

Lo que nos fascina de las ilusiones es que -en su condición de puntos fijos entre lo que es real y lo que no lo es- son espacios intermedios y, por ello, llenos de ambigüedad. La ambigüedad nos obliga a aceptar la incertidumbre y la posibilidad de que un problema pueda tener múltiples soluciones, todas ellas igualmente válidas. Esto puede ser desconcertante, pero también es estimulante. Recordemos lo divertido que es cambiar una y otra vez entre las dos interpretaciones del famoso dibujo lineal de la mujer en blanco y negro mientras nos preguntamos: ¿es joven? ¿es vieja?

Las ilusiones, así pues, son herramientas maravillosas para manipular las emociones, para generar sensaciones de deleite y maravilla infantil o de incomodidad y tensión. ¿Cómo olvidar el impresionante uso de líneas y patrones espirales que hizo Saul Bass en su serie de carteles promocionales del filme *Vértigo* de Hitchcock?

Los diseñadores tenemos un cofre de mago lleno de efectos a nuestra disposición, como muestran los trabajos contenidos en estas páginas. La geometría, la acción de la luz sobre una superficie, el juego de líneas y ángulos y la bella claridad de la abstracción: todo puede emplearse con resultados asombrosos para alterar nuestra percepción del espacio, la forma, la información e incluso las marcas.

Además, tenemos acceso a una plétora de técnicas de producción cada vez más sofisticadas en arquitectura, tecnología digital o procesos de impresión. El legendario diseñador gráfico Bradbury Thompson fue el primero en experimentar con sobreimpresiones en los años cuarenta y cincuenta del siglo xx. Thompson creó extraordinarias páginas dobles de profundidad y complejidad deslumbrantes publicadas en revistas y que inspiraron a las siguientes generaciones de diseñadores.

Con independencia de la forma que adopten, las ilusiones invitan a los ojos a entrar y a cuestionarse lo que ven. No podemos ser espectadores pasivos ante unas imágenes tan provocativas: somos lanzados a un estado de interés e interacción.

Este es el poder y el influjo de la ilusión.

M. C. Escher escribió que «el que se asombra descubre que el mismo asombro es algo asombroso». Siempre hemos pensado que el mejor diseño es el que desafía nuestras suposiciones acerca de lo que creemos y cambia nuestra visión de la sociedad y de nosotros mismos. En *Optical Illusions* tenemos una poderosa herramienta que puede ayudarnos a hacer precisamente eso y que con sus cualidades mágicas y cautivadoras puede además insuflarnos un profundo sentido de maravilla hacia el mundo que nos rodea.

Lines & Waves
/////////////////////////////////////

Overlapping
///////////////////////////////////////

2D or 3D

Spatial Experience

////////////// LINES & WAVES //////////////

Parallel contour lines are the basic elements to create optical illusions. In the op-art movement, black and white wavy lines were arranged closely to create sharp contrast and embody the artwork with dynamic visual perception. Nowadays, based on new founding on how our retina works, designers employ more colors in this game, creating after-images of certain colors.

Lines and waves are often employed to create a strong visual appeal. By emphasizing information within distorted lines, the maze can effectively convey the information in a playful manner.

Boomerang //

This identity was designed for an event reuniting professionals of the web industry in Montreal. Playing and deconstructing the burger and menu icon into lines, byHaus utilized these elements to create opt-art and hypnotic effects reflecting the theme of the conference in the name of "Experience".

Design Agency byHAUS
Designer Philippe Archontakis, Martin Laliberté
Animation Developer Samuel Jacques, Amélie Tourangeau
Music Underground productions
Client Éditions Infopresse

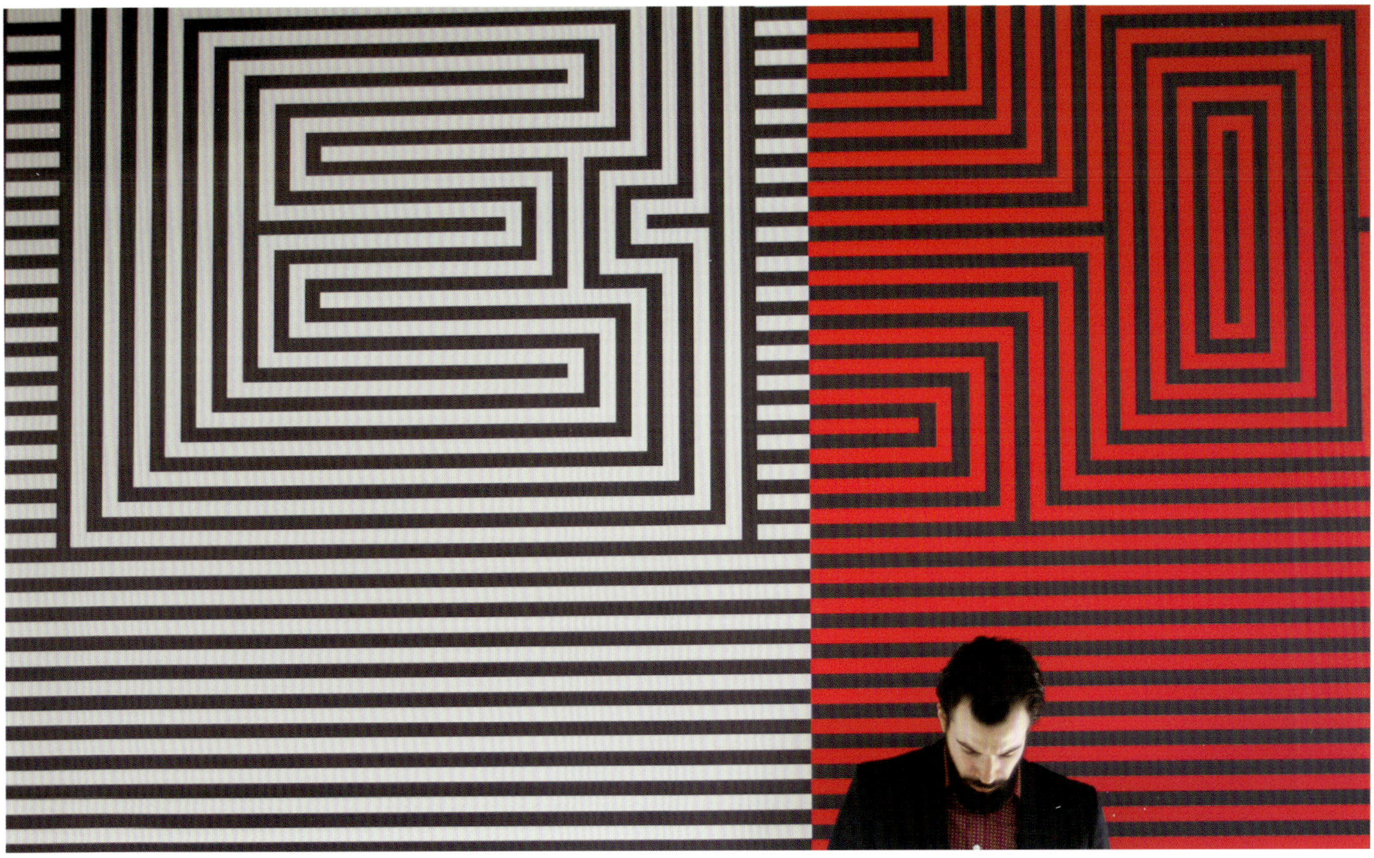

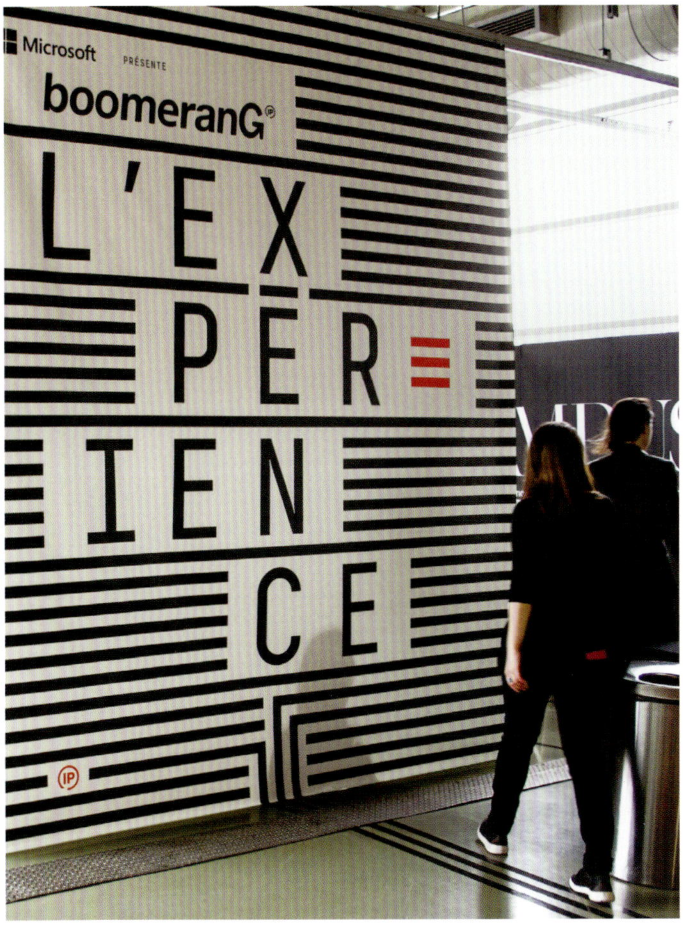
Microsoft
PRÉSENTE
boomeranG
L'EX
PÉR
IEN
CE

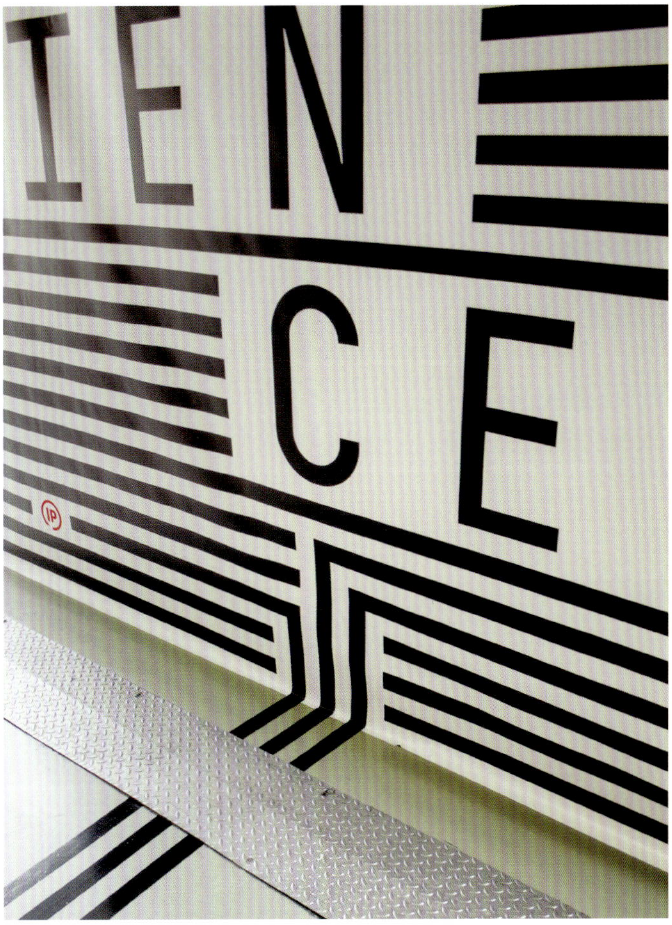
IEN
CE

Uzuri //

Uzuri is a premium make-up brand, using 100% natural organic ingredients, which appeals to the increasing number of women whom desire high-quality products with the added benefits of natural ingredients and an ethical guarantee.

Chloë Galea created a clean and confident logotype, brand identity, and a full packaging range. Inspired by optical illusionary art, a series of monotone patterns were created from scratch. These patterns lead to a striking and original packaging suite that is bold enough to stand out from the competitive beauty market.

Designer Chloë Galea

UZURI
UZURI
Foundation
natural / illuminating
/ medium coverage
summer sun
UZURI
UZURI
UZURI

UZURI
UZURI
PRIVATE INVITE

The Nordic //

In order to immerse customer into the new culinary experience characterized by various seafood, farms, and forests, farm and forest, The Nordic aims to make known the Nordic product and variety, as well as their cultural context from which they are derived. The design represents the minimalist, timeless and contact of the Nordic culture by using a color scheme of blue and black. The pattern takes inspiration from Scandinavian geometric patterns, creating a powerful contrast and highlighting the natural environment of Scandinavia.

Designer David Massara

THE NORDIC
20%
*
TheNordic.ch

THE NORDIC

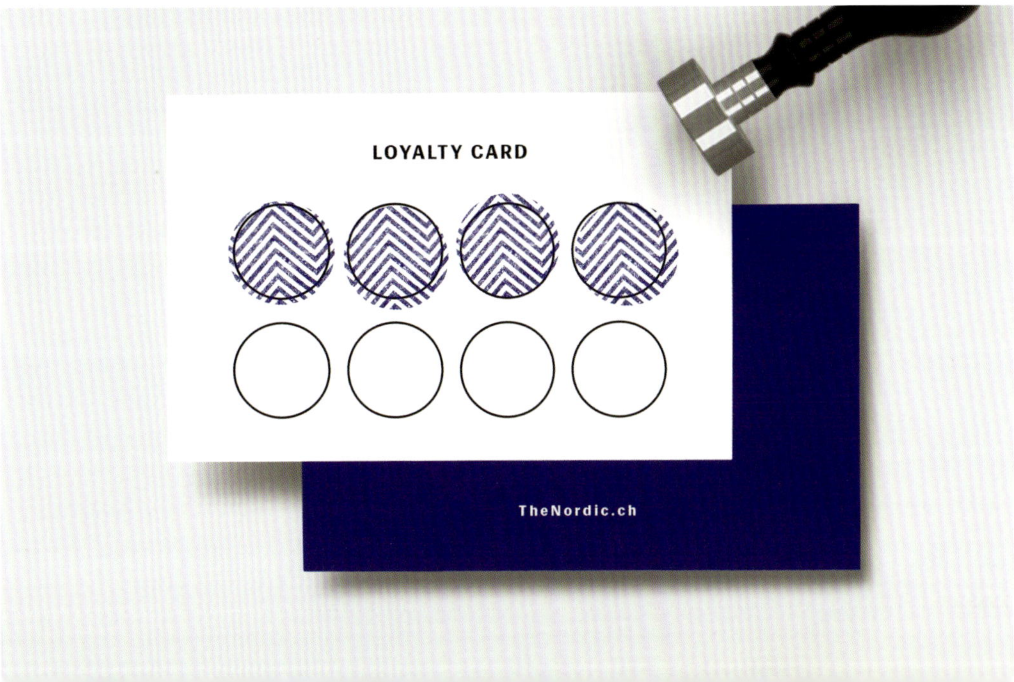
LOYALTY CARD
TheNordic.ch

THE NORDIC
THE NORDIC

Cirkulationscentralen //

This project, inclusive of a visual identity and web design, was a proposal for the art gallery and studio in Cirkulationscentralen (CC) in Malmö. The identity is based on a geometric cube shape which can be applied in many different ways on print and web material. The variation of the cube is determined by different contents filled in, such as pictures, patterns, or color fields, which are created by the members of the studio. The cube can also be used in animated visuals at night clubs in Malmö to market CC.

Designer Anna Lindner

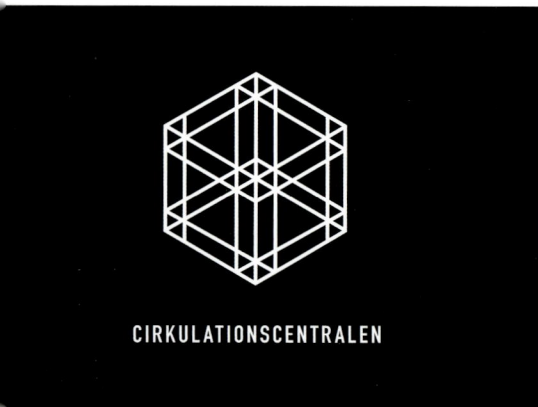

CC ON THE WALL:
ANDREAS ALBRECHTSEN
7-28 APRIL 2013
CIRKULATIONSCENTRALEN
CIRKULATIONSCENTRALEN
CIRKULATIONSCENTRALEN

JOANNA THEDE:
REFLECTIONS
7-28 APRIL 2013
CIRKULATIONSCENTRALEN
CIRKULATIONSCENTRALEN

SPRING 2013
1/2-24/2
GOSIA BOJKOWSKA (SE)
ARKITEKTONIK
1/2-24/2
ANDREAS ALBRECTSEN (SE)
REAL TIME
5-28/4
CHARLOTTA ÖSTLUND (SE)
EN LITEN SKOGSTABLÅ
15-17/2
SUPERMARKET ART FAIR
STOCKHOLM
1-24/2
MACIEJ KALYMON (PL/SE)
JOHN DAILY (US/SE)
TRASH IS FREE
3/5-18/8
MALMÖ NORDIC
2-31/3
MICHAEL STRASSER (AUT)
MUSHROOMING
CIRKULATIONSCENTRALEN

KAPELLO HAIR

Leading the charge in innovation and ethical sourcing, Kapello Hair is at the forefront of the premium hair extensions industry in the UK. To showcase their new brand mark, a suite of branding collateral was developed to aptly reflect their positioning as a modern, luxury salon product.

Designer Cindy Forster

Show Up ///

Show Up is a boutique photography studio that specializes in fashion photography.

The initial idea of Show Up was that fashion photographers are always there at the show to capture the peak of fashion. The 60's optical art movement and refraction of light worked together to create a synergy that reflects both fashion and photography.

Using the optical art's emphasis on lines and sharp contrasts coupled with how light refraction transforms pure white light into the entire spectrum of color, the new Show Up design expresses how photography captures trends and refracts it into the beauty of fashion.

Design Agency Shine Visual Lab
Design Director Tan Wee Bing
Art Director Yap Weng Nam
Designer Yap Weng Nam

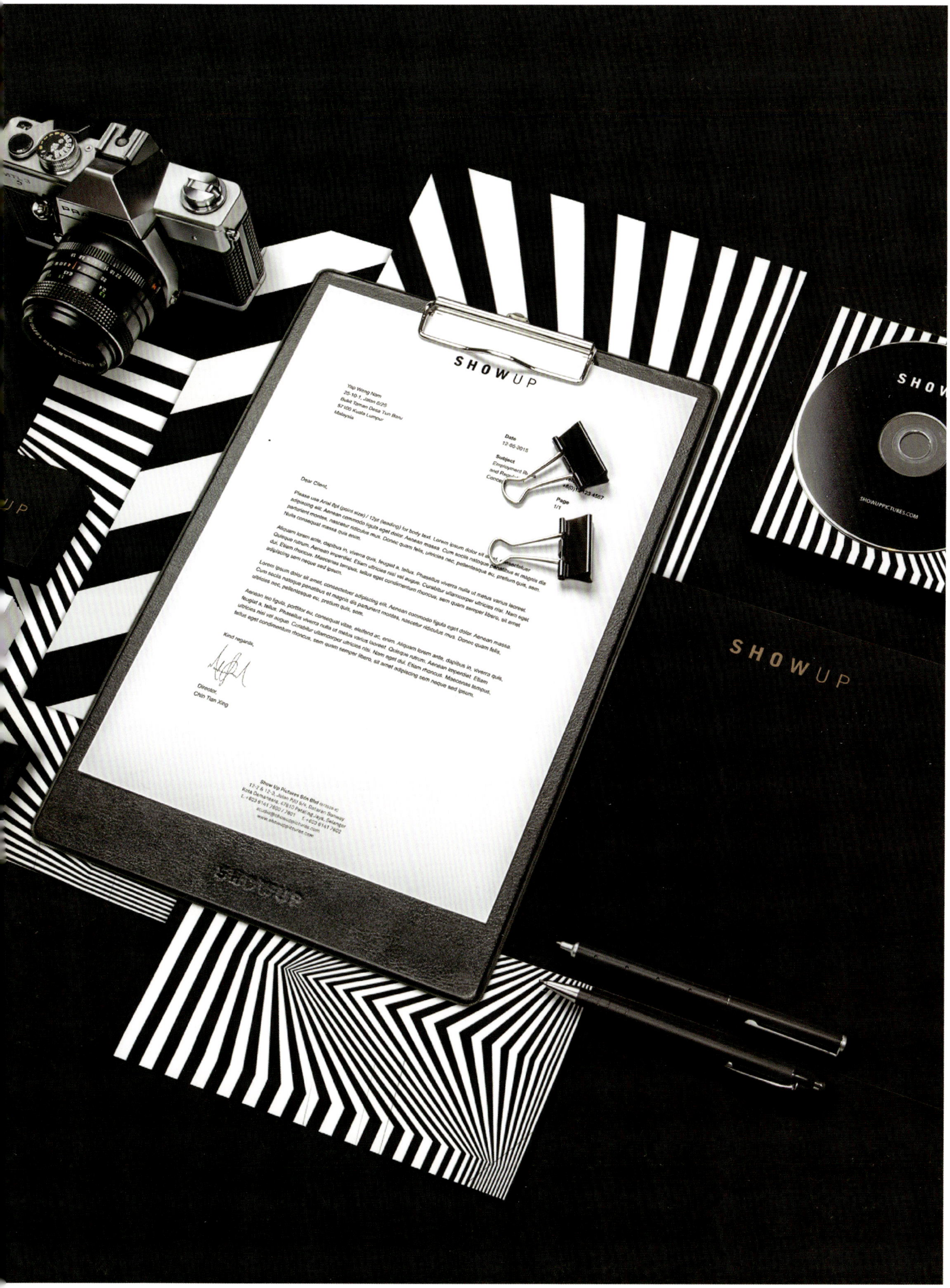
SHOWUP
SHOWUP
SHOWUPPICTURES.COM
SHOWUP

Yu Wei Si ///

Brand design for Yu Wei Si, a rain companion.

Designer David Hong

RAIN COMPANION

—Yu·Wei·Si—

David Hong / Manager
Q 564844419
M 15989277777
W weibo.com/kfm252
E 564844419@qq.com

Musée de la magie

**11 rue Saint Paul
75004 Paris
Métro Saint-Paul, Pont
Marie ou Sully-Morland**

**Ouvert toute l'année
Le mercredi, le samedi
et le dimanche
De 14 à 19 heures**

**+33 1 42 72 13 26
museedelamagie.com**

Museum of Magic //

The aim of this project was to instill some sort of magic into the entire identity. Valentin Noguès and Myriam Cordoba used optical illusions to represent this magic through a combination of patterns and letters, which drew inspirations from the "Op-art" movement. The whole identity for the Museum of Magic is a magic tricking itself.

Designer Valentin Noguès, Myriam Cordoba

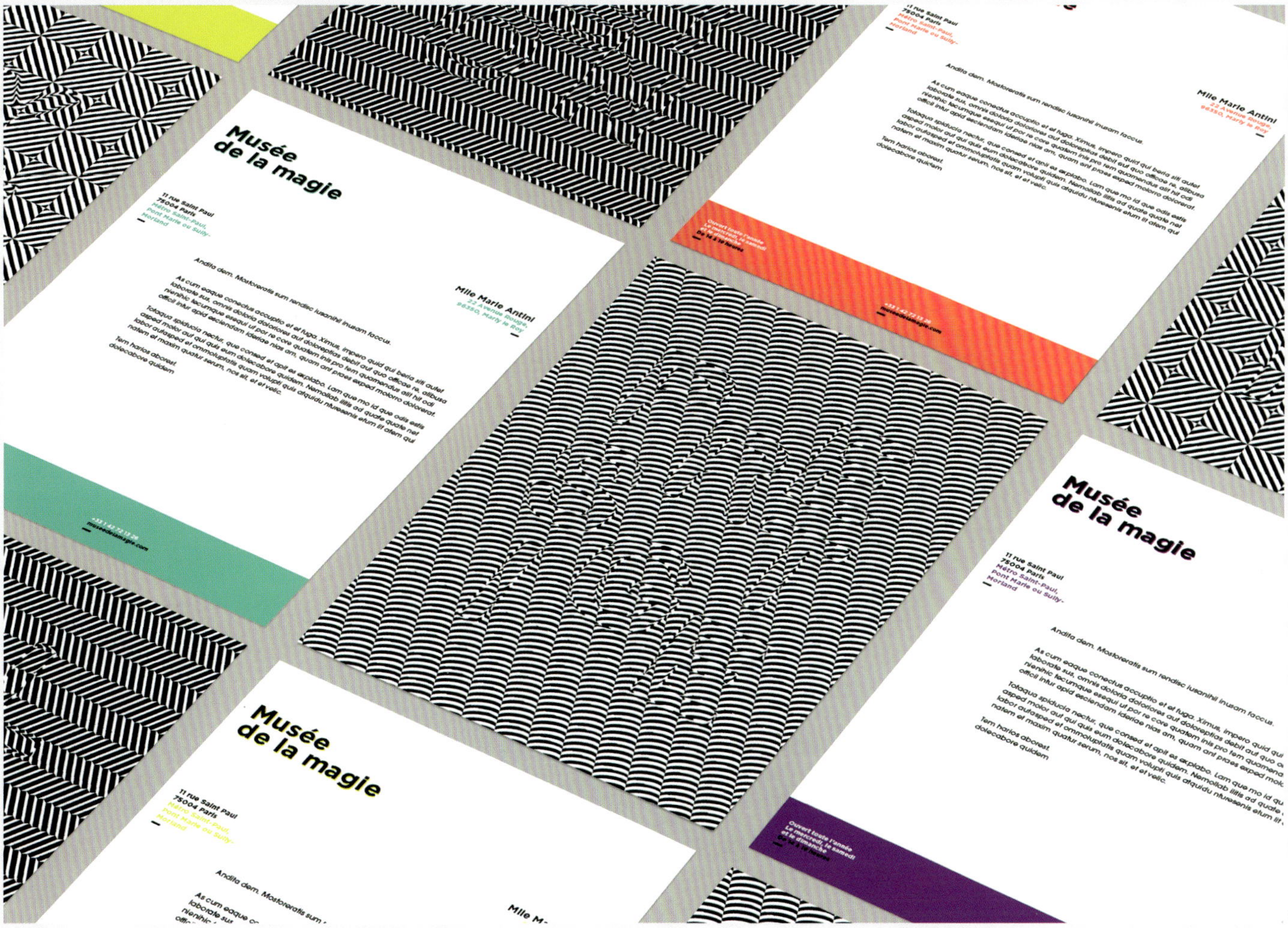
Musée
de la magie
11 rue Saint Paul
75004 Paris
Mlle Marie Antini

France
Musée
de la magie
Postes
20g
France
Musée
de la magie
Postes
50g
France
Musée
de la magie
Postes
100g
France
Musée
de la magie
Postes
250g

Dimétrica //

Dimétrica is a 3D laser scan service provider company located in Guadalajara. The services of this company include 3D scan, topographic survey, among many others.

The identity was created from the inspiration of topographic lines and a strong typography. The color palette is black and white so as to keep it simple and elegant.

Design Agency Menta Picante

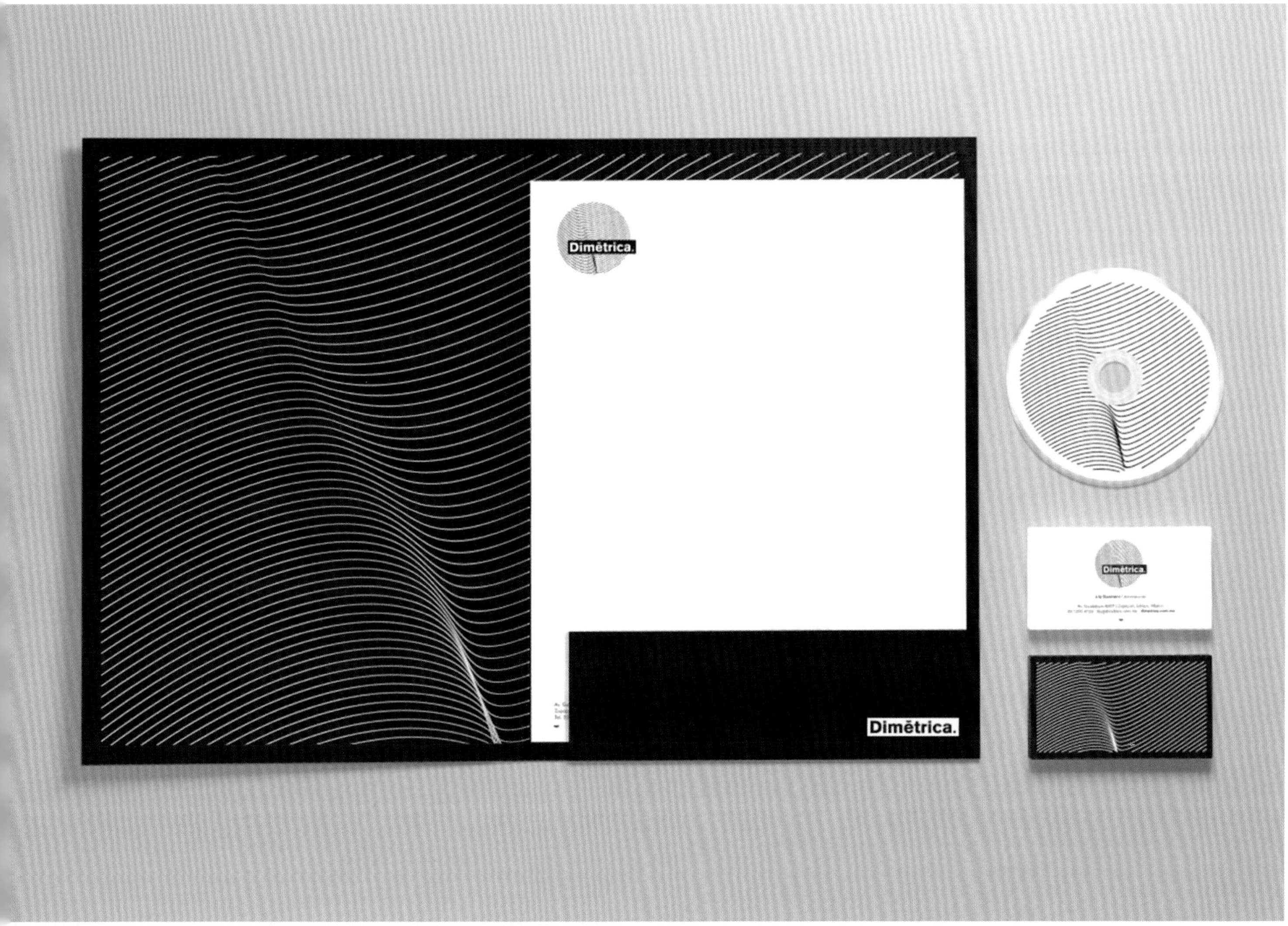
Dimĕtrica.
Dimĕtrica.
Dimĕtrica.

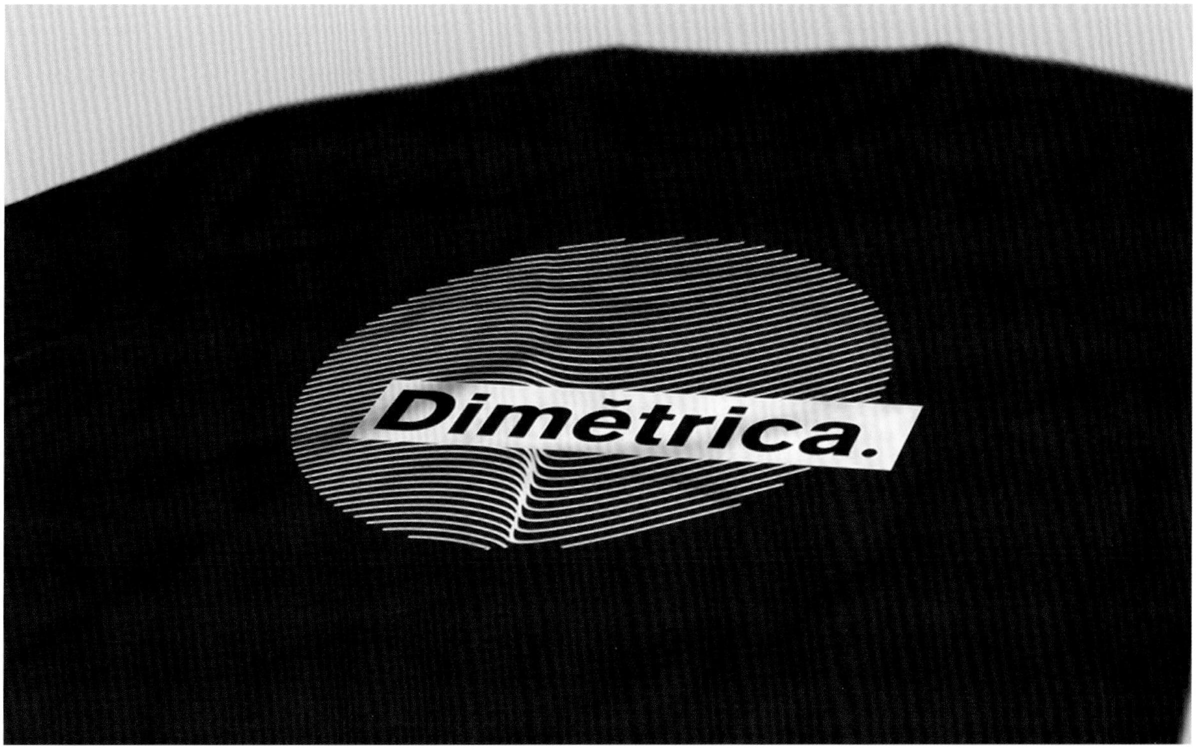
Dimĕtrica.

SINT LUCAS ANTWERPEN PRESENTS

HARRY PEARCE (UK) — JULIEN VALLÉE & EVE DUHAMEL (CA) — JOOST GROOTENS (NL) — JORDY VAN DEN NIEUWENDIJK (NL) — OLAF BREUNING (CH)
UTA EISENREICH & EVA MEYER-KELLER (DE) — THOMAS & LAWRENCE SLATER (UK) — DIMITRI BRUNI & MANUEL KREBS (NORM) (CH)
STUDIO DUMBAR (NL) — TIM FENDLEY (UK) — JAMES LANGDON (UK) — LIEVEN DE CAUTER (BE) — JOHANNA BENZ (DE) — TYPERADIO (NL)
CECILIA AZCARATE (ES) — STUDIO FLUIT (BE) — PAUL COX (FR) — VINCENT HAGNAUER (NL) — ROBIN SCHIJFS (NL) — MONIKER (NL)
BENNY VAN DEN MEULENGRACHT-VRANCX (BE) — OEKIE SEGERS (BE) — KASTAAR (BE) — ELINE WILLEMARCK (BE) — JANE COPPIN (BE)
PETRA VAN BRABANDT (BE) — IPPOLITO PESTELLINI LAPARELLI (OMA) (IT) — GROEP JAN EN RANDOALD (BE) — SYNDICAT (FR)

INTEGRATED
2015

BIENNIAL
INTERNATIONAL
ART & DESIGN
CONFERENCE

26 & 27 NOVEMBER 2015
DESINGEL ANTWERPEN

TICKETS
INTEGRATEDCONF.ORG

SINT LUCAS ANTWERPEN | K|d G | deSingel Internationale Kunstcampus | wetransfer | PAPYRUS | GR

SINT LUCAS ANTWERPEN

HARRY PEARCE (UK) — JULIEN VALLÉE & EVE DUHAMEL (CA) — JOOS
UTA EISENREICH & EVA MEYER-KELLER (DE) — THOMAS & L
STUDIO DUMBAR (NL) — TIM FENDLEY (UK) — JAMES LANGDON
CECILIA AZCARATE (ES) — STUDIO FLUIT (BE) — PAUL COX
BENNY VAN DEN MEULENGRACHT-VRANCX (BE) — OEKIE SEC
PETRA VAN BRABANDT (BE) — IPPOLITO PESTELLINI LAPA

INTEG

BIENNIAL INTERNATIONAL
ART & DESIGN CONFEREN

TICKETS
INTEGRATEDCONF.OR

Integrated 2015

Design Agency Mirror Mirror

Mirror Mirror designed the visual identity and complete communication rollout – including posters, flyers, website, motion video, audio production and assorted merchandise – for Integrated 2015, the 5th edition of the buzzing art & design conference format organized by St Lucas School of Arts Antwerp. Each design showed a different iteration of the same seemingly random optical illusions, a controlled arbitrariness applied throughout all platforms and media.

The – sometimes distressed – optical art is a metaphor for the disorienting and contrasting views on art & design that will clash before their eyes, representing the dazzling spectrum of inspiration and opportunity that emerges from within this whirling debate.

SENTS

RATED
2015

26 & 27 NOVEMBER 2015
DESINGEL ANTWERPEN

SINT LUCAS ANTWERPEN PRESENTS

HARRY PEARCE (UK) — JULIEN VALLÉE & EVE DUHAMEL (CA) — JOOST GROOTENS (NL) — JORDY VAN DEN NIEUWENDIJK (NL) — OLAF BREUNING (CH)
UTA EISENREICH & EVA MEYER-KELLER (DE) — THOMAS & LAWRENCE SLATER (UK) — DIMITRI BRUNI & MANUEL KREBS (NORM) (CH)
STUDIO DUMBAR (NL) — TIM FENDLEY (UK) — JAMES LANGDON (UK) — LIEVEN DE CAUTER (BE) — JOHANNA BENZ (DE) — TYPERADIO (NL)
CECILIA AZCARATE (ES) — STUDIO FLUIT (BE) — PAUL COX (FR) — VINCENT HAGNAUER (NL) — ROBIN SCHIJFS (NL) — MONIKER (NL)
BENNY VAN DEN MEULENGRACHT-VRANCX (BE) — OEKIE SEGERS (BE) — KASTAAR (BE) — ELINE WILLEMARCK (BE) — JANE COPPIN (BE)
PETRA VAN BRABANDT (BE) — IPPOLITO PESTELLINI LAPARELLI (OMA) (IT) — GROEP JAN EN RANDOALD (BE) — SYNDICAT (FR)

INTEGRATED
2015

BIENNIAL INTERNATIONAL
ART & DESIGN CONFERENCE

26 & 27 NOVEMBER 2015
DESINGEL ANTWERPEN

TICKETS
INTEGRATEDCONF.ORG

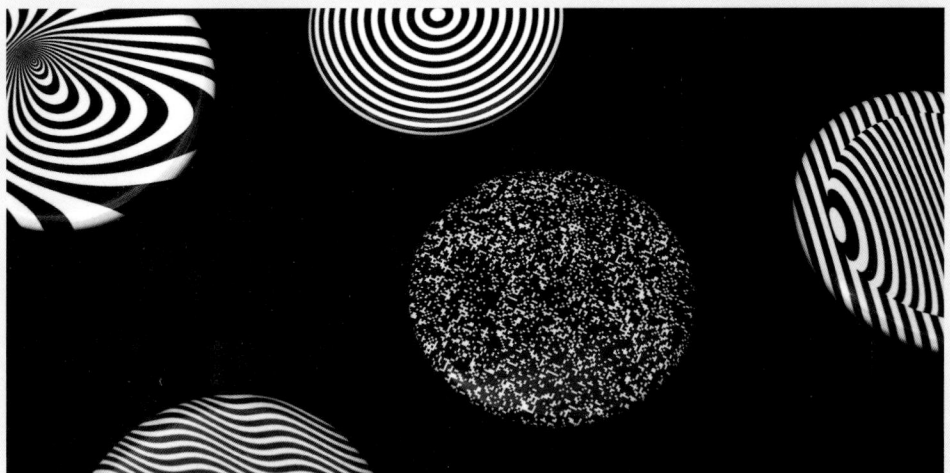

The Pointe

The Pointe is essentially a large studio space that changes uses ranging from dance lessons to corporate events to small concerts. Drew Watts and his design team were tasked with creating a new brand that would highlight the industrial nature of the space as well as generate interest in the local arts and music culture. Their concept was to create a brand that, like the space itself, is continuously changing and evolving. The circle transforms into the letter "P" which regularly changes positions, much like the furnishings in the studio. The icons shift on a grid system throughout the branded elements revealing information.

Designer Drew Watts

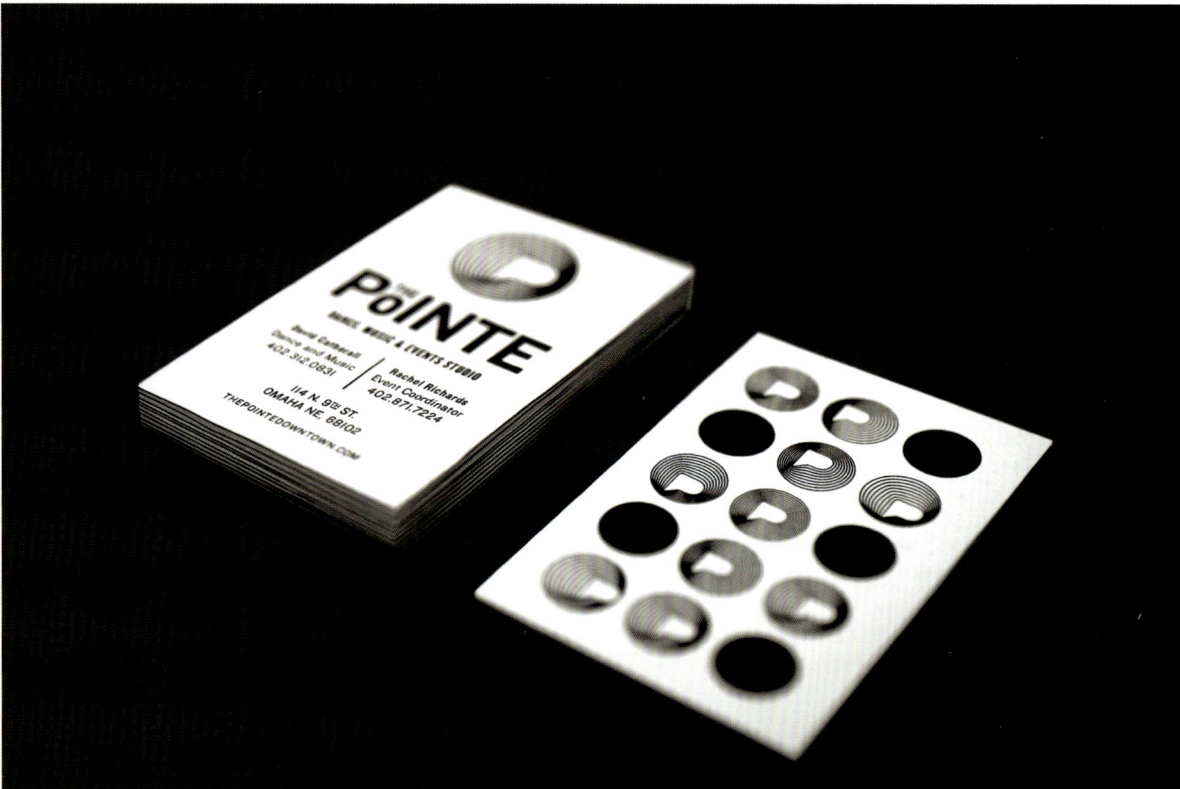

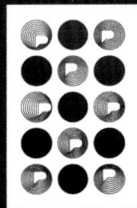

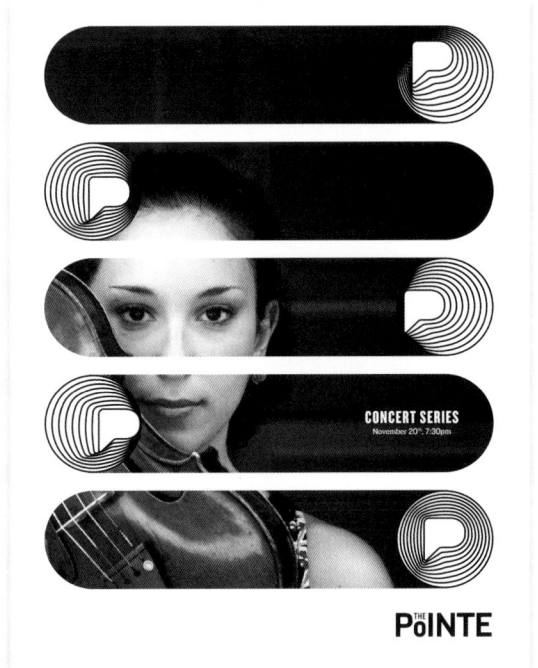

From the Studio of Johnny Helvete ///////////////////////////////////////

This visual identity, shaped to seduce clients with hypnoses, is based on strong contrast and lines for a look book of generic visual identities called *From the Studio of Johnny Helvete*. This project was not only about visual expressions, jargons, and trends within visual identities but also about designers' ability to visualize concepts without explanatory texts.

Designer Gustav Karlsson Thors

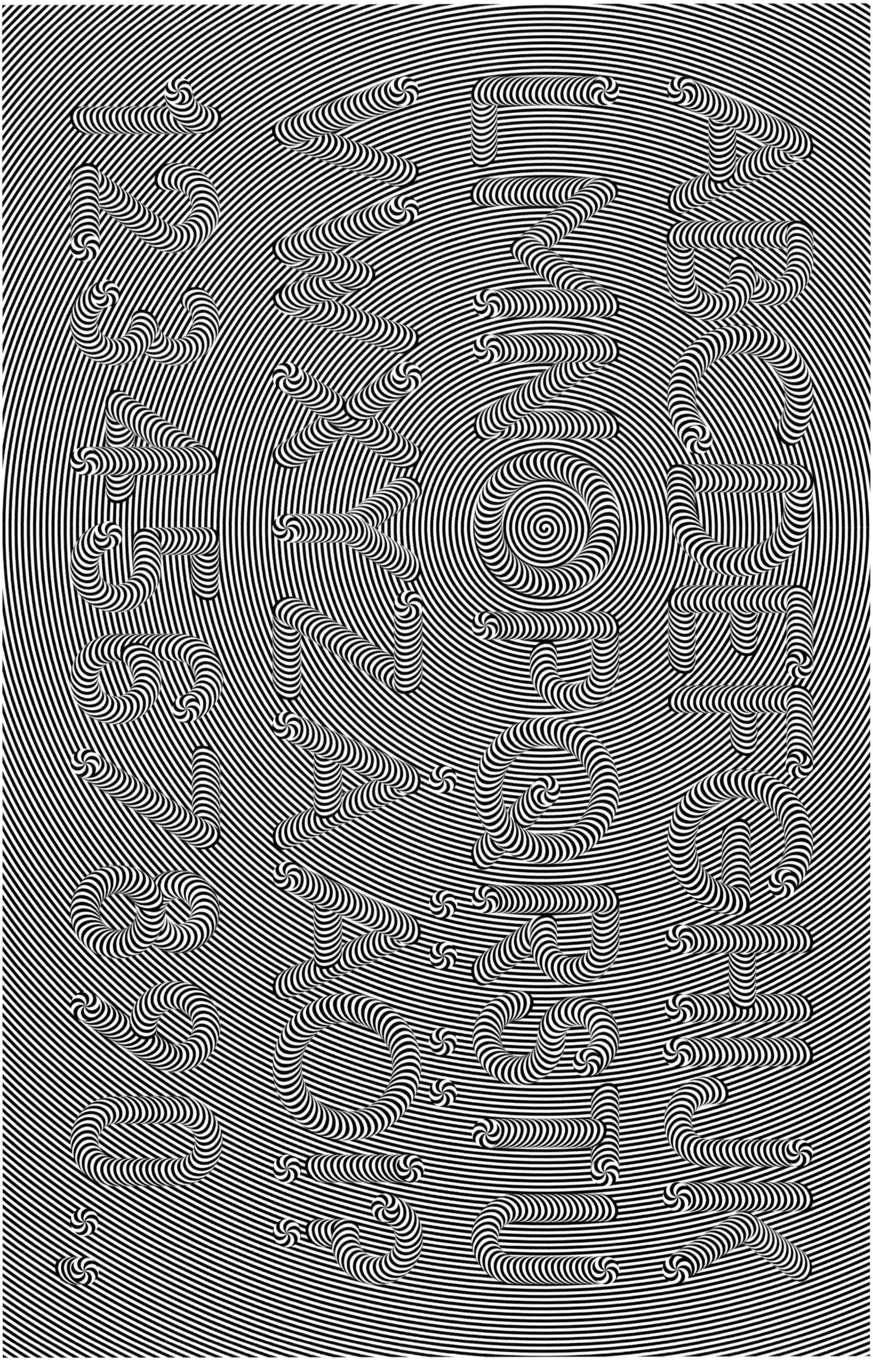

CULTUR∃ management ///

This is a branding design for CULTUR∃ Management, an enterprise agency of DJs/Music producers, record label and event planner.

In the search for the essence of electronic music is impossible not to encounter the binary numbering system, the labyrinthine circuit boards and the black and white piano keyboards. Music and the roots of all electronic devices was the inspiration for the visual identity system for CULTUR∃ Management. Combining the use of Optical Art, highly energetic use of color, a contemporary geometric typography, and the inverted "E" – the mathematical symbol of existence – the identity of CULTUR∃ is a synthesis of values as vanguard, youthfulness, and energy.

Design Agency
Pornographitti Design
Explicito

T-SHIRT
I ♥ E-MUSIC

COVER ART
Colma - Cards On The Deck EP [culturemusic]

COVER ART
Strival - Money In The Bank EP [culturemusic]

COVER ART
Handerson - Time EP [culturemusic]

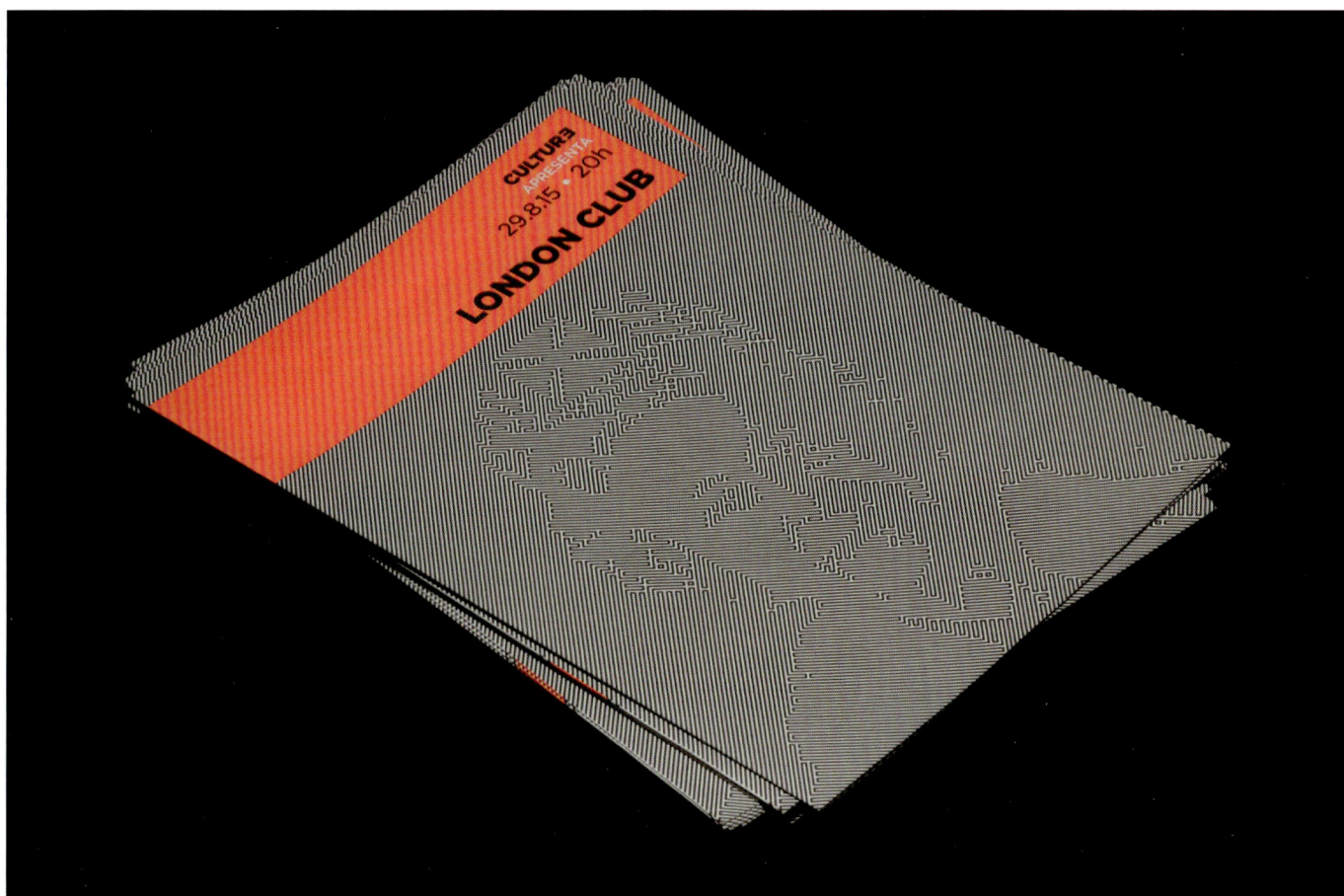

CULTURE
APRESENTA
29.8.15 • 20h
LONDON CLUB

Al Este de Lima 2014

Dedicated to East European films, Al Este de Lima is a film festival celebrated yearly in Lima, Peru and Rouan, France. 2014's edition featured stories about dreams. Infinito Consultores used high contrast moving lines as a way to resemble the mesmerizing voyage a dream can generate.

Design Agency Infinito Consultores
Design Director Alfredo Burga
Art Director Paola Vecco
Designer Thalia Echevarria

AL
ƎTƧE
DE
LIMA

V FESTIVAL
DE CINE
DE EUROPA
CENTRAL Y
ORIENTAL

AL
ƎTƧE
DE
LIMA

EXO

The design of the logo and the visual identity were first imagined through a system which enabled Murmure to play with the graphic sphere as a singular architectural element. This notion of volume lies on principles of perspective which are created by convergence lines. The choice of black and white highlights the graphic power of the material, the volume and its contrasts. The elements are cut through shapes so it reinforces the effect of depth: they bring the necessary discontinuity and become a constituent part of the visual identity.

Design Agency
Murmure

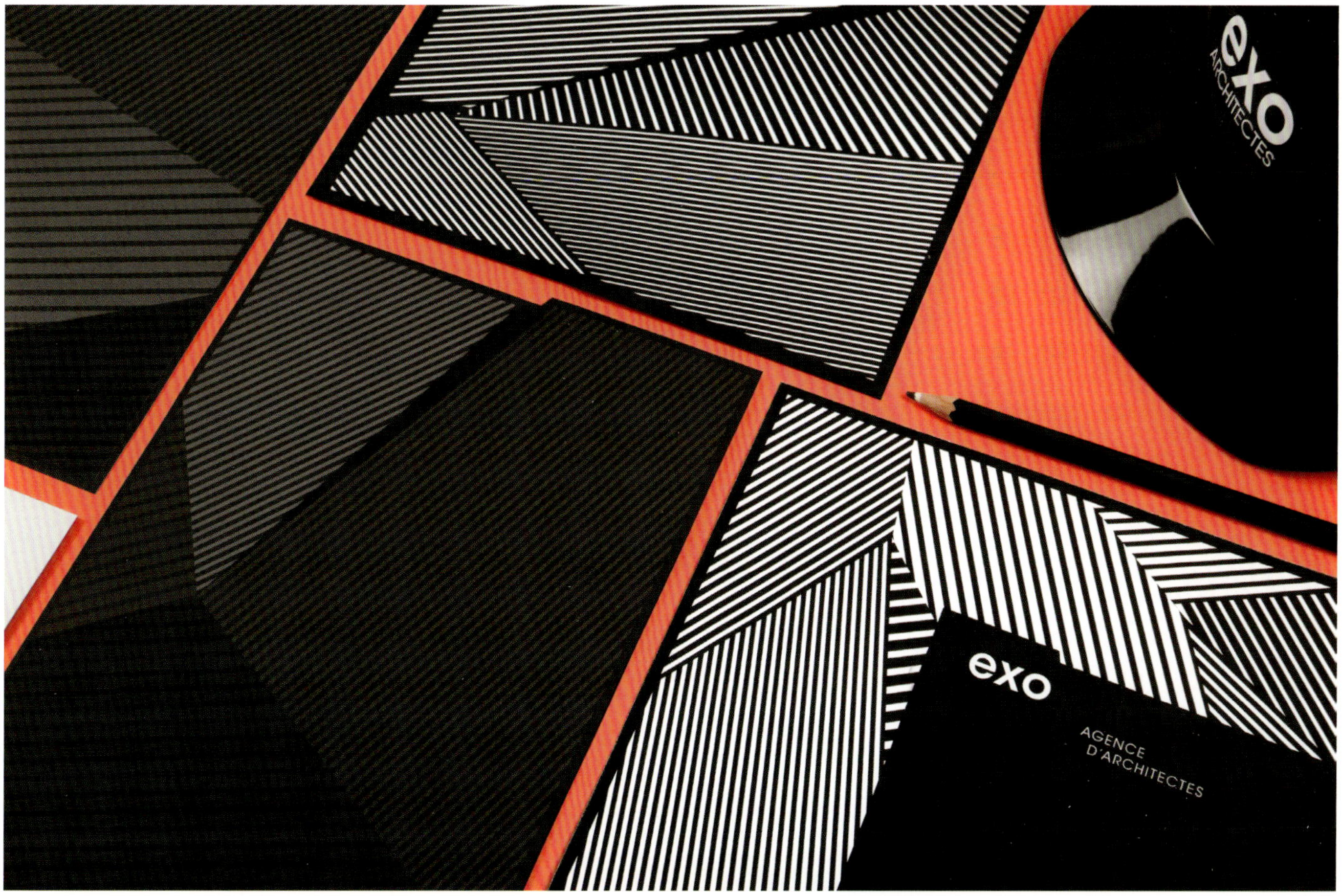
exo
ARCHITECTES
exo
AGENCE
D'ARCHITECTES

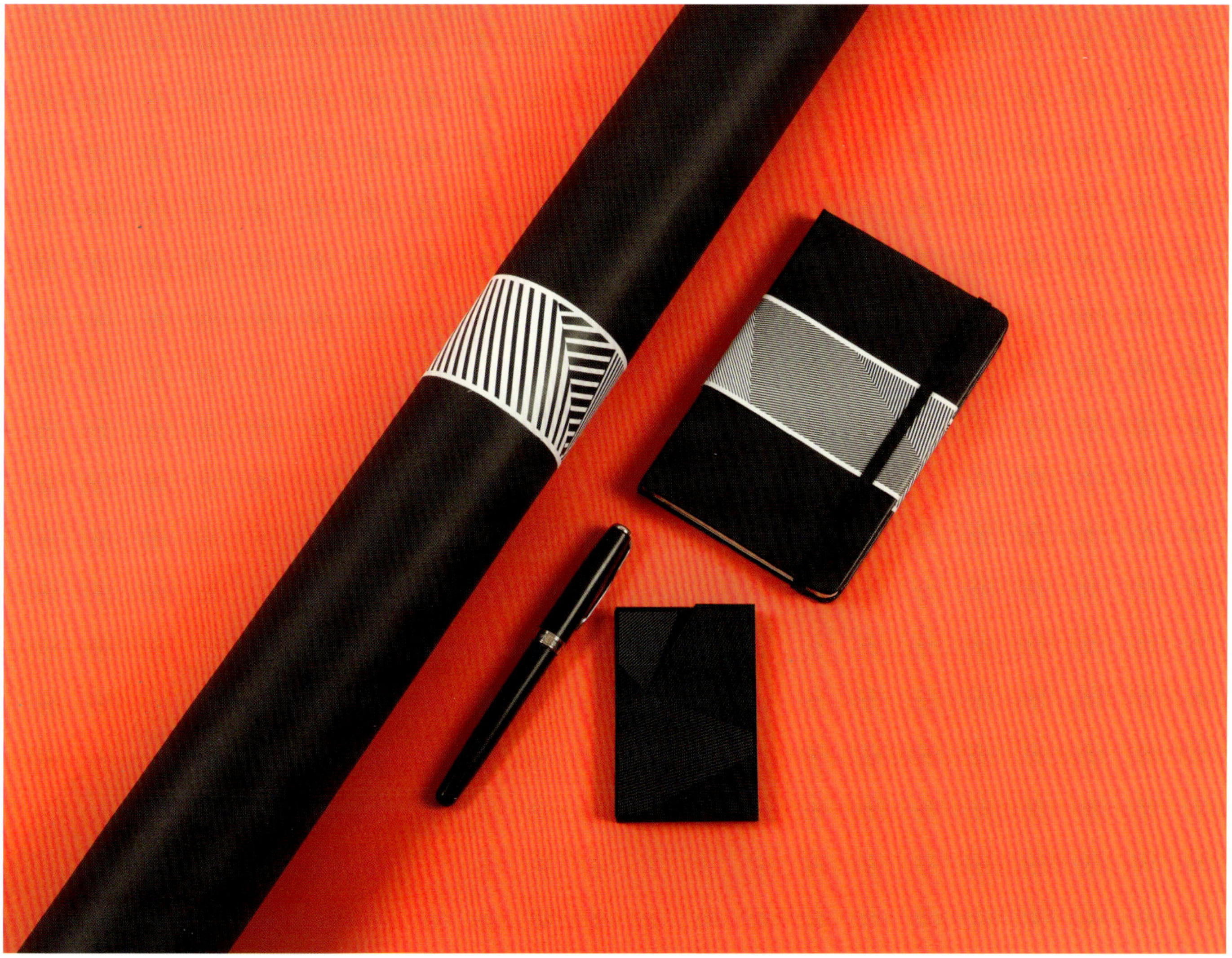

Red Bull Music Academy

The Red Bull Music Academy hosts musical events throughout the world. One of the events on March 16 and 17, 2015 at the concert hall of Cargö, Caen featured an edgy musical line-up. Murmure designed for this Red Bull Music Academy an electric blue graphic pattern emphasized by an elegant typographic composition. Moreover, Murmure used a vibrant visual identity using a graphic pattern enhanced by a blue Pantone which is underlined by an intricate typographic composition announcing the line-up.

Design Agency
Murmure

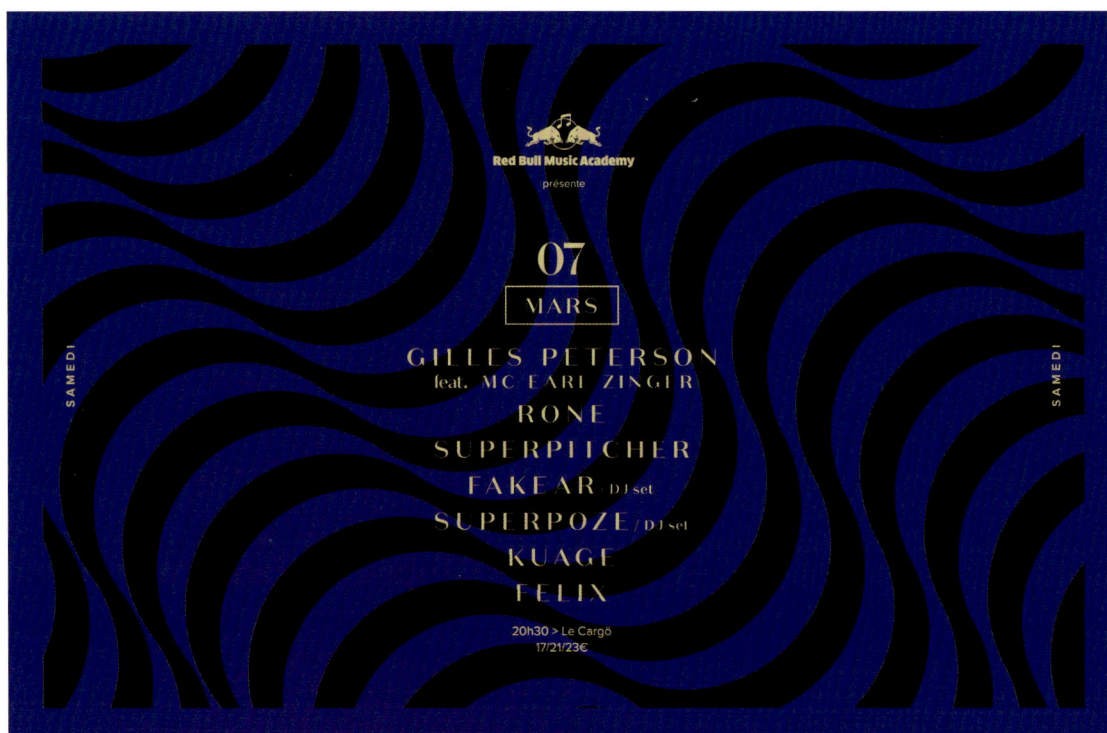

Red Bull Music Academy
06
MARS
DORIAN CONCEPT
ONRA
FULGEANCE
07
MARS
GILLES PETERSON
RONE
SUPERPITCHER
TAKLAR
SUPERPOZE
KUAGE
FELIX
CARGÖ
TRAX
RECORDED LIVE

Red Bull Music Academy
présente
07
MARS
Lecture
GILLES PETERSON
Gratuit - Uniquement sur inscription auprès de
rbma.caen@fr.redbull.com
SAMEDI
SAMEDI
15h00 > Domaine de Beauregard

Cully Jazz Festival //

With more than thirty years history, this Swiss festival becomes the carnival for the jazz amateurs. Around 65,000 festival-goers invade the street, the vaults and the docks of Cully. The festival offers diversified choices and discovers new talents in jazz, while it never forgets the fundamental roots that attract the audience in jazz through more than 100 concerts in 9 days. For the 33rd festival, David Massara brought a new graphic structure that created a powerful identity and a visual coherence. He conveyed modernity in the symbol of jazz, and the dynamic effect, and emotion in different supports.

Designer David Massara

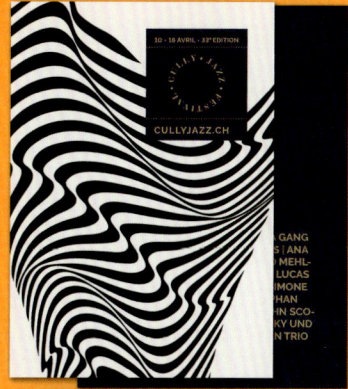

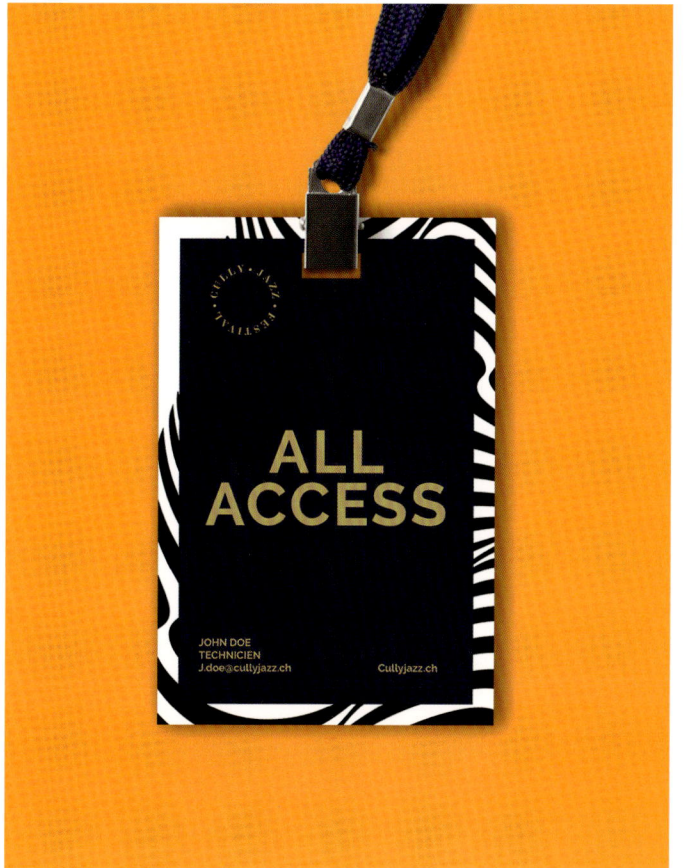

Belle Epoque

Belle Epoque is a French Patisserie on Upper Street in London. The identity was based on the drawings by the English Art Nouveau artist Aubrey Beardsley. The logo is relatively simple as the emphasis is on the pattern and photography. The typography links the Art Nouveau period with the Hippie movement of the 60's. Beside the overall print, web, packaging, signage and some interior design, Mind Design developed a photo concept that links the products with the overall identity.

Design Agency Mind Design
Design & Art Director Holger Jacobs
Designer Lena Wallacher
Photographer Metz + Racine

Equilicuá

This project was a new concept including both naming and corporative identity for the leisure service. The focus of the company was to enrich spare time and convey creative and interesting images. Marina Goñi had to communicate apprenticeship along with fun and dynamism in the design.

The name and the identity originated from the concept "learn playing". The logo with small visual puzzle elements was a result from this concept that people have to "discover" the name of the company.

The graphics is composed of a series of optical illusions which are small games to enhance the playful and participative character of the brand.

Design Agency
Marina Goñi
Design Director
Marina Goñi

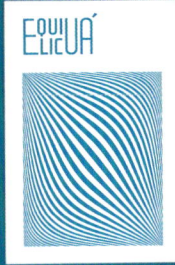
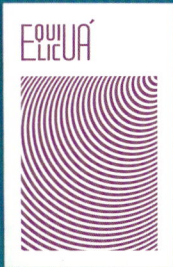

Associació Catalana de la Modaiel Tèxtil ////////////////////////////////////

The Fashion and Textile Catalan Association, a professional collective composed of the main Catalonian companies in this sector, starts a new stage. The Clúster Català de la Moda (Fashion Catalan Cluster) is the new format requiring a new naming proposal as well as a full identity project. Modacc (fashion + the initials of the Catalan Cluster) was the chief solution to upgrade the sector and the cluster format as a complement. The new graphic identity keeps the same blue color as a corporative element and maximizes some new values such as creativity, innovation, and its presence, through a distinctive and variable graphics which resemble the weave.

Design Agency Toormix
Photographer Toormix

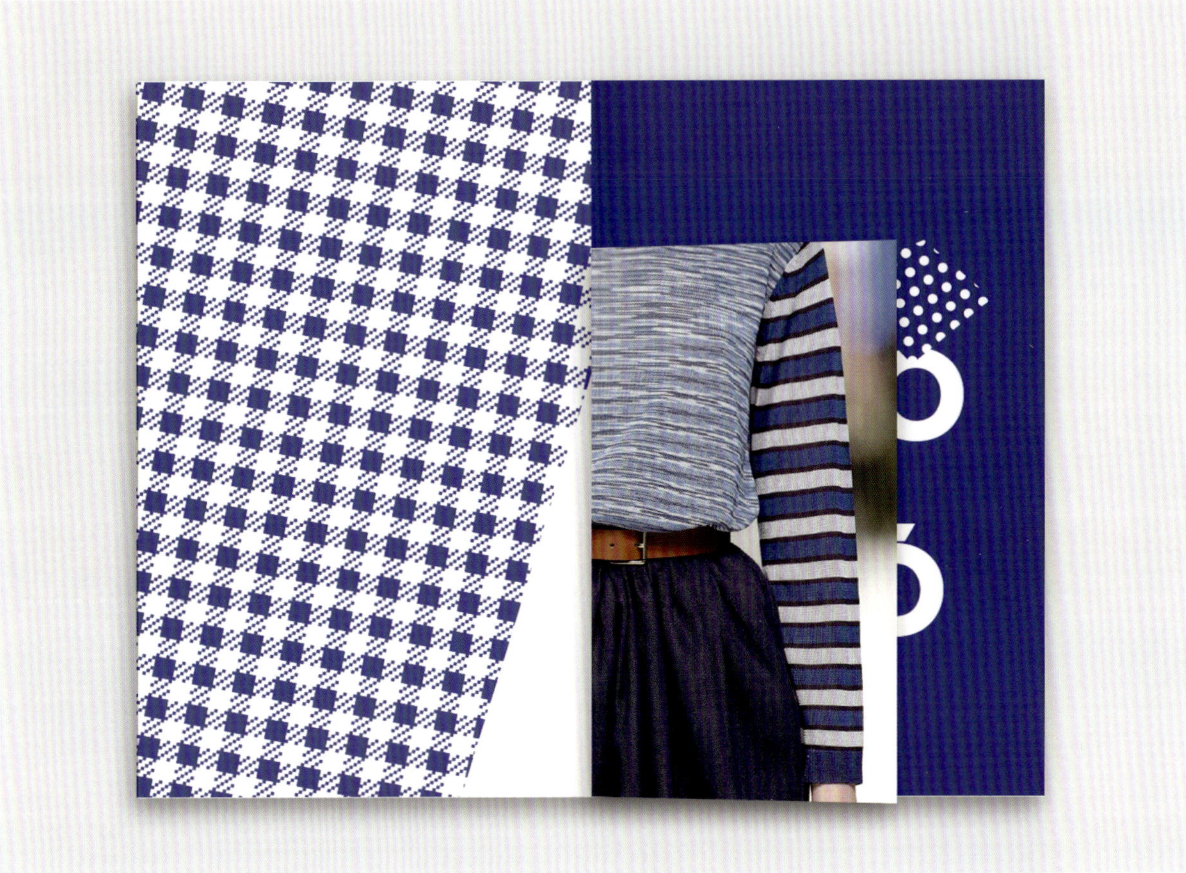

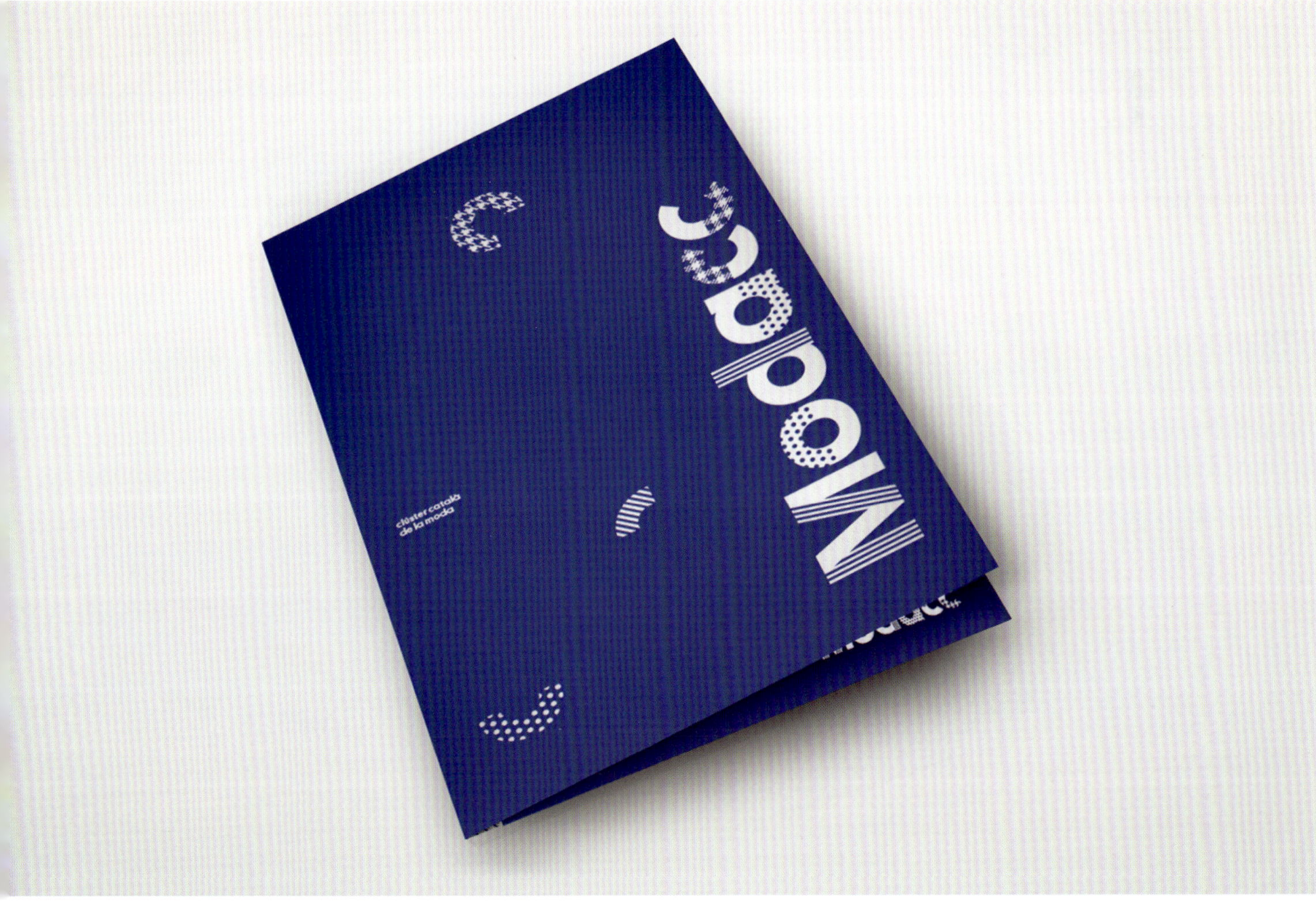
clúster català
de la moda

Minsk ///

The visual style of Minsk expresses the core quality of Minsk and its residents – the ability of critical thinking. With only the width and angle of stripe set as a rule, the visual style is laconic and leaves room for interpretations.

Design Agency INSTID (Institute for Identity)
Design Director Alexander Grand
Designer Maxim Alimkin

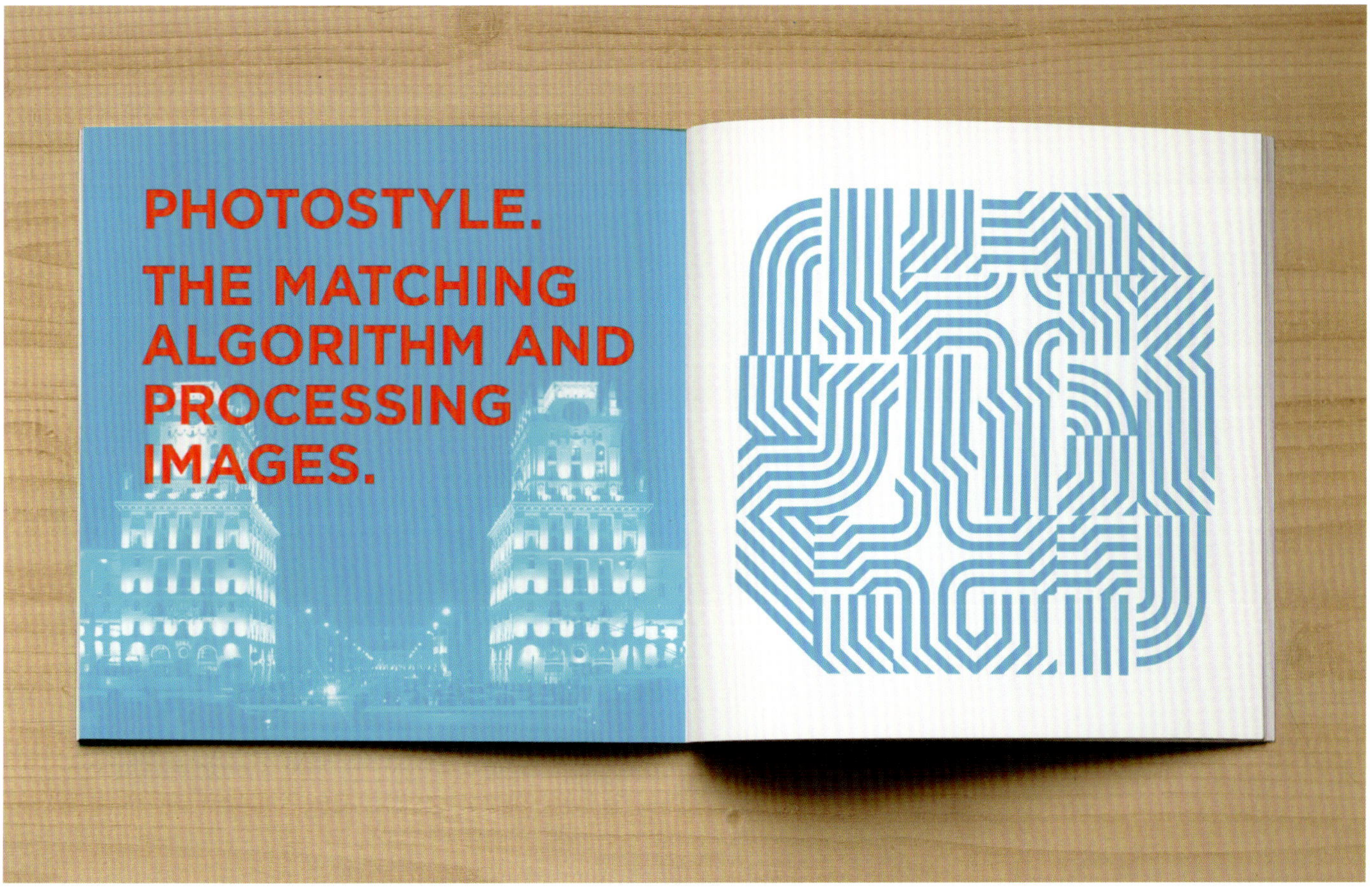
PHOTOSTYLE.
THE MATCHING ALGORITHM AND PROCESSING IMAGES.

NEED PEOPLE WHO CAN THINK?
Minsk, the closest capital to the EU, is a hub of engineering, software programming, and precision manufacturing. With 34 universities and colleges, 64% of Minsk population hold higher and professional degrees. The six decade history of specialising in engineering reflects in an excellent urban infrastructure, highly skilled and committed workforce, and plentiful opportunities for growing intellect-based business.
THINK MINSK

N3
R—D

(Static)

N3
R—D

(Alive)

Kris Spencer
Founder & Creative Director

kris@n3r-d.com

N3
R—D

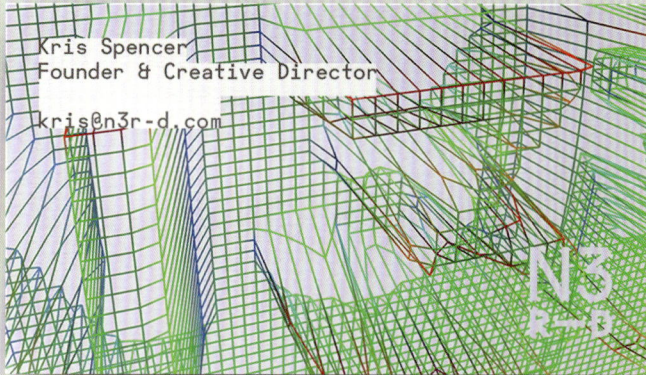

2618 W Sunset Blvd.
Los Angeles, CA 90026

+1 424 324-3263
n3r-d.com

N3R–D //

N3R–D is a design and motion graphics collective based in London, NY, Paris, and Singapore.

They specialize in creating new ways to execute design and moving image for an array of different formats and have become renowned for their work in experimental installations.

The output was delivered with a software which enabled designers to create random glitch compositions from photos they imported using a playful UI that allow mixing and matching different actions to create unique graphics.

Design Agency
WeLoveNoise
Designer Luke Finch

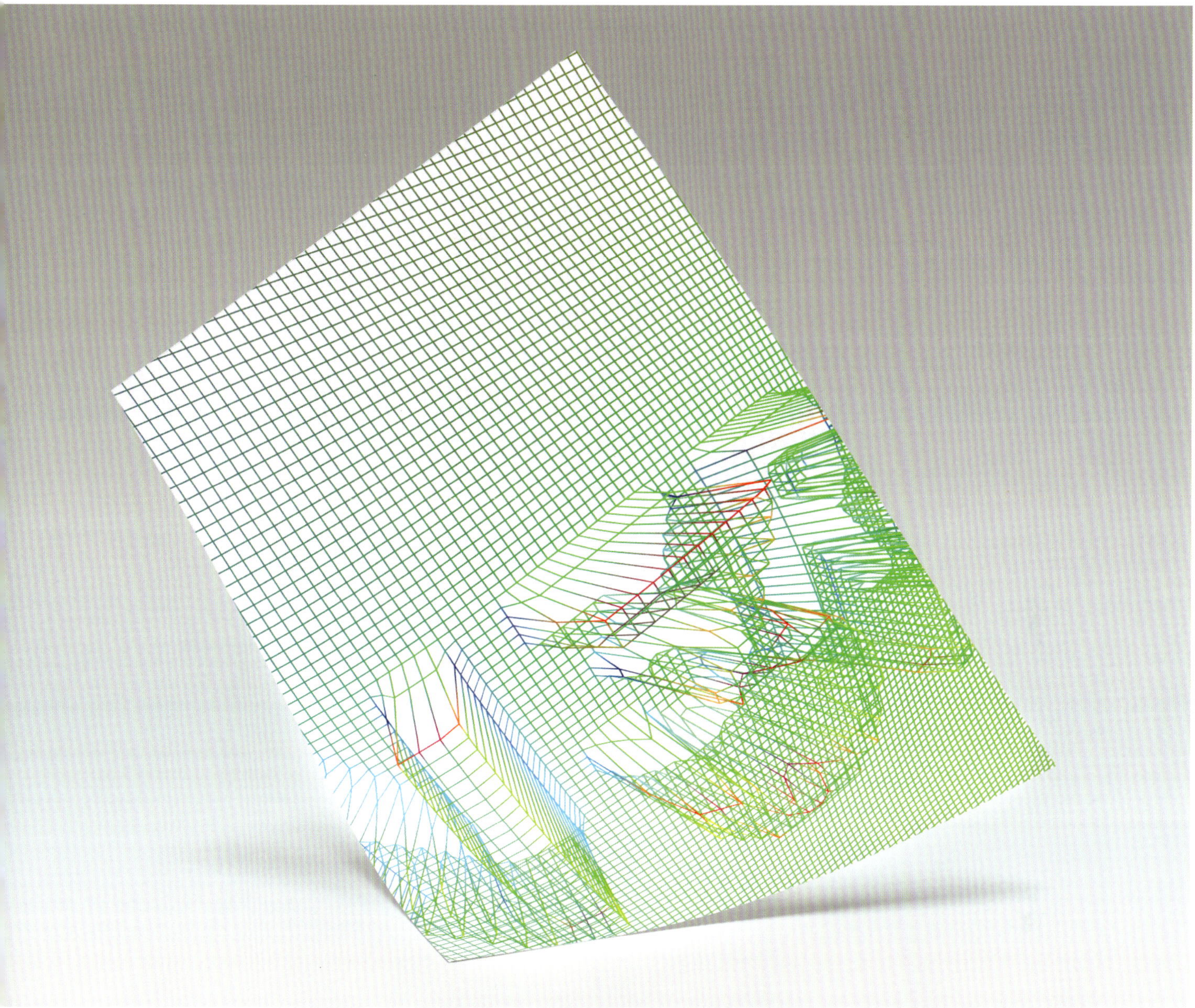

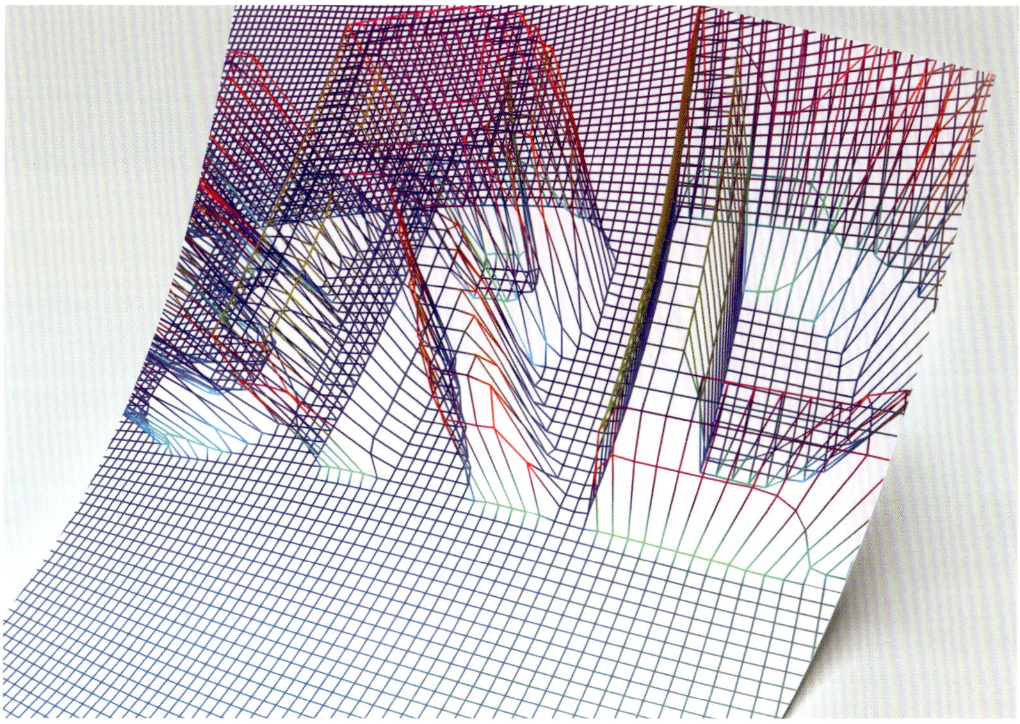

Al Este de Lima 2013

In 2013, the theme of this film festival was dark stories. Infinito Consultores found the use of glitch as a way to resemble mistakes within beauty.

Design Agency Infinito Consultores
Design Director Alfredo Burga
Art Director Franco Zegovia
Designer Maria Jose Vargas

16-25
DE MAYO
2013
ALESTEDELIMA.COM
CUARTO
FESTIVAL
DE CINE
DE EUROPA
CENTRAL
Y ORIENTAL

AL
ESTE
DE
LIMA

Conservatoire de Musique et de Danse //

At the Conservatory of music and dance Levallois, the signage system circulates throughout the building as an undulating frame evoking the rhythms and movements and dedicating artistic disciplines to the place. The words appear in a kinetic typography created by mesh effect that cancels outline of the letters while maintaining readability.

Design Agency Des Signes
Designer Avec Florence Bourel

MAURICE DURUFLÉ
HENRY PURCELL
PARTOTHÈQUE
SALLE DES PROFESSEURS

Keshet – Beauty of Refraction //

Keshet is a distribution firm in Singapore focusing on beauty products. The name, meaning "rainbow" in Hebrew, drives the core direction of the firm's identity. Using parallel lines to symbolize light spectrums and hints of the seven colors of a rainbow within its visual elements, Keshet's design is both an inconspicuous portrayal of a rainbow and also the vibrancy of beauty products. The logogram "K" has a dynamic function where it can be used as key graphic and visual elements for all the design applications.

Design Agency Sciencewerk®
Creative Director Danis Sie
Designer Adji Herdanto
Photographer Evelina Kristanti
Copywriter Devina Sugono

Cartisane //

Cartisane is a furniture upholsterer which wanted to extend its activities to interior design. This artisan has invited Murmure to guide its image towards this direction by providing a feminine and contemporary visual identity. Drawing on its knowledge and playing on the optical effects created by different sizes and crossing threads, Murmure made a set of graphic patterns from different sewing techniques. The roundness of the logo and typographic refinement combine with geometric and technically strong graphic patterns, which symbolize the harmony between creativity and know-how.

Design Agency
Murmure

Typo en Mouvement

A project playing with graphic vibrations to evoke the movement.

Design Agency Des Signes

LE LIEU DU DESIGN
PRÉSENTE

TYPO
EN
MOUVEMENT

TYPE IN MOTION

EXPOSITION
20 NOVEMBRE 2015
5 MARS 2016

ENTRÉE LIBRE
11, RUE DE CAMBRAI
PARIS 19e

LELIEUDUDESIGN.COM

le lieu
du design
île de France

MAIRIE DE PARIS

Une exposition du Museum für Gestaltung Zürich

Museum Gestaltung Zürich   frac île-de-france   vitra.   libération   A NOUS PARIS   étapes: FLUENCIA   socialter   nova LE GRAND MIX

conception graphique : DES SIGNES Muchir Desclouds

Rítmia. Music Therapy //

Based on a graphic expression of the rhythmic exercises that Celia develops, Atipus designed an identity for social music therapist and educator Celia Castillo. The basic aim was to provoke different moods in their patients.

Design Agency Atipus
Designer Albert Estruch
Client Celia Castillo. Rítmia

Música
activa!
Musicoteràpia
a la tercera
edat
Rítmia
Centre Cívic Ateneu Fort Pienc
Desembre 2012
Rítmia
Tallers — (2012)

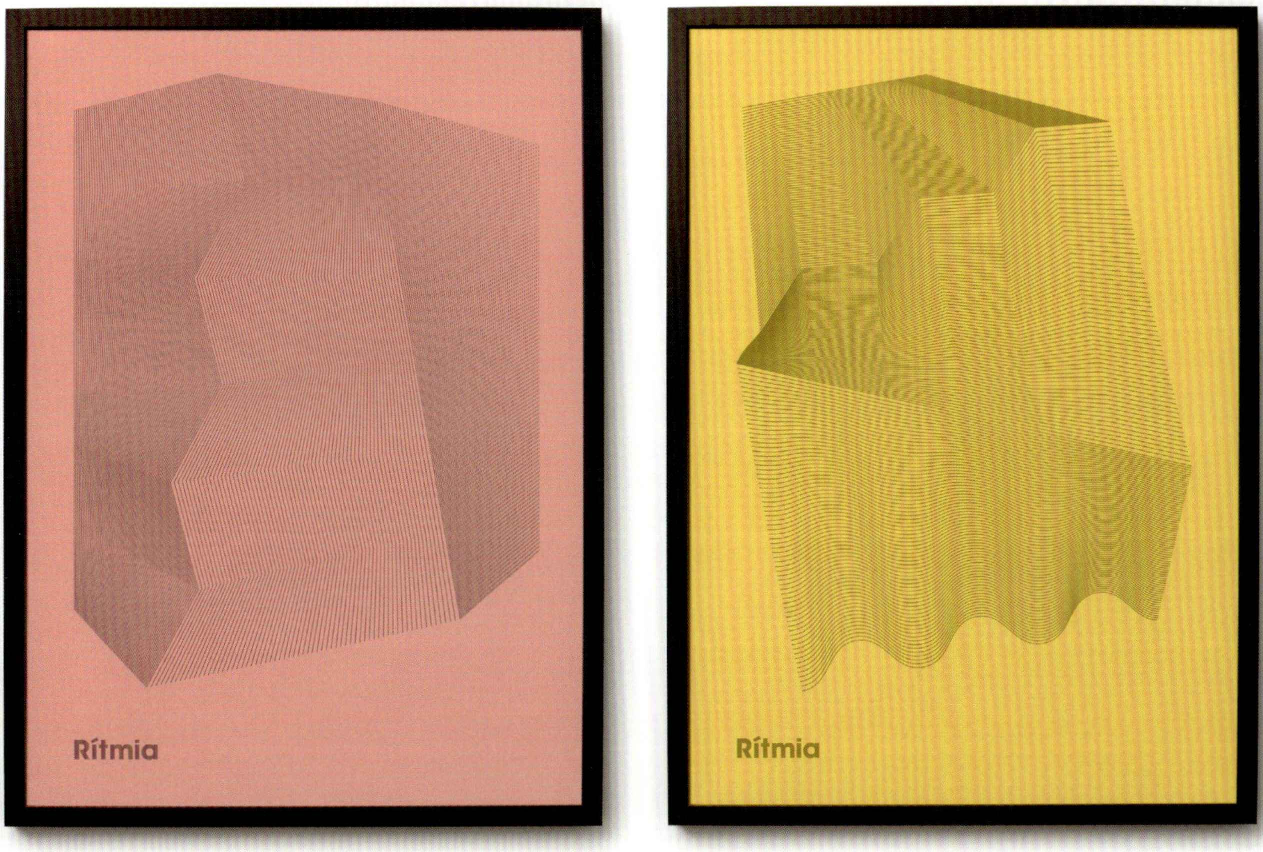
Rítmia
Rítmia

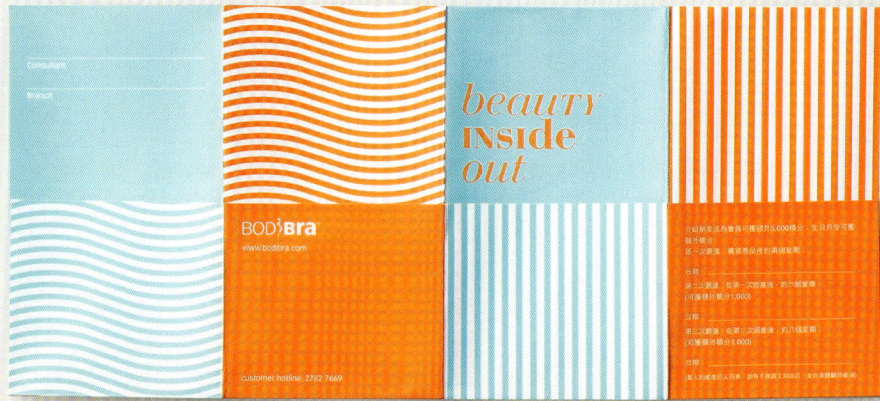

beauty
INSIDE
out

BODiBra
www.bodibra.com

customer hotline: 2702 7669

瘦肉的目的及方向
因大部分客人回家後會忘卻穿著方法，所以請客人必須依時回店，調教肩帶及跟進美體進度，才能得到理想的效果。

穿著束褲的方法
產品的保養

BODiBra

BodiBra ///

A new identity designed by Raymond Ng for BodiBra, a lingerie chain store in Hong Kong renowned for its body-correcting bras.

The mission was to deliver a younger, more modern, and confidence images to its customers. Designer began with a vivid color palette to send out positive vibes to the customer.

For all communications, they utilized the beauty of geometric graphics, curves, and vertical straight lines in particular, both of which symbolize the proper function of the correct bra – to reshape a woman's body curve and straighten her spine.

Design Agency
A Green Hill
Designer
Raymond Ng

BODiBra
May Tsang 曾美玉
beauty inside out

BODiBra
beauty inside out

OVERLAPPING

The optical illusion realized by overlapping is a result of simultaneous contrast which means colors or images interact with one another and consequently change our perceptions, due to the fact that color will cast a shadow on its complementary color.

The multi-layered images create depth. Heavily patterned and high contrast images enhance our experience and unlock more imaginations. Moreover, because it affects our sense of the color that we see, it also gives us a richer color experience.

Central Avenue Type Specimen

StudioMakgill were initially commissioned by Birmingham City Council and Standard 8 to create the identity and graphics for an exhibition celebrating Birmingham's infamous 1886 exhibition of Local Manufacturers and Natural History. Central to the identity was a bespoke typeface that they created based on the original hand-painted signs from the show.

After working with this typeface almost exclusively in black and white, the designers felt that it would be more interesting to explore it in color for the type specimen. Highlighting the awkwardness of the man-made letter forms was a solution. The unbound booklet also works as a series of 4 posters – abstract and bright.

Design Agency
StudioMakgill
Designer
Hamish Makgill

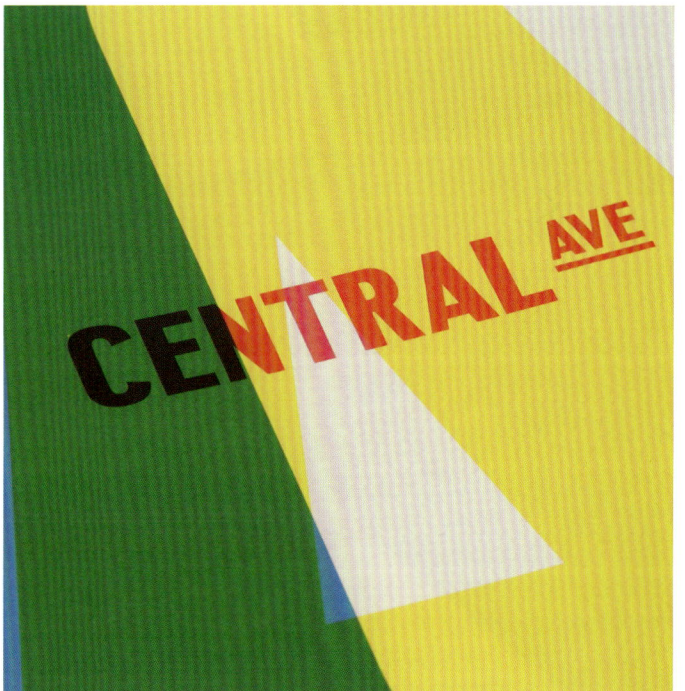

IMPRIMERIE DC

The general concept was designed to be clean, beautiful and colorful. Charles Daoud aimed to show that print could still look cool and flashy if done right, despite bringing a medium viewed as being slowly on the decline. To accomplish this goal, Charles Daoud opted for a dynamic identity system based on geometry and Pop Art that would engage the end user in a rich and fun environment. They developed a full inventory of printed collateral and promotional items including a reversible cubic calendar, a goodie box, full stationery, and much more.

Creative Director Charles Daoud
Art Director Charles Daoud
Graphic Designer
Charles Daoud, Stefanie René,
Kim Peters

Google Mountain View Shuttle

This is an identity and graphic system for the "Google Mountain View Community Shuttle".

WeLoveNoise was ambitious to create a design system that can not only be flexible enough to extend to other cities and countries but still stay true to the principles specifically developed for an individual city.

Design Agency
WeLoveNoise
Designer Luke Finch

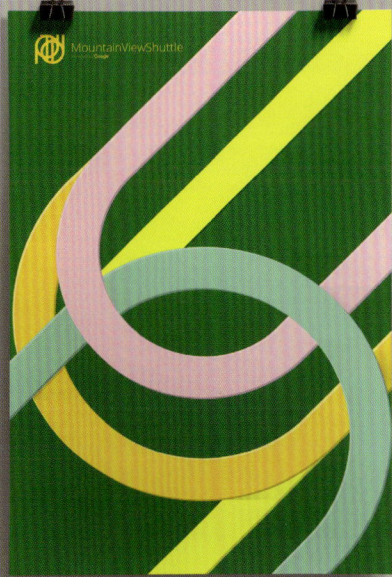

INNÓVATE PERÚ

The National Innovation Program for Competitiveness and Productivity (Innóvate Perú) is one of the main branches of the National Plan of the Ministry of Productive Diversification of Production. Innóvate Perú seeks to increase business productivity by strengthening stakeholder ecosystem of innovation for enterprises, entrepreneurs, and support organizations, and to facilitate the interaction between them.

Design Agency IS Creative Studio
Designer Richars Meza

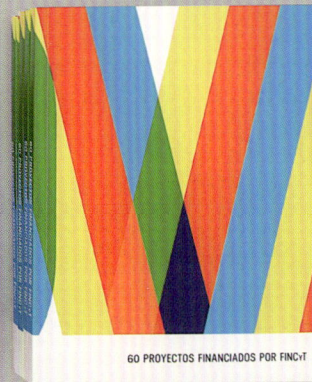

Business Plan

These covers were designed and printed for the 2014 Business Plan of Atelier BangBang. Loyal to its bright colors style, multiple overprints and big typography, all these covers were screen-printed in 2 colors. Binding with elastics with matching colors allows the business plan to be corrected and revised at any time. The business plan of the company explained and demonstrated the company's vision, values, future projects, and commitments.

Design Agency
Atelier BangBang
Designer
Simon Laliberté

TOP-
BILLIN
DJ-
SEKTA

SMUTS:

DISCOBELLE
WOOBANGER

SMUTS PÅ **BABEL**
ONSDAG 25 NOVEMBER **23 - 03**
FRI ENTRE, FRI ÖL INNAN KL 24 SEN 60:-

GRAFISK FORM WWW.CASPERHEIJKENSKJÖLD.COM

Klubb Smuts

The visual identity was designed for Klubb Smuts, a club in Malmoe, Sweden. The overlapping typography is a visualization of the vibrations of music. It resembles the vibrations of the body, when dancing in a club at high audio volume.

Design Agency Casper Heijkenskjöld Atelier
Designer Casper Heijkenskjöld
Photographer Casper Heijkenskjöld

SOLO

J--S-OIN
SAN--ONE
D-SCOBELLE-
CITY CARTEL
WOOBANGER
2C-T-7

SMUTS

GRAFISK FORM WWW.CASPERHEIJKENSKJOLD.COM

SMUTS PÅ **BABEL**
ONSDAG 28 OKTOBER **23 - 03**
40:- INNAN KL 24 SEN 60:-

SMUTS

BOK BOK

SPOEK-
MATHAMBO
D-SCOBELLE
WOOBANGER

GRAFISK FORM WWW.CASPERHEIJKENSKJOLD.COM

SMUTS PÅ **BABEL**
ONSDAG 30 SEPTEMBER **23 - 03**
40:- INNAN KL 24 SEN 60:-

NADA-STROM

FET ELECTRO
TUNGA BASGÅNGAR
SKRUVADE BEATS
HIPHOP OCH TECHNO

DUBSIDED RECORDS, US

STAFFAN

80:-
60:-
FÖR STUDENTER

BACKLASH, DRAMA

WOOBANGER

SMUTS

MIHIN CREW

DANNY THE DOG
NISSMO
VJ, SMUTS

LÖRDAG
25
APRIL

BASÄNGKAJEN 8
GAMLA KAJPLATS 305
22 - 03

PARIS MUSÉES 2013 / 2014

PARIS MUSÉES is an institution composed of 14 museums in Paris. They intended to express a new image through the recreation of a new visual identity. Des Signes employed overlapping square propositions as the main visual to imply the variety of the network of museums and exhibition in Paris.

Design Agency Des Signes

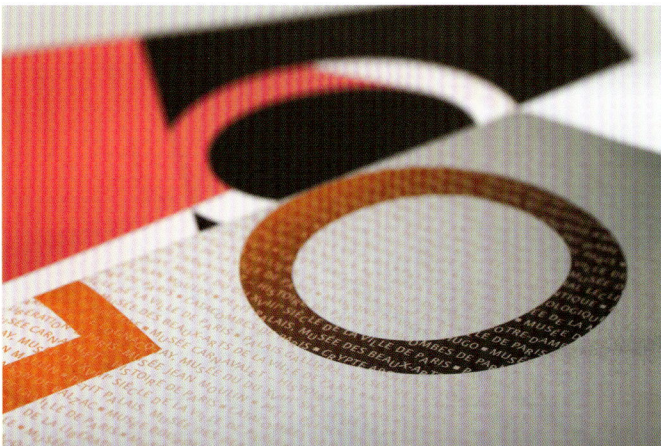

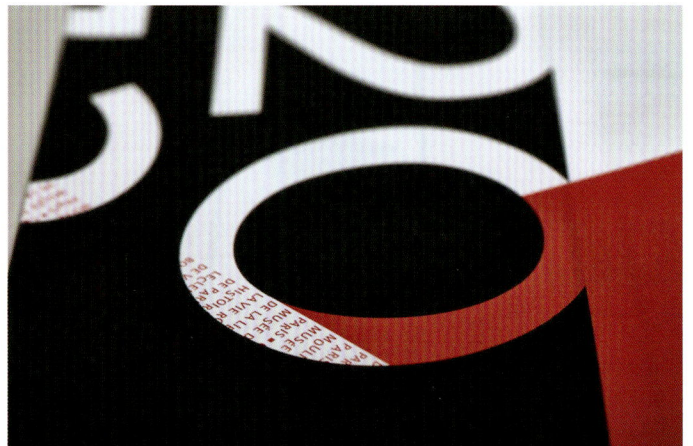

Folkeklubben: Nye Tider

Folkeklubben is a Danish folk band based in Copenhagen. Studio WAAITT has been developing their album artworks since their first release. To visualize the music that has an old school feel, they chose the retro look composed of overlapping elements and old style color scheme to convey it. The overlapping typographic album title and singers' images help create a time eclipse to serve the theme.

Design Agency WAAITT
Designer Jess Jensen
Photographer Anders Rimhoff

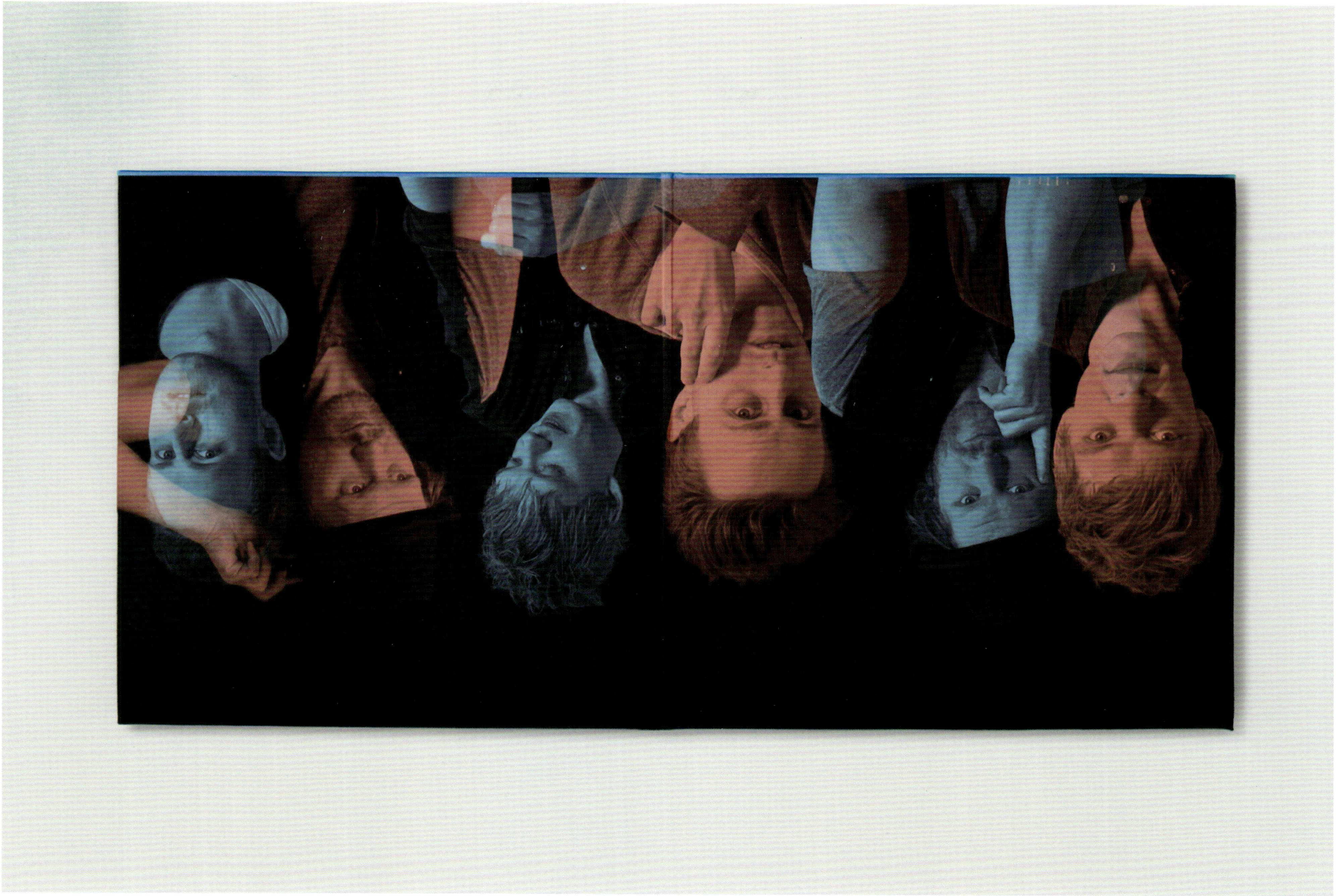

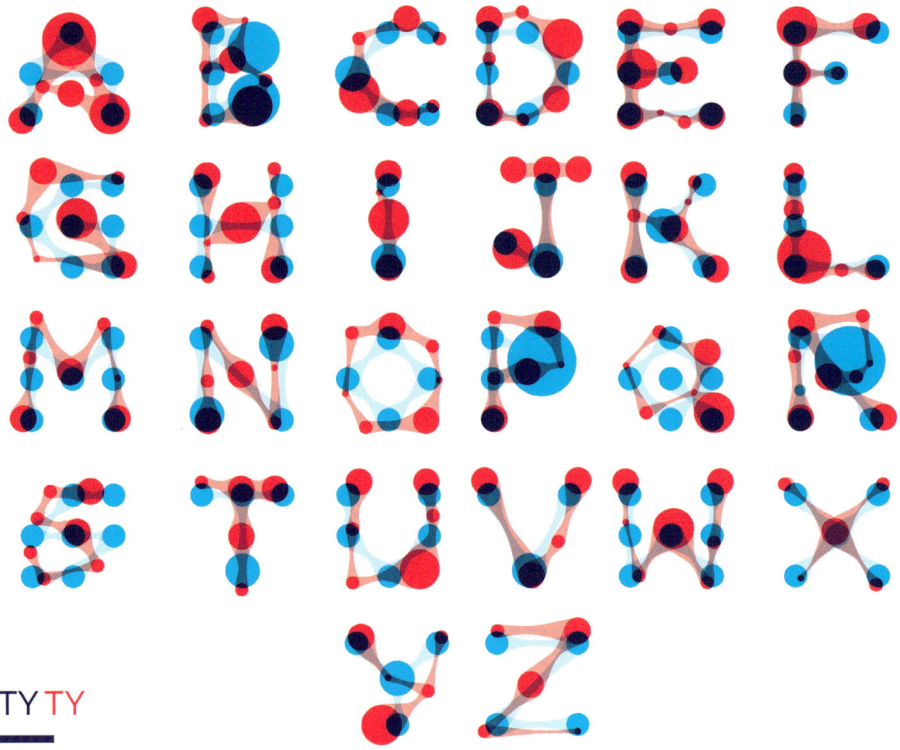

ACTY **TY**

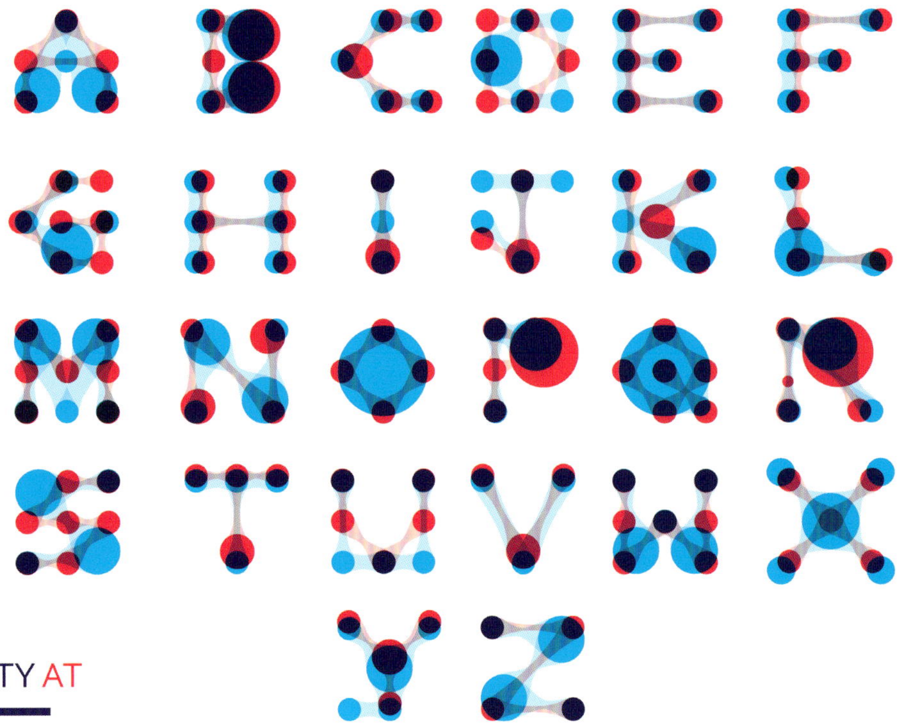

ACTY **AT**

ACTY Typography

A smell is a mixture of several fragrances, but also a molecule. From this idea Aurélien Hervé and his teammates created a molecular typography composed of several elements, just like the odor.

They each created their own typography and then mixed them up. This principle allows rich combinations for each letter.

Designer Aurélien Hervé, Chloé Méot, Tian Bai, Yili Sun

la typographie moléculaire

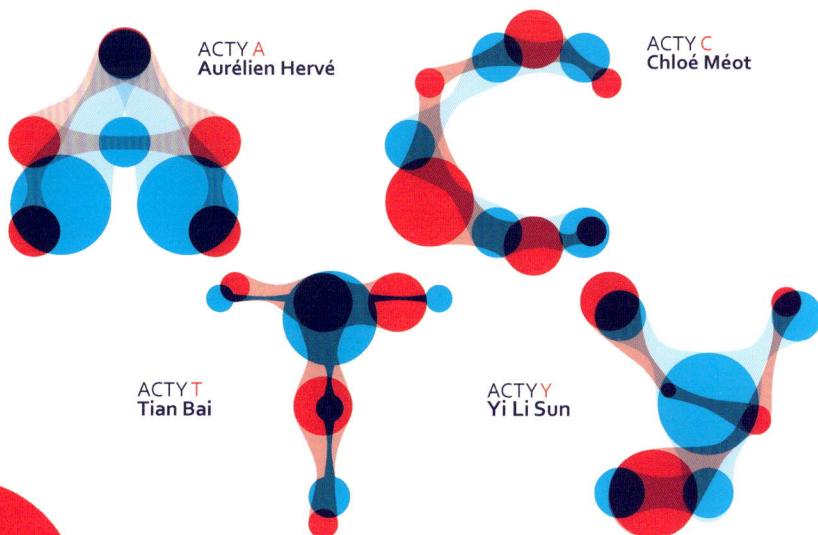

ACTY A
Aurélien Hervé

ACTY C
Chloé Méot

ACTY T
Tian Bai

ACTY Y
Yi Li Sun

	C	T	Y	A
C	CC	TC	YC	AC
T	CT	TT	YT	AT
Y	CY	TY	YY	AY
A	CA	TA	YA	AA

Dialekt Kunstverein

Gold & Wirtschaftswunder developed the corporate design for the Dialekt Kunstverein Art Institution. This institution promotes young artists from all over Europe, and organizes exhibitions and art events. The main components of the Corporate Design are the logo. "D," the first letter of the brand name, became the component of the logo, which stands for "Dialect". And the complement element "/" reflects the projects bring together artists from different national and artistic backgrounds. Also it is also visible from all stationery for Dialekt Kunsverein that is multi-layered of varied color and design elements.

Design Agency
Gold & Wirtschaftswunder
Design Director
Julia Kühne, Christian Schillert

DIALEKT KUNSTVEREIN MITGLIED WERDEN*
An den
DIALEKT KUNSTVEREIN
HEILBRONNER STRASSE 7
D-70174 STUTTGART

DIALEKT KUNSTVEREIN
HEILBRONNER STRASSE 7
70174 STUTTGART
T +49.711.99 78 19 58
F +49.711.99 78 19 61
KONTAKT@DIALEKT.ORG
WWW.DIALEKT.ORG

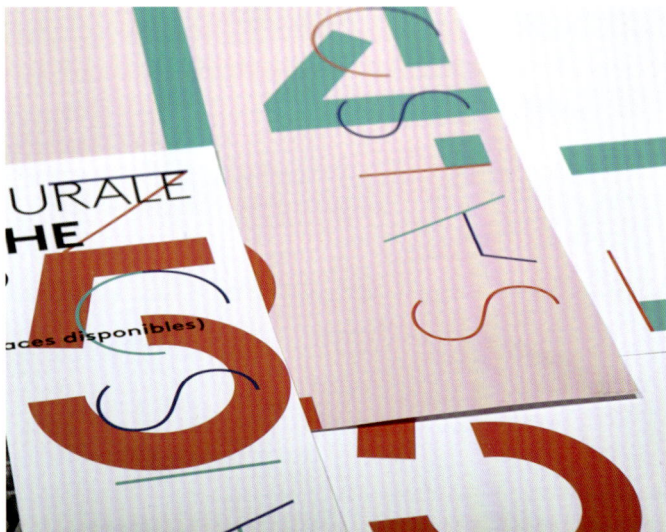

Saison 2014/2015 CNSMD de Lyon

Des Signes realized the new program of the 2014/2015 season for the National Conservatory of Music and Dance of Lyon. They formalized the new identity, with a layout and an increasingly dynamic color code and dancing types.

Design Agency Des Signes

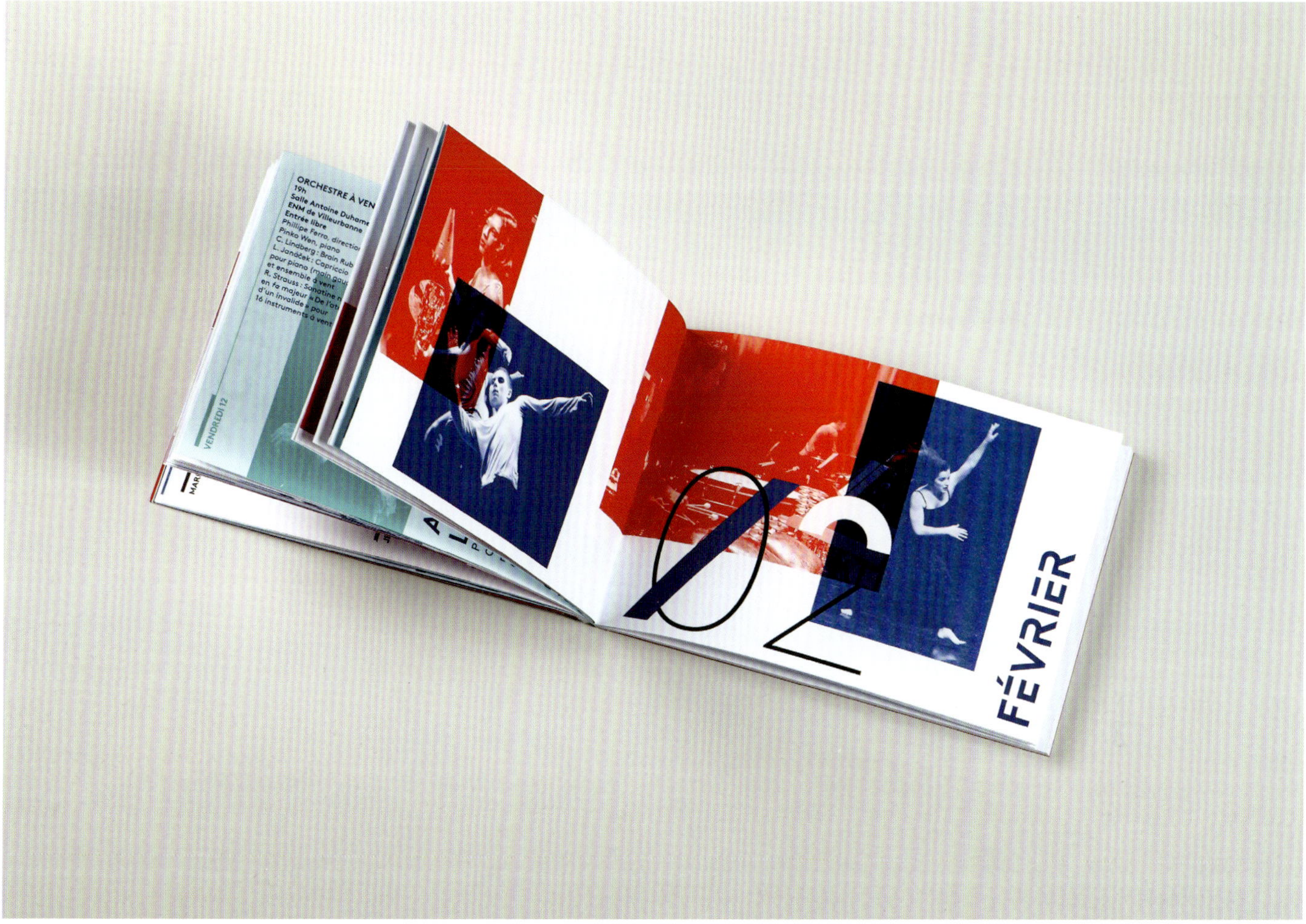
FÉVRIER

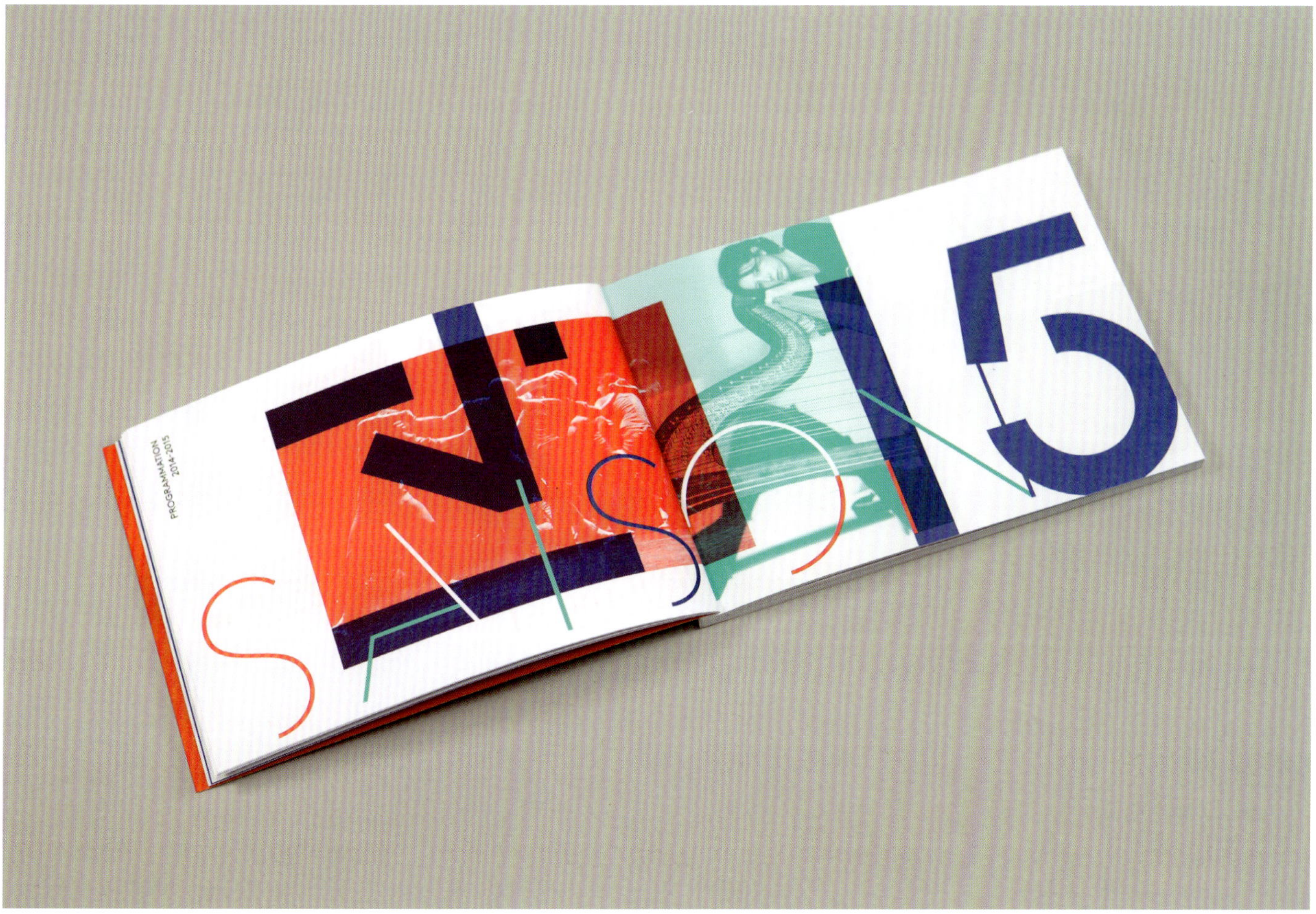
PROGRAMMATION
2014-2015

Readux

New German
Fiction
Prizewinner

Dear A.

Translated by Donal McLaughlin

Inga Machel

Readux Cover Design

Stahl R designed the book cover for the new series of Readux Books. The concept was based on their design research project on the experimental visualization of data by using character systems. They created a visual synopsis for each books, represented in three levels and indicated varied meanings.

Design Agency Stahl R
Design Director
Susanne Stahl, André Gottschalk
Art Director Susann Stefanizen

Readux

New German Fiction **Prizewinner**

The Last Hous

Translated by Katy Derbyshire

Dear /

Translated by Danial McL

Judith Ke

Inga Machel

Read*ux*

The Wall, the City, and the World

Eliot Weinberger

Judith Keller

Readux Books
Series Nº4

The Last House
Judith Keller

Dear A.
Inga Machel

Three texts straddle the line between essay and poetry as they examine the ways in which humanity builds civilizations — and tears them apart. "The Wall" presents a protocol of interactions along the Berlin Wall in the late 1960s. "The City" zooms out to examine the city as social unit. "The World" is dedicated to the myths that humanity creates to come to terms with itself. In their sweeping scope, the pieces illustrate Weinberger's characteristic sincerity and intelligence.

ISBN 978-3-944801-26-1
50500 >

9 783944 801261

Second Home

Second Home is a curated community that brings together companies and freelancers to foster new inventions and partnerships. The identity represents the crossover between life and work, art and science, and knowledge and invention created by a shared environment. It consists of twelve logos made of overlapping circles. The word mask sits on the overlapping section, representing the space where new ideas happen. The logos feature a range of colors, reflecting the diversity and energetic spirit of Second Home's members.

Design Agency Pentagram
Design Director Marina Willer
Art Director Marina Willer
Designer Inn Osborne, Hiromi Suzuki
Project Manager Lucie Garnier
Photographer Nick Turner for Pentagram

Talks work

Every Thursday
6.30 – 9.00pm

secondhome.io/talks
#shtalks

SECOND
HOME

Second Home
68 Hanbury Street
London E1 5JL
+44 (0)7966 478 586
www.secondhome.io

SECOND
HOME

DESIGN
WEEK

SHOW
+
TELL

09:05	Buses depart from The Argonaut + 601 Townsend
10:00-12:00	Oxfam Design Review
12:00-01:00	Lunch
12:05	Bus departs from 601 Townsend*
01:00-05:00	Show + Tell
05:15	Bus departs to 601 Towsend*
05:30-10:30	XD Team Dinner
08:15-11:15	Shuttles run between SFWM + The Argonaut + 601 Townsend

*For guests who are only attending Show + Tell

XD

2016

Adobe XD Design Week 2016

Each year Adobe Design gathers all of its designers, researchers, engineers, and other team members together in San Francisco for a week-long event where people share their work and experiences, build relationships, and plan for the next year. The theme for 2016 was *Convergence* – representing coming together to build something bigger and better across products, services, and organizations. The Adobe Design Brand team took on the task of creating an appropriate brand system to support the goals and needs of the event.

Design Agency
Adobe Design
Design Director Shawn Cheris
Designer Anny Chen

Poster 1 (top left):

2016

DESIGN WEEK

XO

Poster 2 (top right):

08:30   Buses depart from The Argonaut + 601 Townsend
10:00–10:15   Kick-Off with the Oxfam Team
10:15   Design Challenge Begins
11:00   First Design Critique Walk-Thru
12:00–01:00   Lunch
02:00   Second Design Critique Walk-Thru
05:00   Presentation Submission Deadline
Buses depart to The Argonaut + 601 Townsend

DESIGN WEEK

OXFAM DESIGN

CHALLENGE

XO

2016

Poster 3 (bottom left):

08:30   Buses depart from The Argonaut + 601 Townsend
10:00–10:15   Kick-Off with Bryan Lomkin + Phil Clevenger
10:15–12:00   XD Design Week Pop-Ups
12:00–01:00   Lunch
01:00–04:00   Speakers Take the Stage
04:00–05:00   Team Time
05:00   Buses depart to The Argonaut + 601 Townsend

DESIGN WEEK

MAKE MAKE

CREATE

INSPIRE

XO

2016

Poster 4 (bottom right):

2016

DESIGN WEEK

XO

Edut

Edut is an educational content making platform for adaptive learning, which provides optimized content for each person with diversified educational contents. enhanced Inc. make an analogy of this service as an abstract diagram with dots placed as the diverse contents.

Rather than using a static logo, their solution intended to make the symbol express both static and dynamic. They believed Moire effect can best translate adaptive learning into a graphical language. The static yet seemingly dynamic layers of dots personify the adaptive learning. Patterns and color changes created the logos with simple shapes but still visually unique. Also the Moire represents "Educe", the origin of the word Edut, which means drawing out each student hiding talent and potential.

Design Agency
enhanced Inc.
Designer
Hiromi Maeo

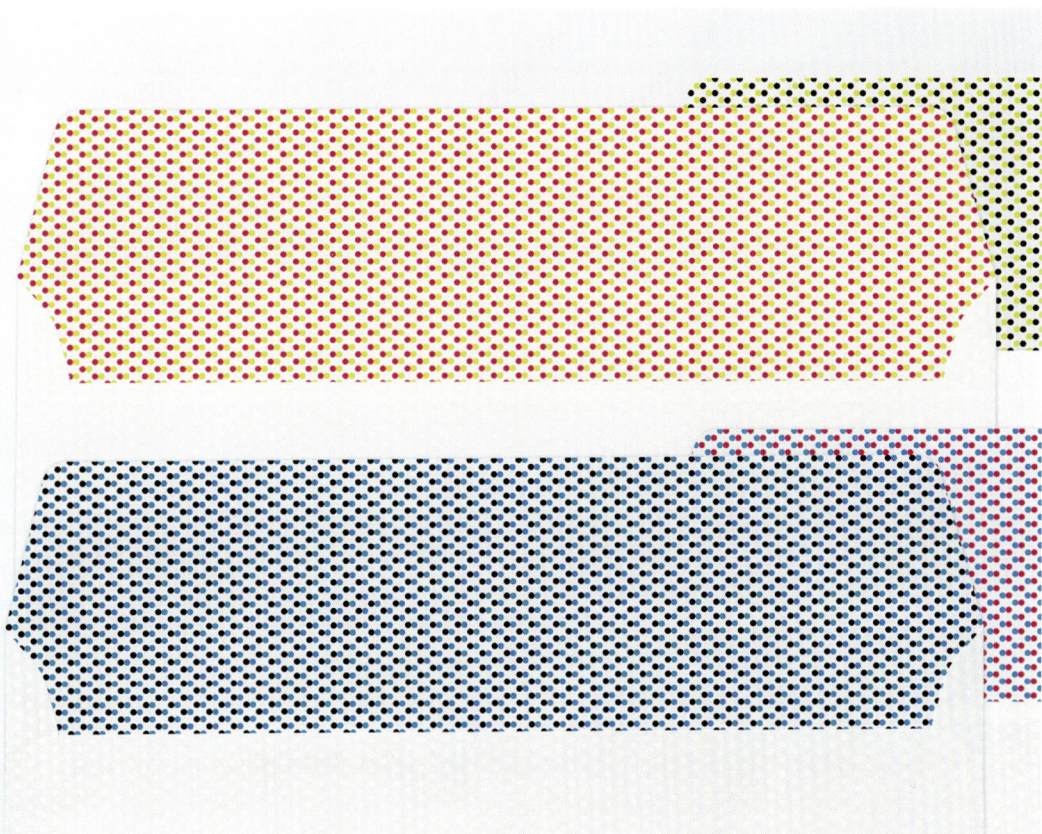

MAIO

The identity system created for MAIO was realized by the flexible use of tape, which can be applied in any media, to reflect their varied creations executed in the common way. Three different tapes were designed and printed on elegant paper, featuring patterns of the logo and the company's information. In this way they can be used as letterhead, business card, greeting cards or envelopes without printing out.

Design Agency TwoPoints.Net

MAIO
M 669315173
W maio-maio.com
MAIO
A Bruniquer, 23
08012 Barcelona
M 669315173
W maio-maio.com

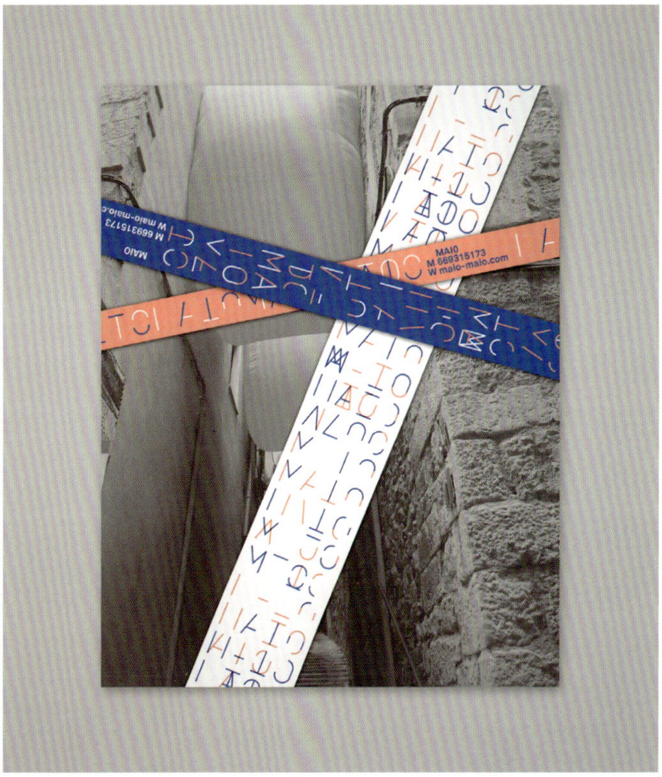
MAIO
M 669315173
W maio-maio.com

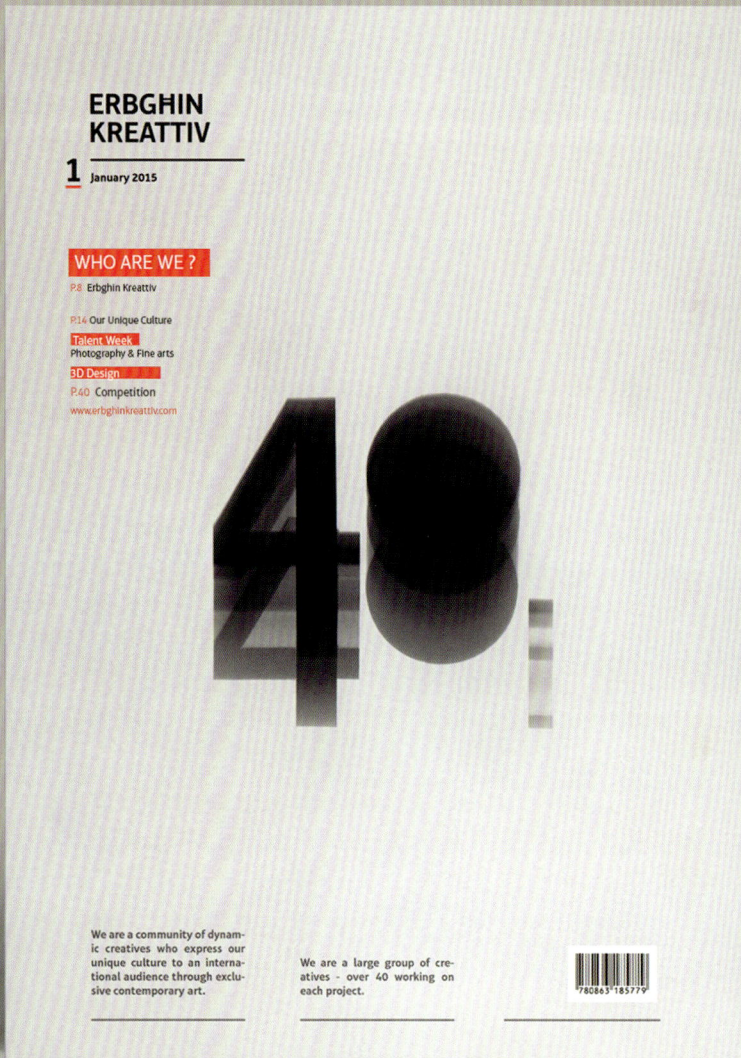

Erbgħin Kreattiv Magazine Covers

This project is a proposal for Erbgħin Kreattiv magazine. Andrew Carter experimented with varied forms of 40 to produce playful covers for different issues.

Designer Andrew Carter

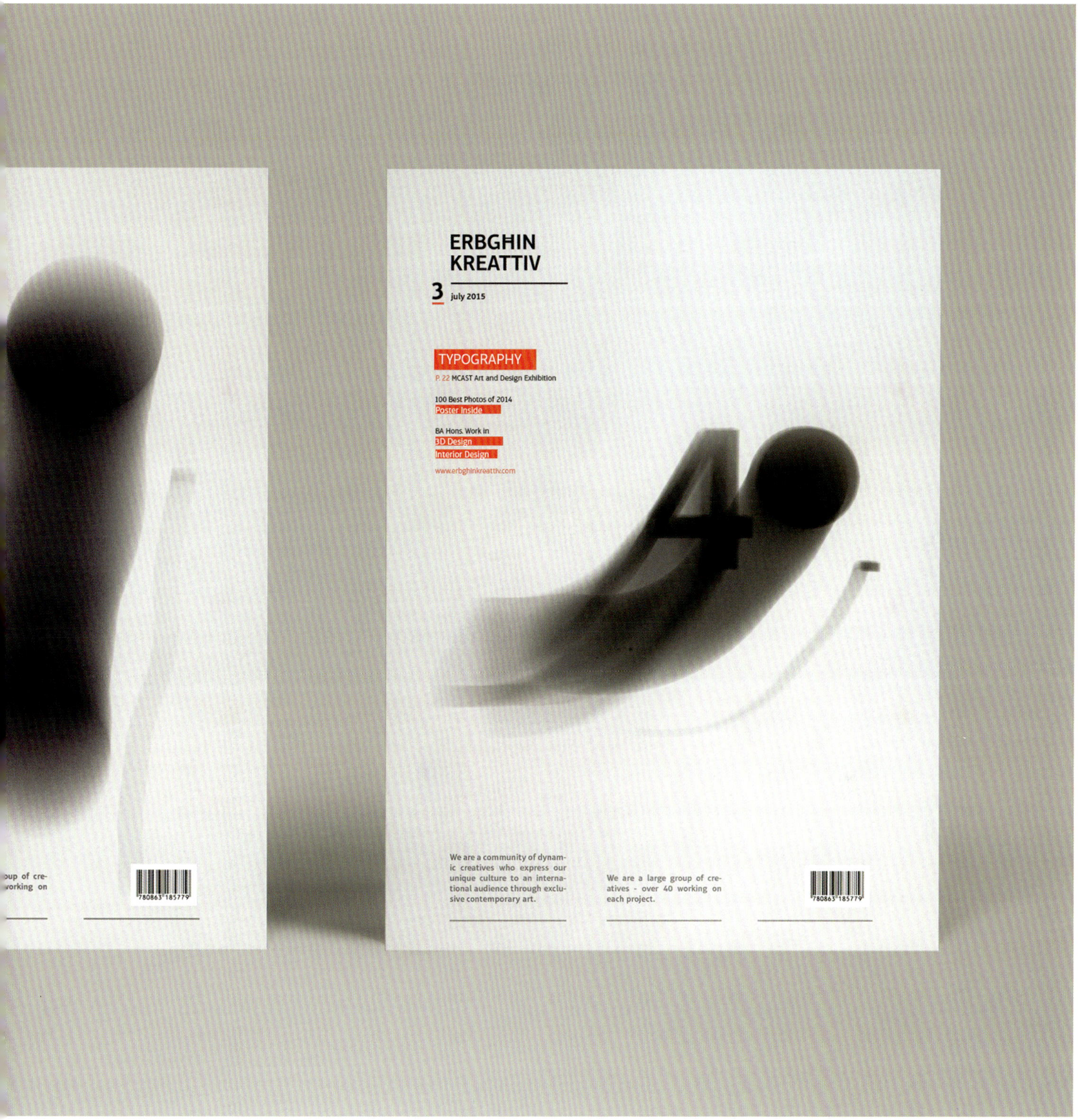

**ERBGHIN
KREATTIV**

3 july 2015

TYPOGRAPHY

P. 22 MCAST Art and Design Exhibition

100 Best Photos of 2014
Poster Inside

BA Hons. Work in
3D Design
Interior Design
www.erbghinkreattiv.com

We are a community of dynamic creatives who express our
unique culture to an international audience through exclusive contemporary art.

We are a large group of creatives - over 40 working on
each project.

oup of cre-
working on

Living Room

Living Room is an annual live art event that sees the Auckland CBD showcase energetic and spontaneous performance art. 485 Design wanted the artwork to be simple but remain abstract and attracting. By blending and overlapping images of different performances, they created a kaleidoscope of diversified art and performance, showing that performance art blended with a twist. In this way the visual identity invites the public to feel the movement, see the artistic performance, and enjoy the creative spectacle on show in the city.

Design Agency
485 Design
Designer
Nathan Chambers

Art + *Performance* in the City
26 Oct - 4 Nov · Aotea Square
www.aucklandcouncil.govt.nz/events

BRITISH COUNCIL

Waitematā Local Board

Couch potatoes no more!

This year's Living Room invites you to the city centre for a bold infusion of art and performance. Aotea Square and surrounds are energised with fresh, quirky, fun, interactive and slightly alternative acts, rolling out each lunchtime and evening.

Assembled by award-winning choreographer MaryJane O'Reilly, Living Room offers fresh twists on everything from BMX to kapa haka and hip hop, marching girls, go-go dancing and more.

Living Room, brought to you by the Waitematā Local Board, is an annual 10-day public art event featuring artists from overseas and outstanding local talent in a series of performances that will bring the city centre alive.

BRITISH COUNCIL

Waitematā Local Board

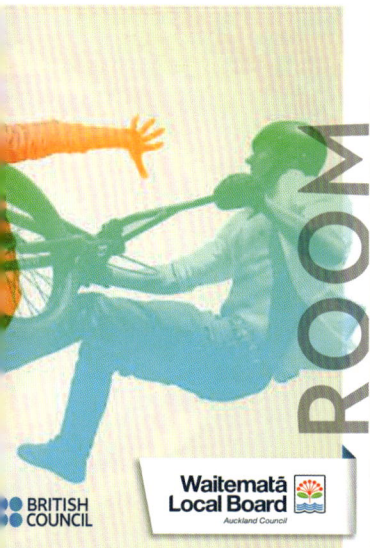

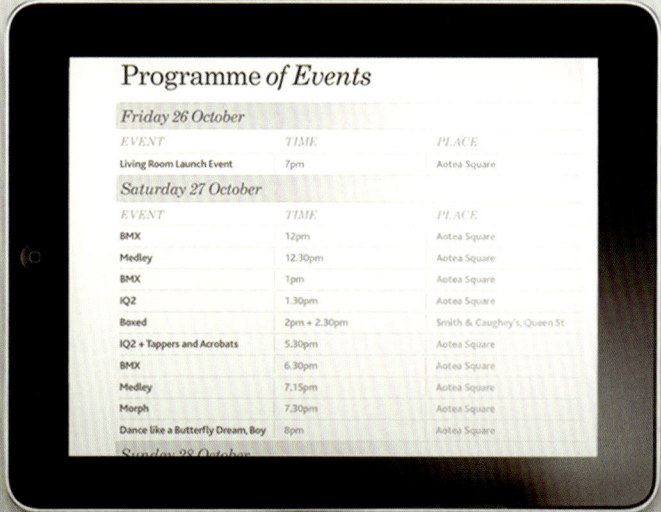

Programme of Events

Friday 26 October

EVENT	TIME	PLACE
Living Room Launch Event	7pm	Aotea Square

Saturday 27 October

EVENT	TIME	PLACE
BMX	12pm	Aotea Square
Medley	12.30pm	Aotea Square
BMX	1pm	Aotea Square
IQ2	1.30pm	Aotea Square
Boxed	2pm + 2.30pm	Smith & Caughey's, Queen St
IQ2 + Tappers and Acrobats	5.30pm	Aotea Square
BMX	6.30pm	Aotea Square
Medley	7.15pm	Aotea Square
Morph	7.30pm	Aotea Square
Dance like a Butterfly Dream, Boy	8pm	Aotea Square

Sunday 28 October

EVENT	TIME	PLACE
Dance like a Butterfly Dream, Boy	8pm	Aotea Square

Sunday 28 October

EVENT	TIME	PLACE
BMX	12pm	Aotea Square
Medley	12.30pm	Aotea Square

UNA
NOCHE
EN EL
MUSEO

Shawn Levy

15.11   cny   20 hs

CNY

CNY – Una noche en el museo (Night at the musuem) was a university project finished by Emilia Ferraresso. The idea was to create a visual identity for the fictional New York Film Festival. The objective was to choose one film to create its respective identity. The communicational purpose was to bring to life inanimate elements found in a museum through a classic and elegant design. The overlapping images indicate the ridiculous yet fantastic experience in this movie.

Designer & Illustrator
Emilia Ferraresso

UNA NOCHE EN EL MUSEO

Shawn Levy

CINE DE NUEVA YORK

제4회 서울레코드페어
4TH RECORD & CD FAIR IN SEOUL
2014. 6. 28. 土 - 29. 日 12PM - 8PM
무료입장 FREE ENTRANCE

레코드페어 한정반:
언니네이발관 <가장 보통의 존재>
V.A.: ILLIONAIRE RECORDS <11:11>
노브레인 <청년 폭도 맹진가> 2LP
DJ SOULSCAPE <180 GRAM BEAT>
김목인 <음악가 자신의 노래+1>

WWW.RECORDFAIR.KR

PLATOON
KUNSTHALLE

#97-22 · NONHYEON-DONG · GANGNAM-GU · SEOUL · REPUBLIC OF KOREA
TEL: +82-(0)2-3447-1191~7 · FAX: +82-(0)2-3447-1198
WWW.KUNSTHALLE.COM · OPENING HOURS: MON — SAT. 11 AM — 1 AM

5th Record & CD Fair in Seoul

Record & CD Fair in Seoul is a domestic sale event to embody record labels, musicians and music fans. Studio fnt was commissioned to make the art direction for the visual language and graphics of the entire event, including teaser and main posters, banners, postcards, fliers, web banners, leaflets, signage, etc.

The challenge was to attract new audience while maintain the retro look of the vinyl records. Moreover, the event brings together many different vendors, so it was important that the main graphics were strong enough to bring together the individual labels. Finally, the contemporary identity was created by simply using a solid black color of vinyl records to repeatedly appear as graphic motifs. It also helped them to minimize the cost of production.

Design Studio
Studio fnt

제4회 서울레코드페어
4TH RECORD & CD FAIR IN SEOUL
2014. 6. 28. 土 - 29. 日
12PM - 8PM
무료입장
FREE ENTRANCE

레코드페어 한정반:
언니네이발관 <가장 보통의 존재>
V.A.: ILLIONAIRE RECORDS <11:11>
노브레인 <청년 폭도 맹진가> 2LP
DJ SOULSCAPE <180 GRAM BEAT>
김목인 <음악가 자신의 노래+1>

WWW.RECORDFAIR.KR

DOORLY & FRIENDS... ANNIE MAC & MIKE SKINNER DJ SET & DUSKY & HEIDI & JUSTIN MARTIN & HUXLEY & SONNY FODERA & THE CUBAN BROTHERS & ARTWORK & HAUSWERKS & TAN DEM & MAT FORMAT & **FRIENDS & FRIENDS & FRIENDS**

SAT. 9TH JULY
BROWNSTOCK FESTIVAL @ THE GOOD SHED
MORRIS FARM - ESSEX - UK - CM3 6SG

DOORLY & FRIENDS @ PIKES
MONDAYS @ IBIZA ROCKS HOU
WITH **VERY VERY SPECIAL SECR**

4TH, 11TH, 18TH OF JULY & 19TH S
POOL PARTY/DINNER & ALL NIGHT D
GUESTLIST ONLY: **EVENTS@IBIZAR**

Doorly & Friends

Doorly & Friends is a live music show held by the singer Doorly. It was the first time that Pornographitti Design Explicito designed for an international customer. But they gave out an absolutely impressive design that can be used as motion graphics or print design. The artistic and bold visuals attempt to cast a great impact on its audience.

Design Agency
Pornographitti Design Explicito

DOORLY & FRIENDS... CLAUDE VONSTROKE & DERRICK CARTER & WILL TRAMP & TAN DEM & NICOLA BEAR & JAY NEWMAN & **FRIENDS & FRIENDS & FRIENDS**

FRI. 15TH JULY
BEAT-HERDER FESTIVAL @ THE WOODS STAGE
RIBBLE VALLEY - LANCASHIRE - UK

L · FOUR **EXCLUSIVE** PARTIES

KES HOTEL

ST DJ'S & FRIENDS EVERY WEEK

PM – 6AM
ERY
SE.COM

RLE

▰▰▰▰▰▰▰ 2D OR 3D ▰▰▰▰▰▰▰

According to scientists, our brain tends to translate what we see into a real object because of our cognition to the world and our common sense. For example, we tend to regard a two-dimensional ambiguous line drawing as a three-dimensional cube. It is known as Necker Cube illustration or the Impossible Cube Illusion.

This phenomenon is often used to resemble three-dimensional object such as architectures. It can also deliver an image between real and unreal, leaving us a deeper impression and forcing us to think from different perspectives.

K

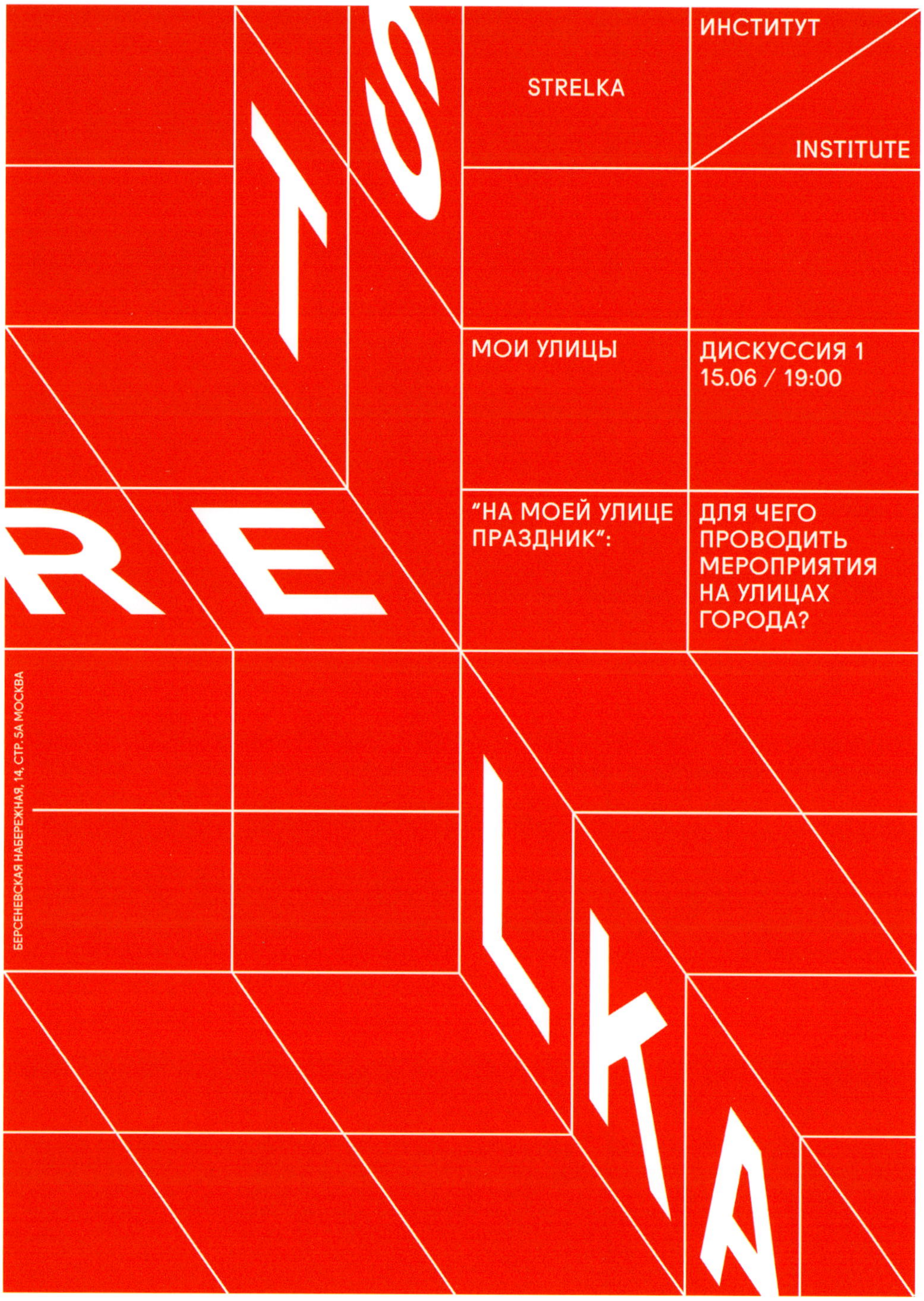

ИНСТИТУТ

STRELKA

INSTITUTE

МОИ УЛИЦЫ

ДИСКУССИЯ 1
15.06 / 19:00

"НА МОЕЙ УЛИЦЕ
ПРАЗДНИК":

ДЛЯ ЧЕГО
ПРОВОДИТЬ
МЕРОПРИЯТИЯ
НА УЛИЦАХ
ГОРОДА?

БЕРСЕНЕВСКАЯ НАБЕРЕЖНАЯ, 14, СТР. 5A МОСКВА

БЕРСЕНЕВСКАЯ НАБЕРЕЖНАЯ, 14, СТР. 5A МОСКВА

My Street

A series of discussions about the streets of Moscow.

Design Agency Strelka Institute
Designer Anna Kulachek

STRELKA

ИНСТИТУТ

INSTITUTE

МОИ УЛИЦЫ

ДИСКУССИЯ 2
14.07 / 19:00

ДЕТИ НА УЛИЦЕ.
БЕЗОПАСНОСТЬ,
ОБРАЗОВАНИЕ,
РАЗВЛЕЧЕНИЕ

ИНСТИТУТ

STRELKA

INSTITUTE

ДИСКУССИЯ 3
27.07 / 19:00

МОИ УЛИЦЫ

УЛИЦЫ МОСКВЫ

ТРАНЗИТ,
ПРОГУЛКИ,
РАЗВЛЕЧЕНИЕ

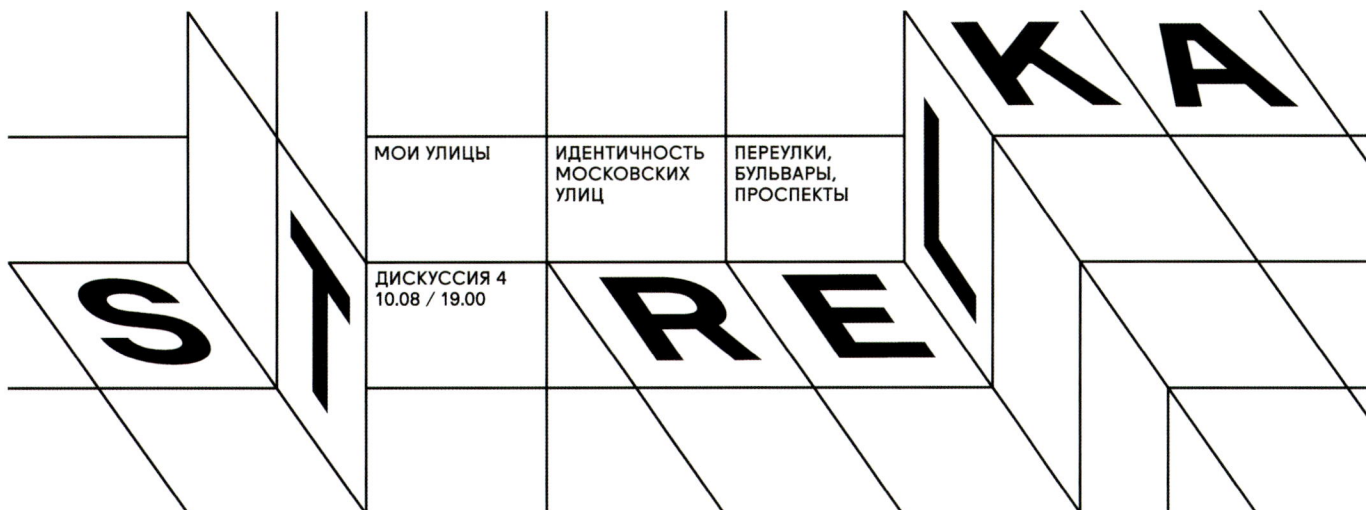

МОИ УЛИЦЫ

ИДЕНТИЧНОСТЬ
МОСКОВСКИХ
УЛИЦ

ПЕРЕУЛКИ,
БУЛЬВАРЫ,
ПРОСПЕКТЫ

ДИСКУССИЯ 4
10.08 / 19.00

TEDx

Ted is a unique platform that gathers and disseminates the best innovations in all areas combined. These events allow audience to hear the speeches of different topics from a series of speakers, broaden their perspective, and exchange ideas.

It is in this perspective that byHAUS made the official identification for the Montreal branch, which formed the colors of the brand constantly diverted around "perspective". It is a visual game that destabilizes surprises and symbolically leads to looking at things from a new angle.

Design Agency byHAUS
Designer Philippe Archontakis, Martin Laliberté
Project Lead Catherine Brosseau
Animation Designer Eltoro studio
Music Underground productions
Camera et stopmotion byHAUS
Vinyl Lamcom
Client TEDx Montréal

TEDx Montreal

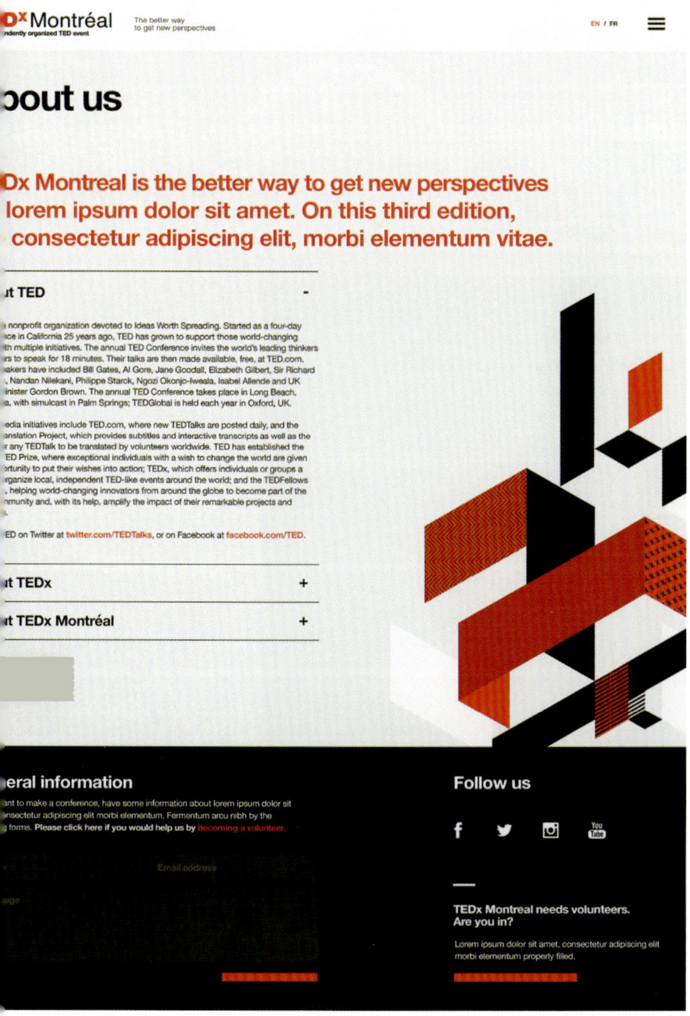
Dx Montréal
The better way
to get new perspectives
EN / FR
bout us
Dx Montreal is the better way to get new perspectives
lorem ipsum dolor sit amet. On this third edition,
consectetur adipiscing elit, morbi elementum vitae.
ut TED
nonprofit organization devoted to Ideas Worth Spreading. Started as a four-day
ice in California 25 years ago, TED has grown to support those world-changing
th multiple initiatives. The annual TED Conference invites the world's leading thinkers
rs to speak for 18 minutes. Their talks are then made available, free, at TED.com.
akers have included Bill Gates, Al Gore, Jane Goodall, Elizabeth Gilbert, Sir Richard
, Nandan Nilekani, Philippe Starck, Ngozi Okonjo-Iweala, Isabel Allende and UK
inister Gordon Brown. The annual TED Conference takes place in Long Beach,
a, with simulcast in Palm Springs; TEDGlobal is held each year in Oxford, UK.
edia initiatives include TED.com, where new TEDTalks are posted daily, and the
anslation Project, which provides subtitles and interactive transcripts as well as the
any TEDTalk to be translated by volunteers worldwide. TED has established the
ED Prize, where exceptional individuals with a wish to change the world are given
rtunity to put their wishes into action; TEDx, which offers individuals or groups a
rganize local, independent TED-like events around the world; and the TEDFellows
, helping world-changing innovators from around the globe to become part of the
nmunity and, with its help, amplify the impact of their remarkable projects and
ED on Twitter at twitter.com/TEDTalks, or on Facebook at facebook.com/TED.
ut TEDx +
ut TEDx Montréal +
eral information
ant to make a conference, have some information about lorem ipsum dolor sit
nsectetur adipiscing elit morbi elementum. Fermentum arcu nibh by the
forms. Please click here if you would help us by becoming a volunteer.
Email address
Follow us
TEDx Montreal needs volunteers.
Are you in?
Lorem ipsum dolor sit amet, consectetur adipiscing elit
morbi elementum properly filled.

Perspectives

TEDx Montréal
Sébastien Tanguay
PARLEZ-MOI DE
design & science
Perspectives

Gamers

Gamers is a logo created for a video game store. The inspiration for the development of this visual identity was the internal networks of command and console video games. On the other hand, the logo was to symbolize the buttons of the controls, and thereby formed the "G" of Gamers with linear strokes and in three dimensions. Finally he opted for two neon colors (red and green) that results from the origin of competition and the need to differentiate the participants.

Designer
Angel J Gonzales Echegaray

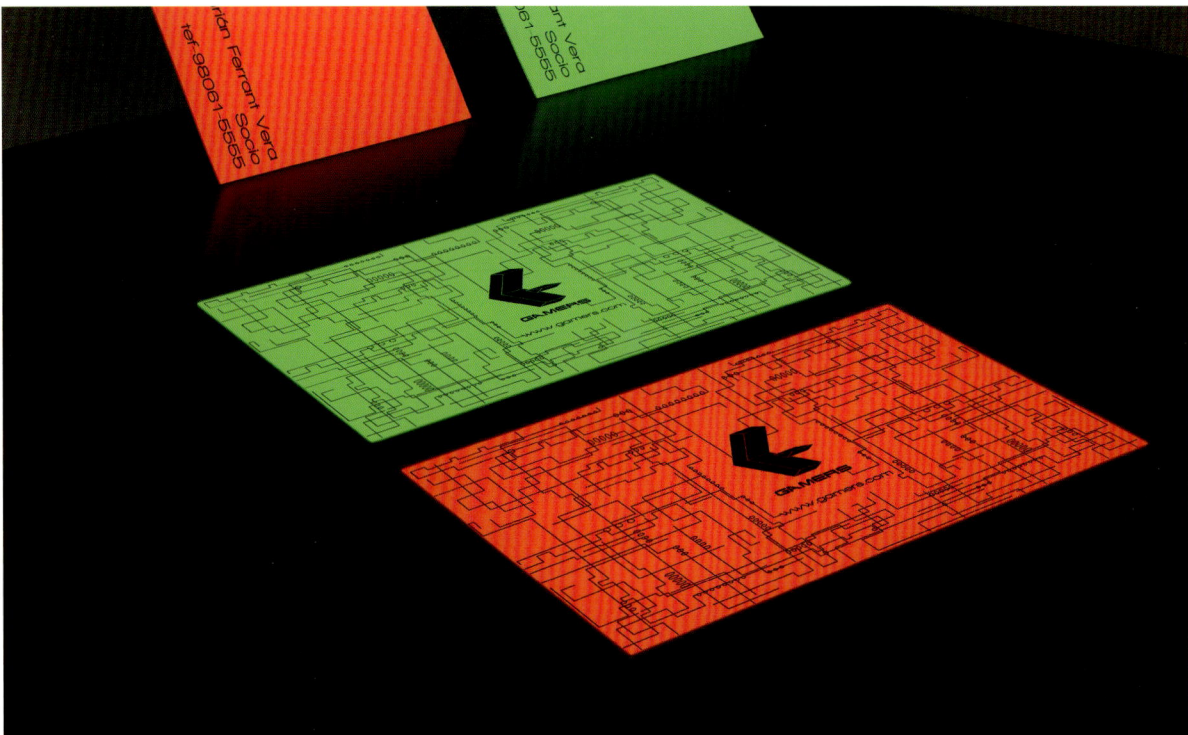

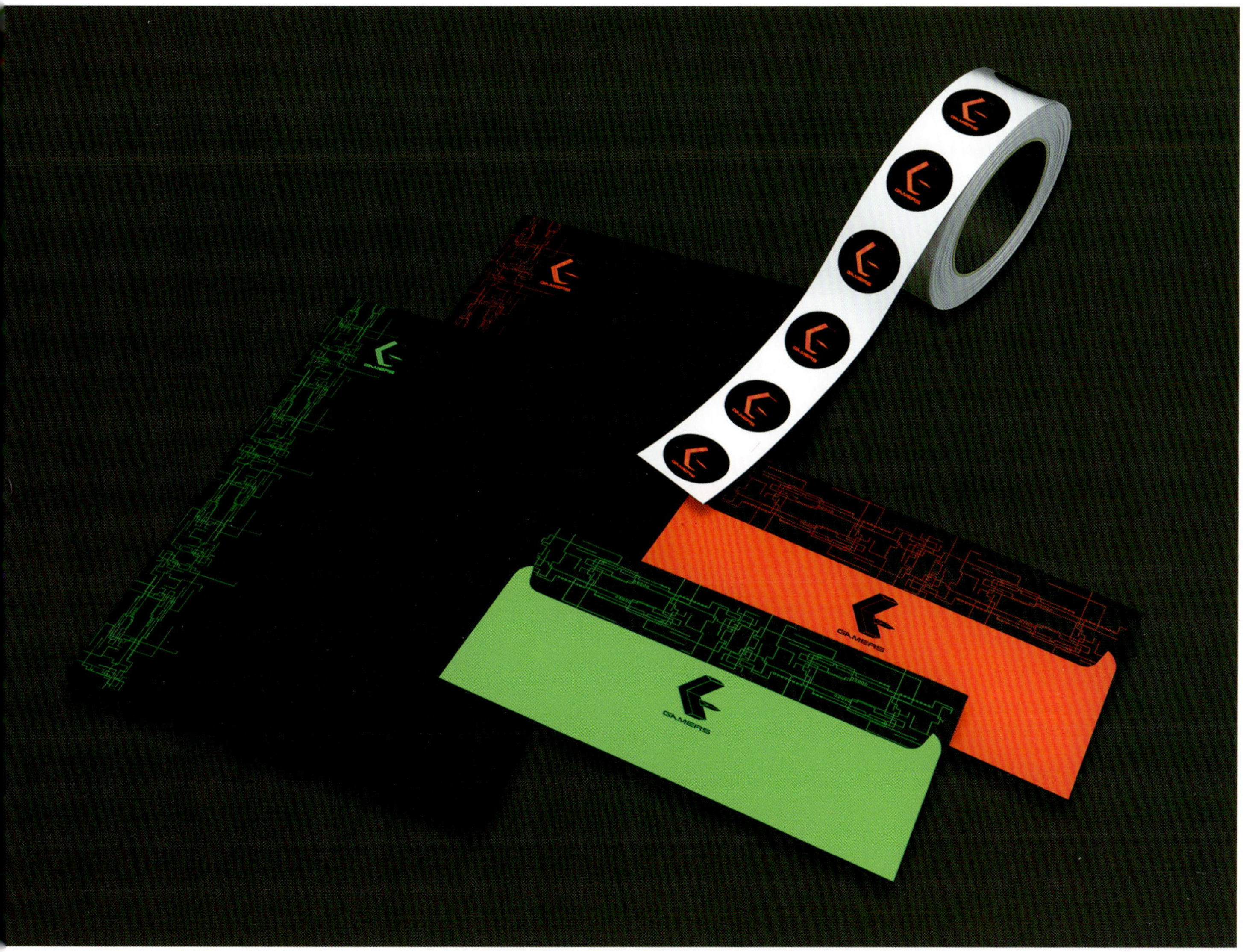
GAMERS

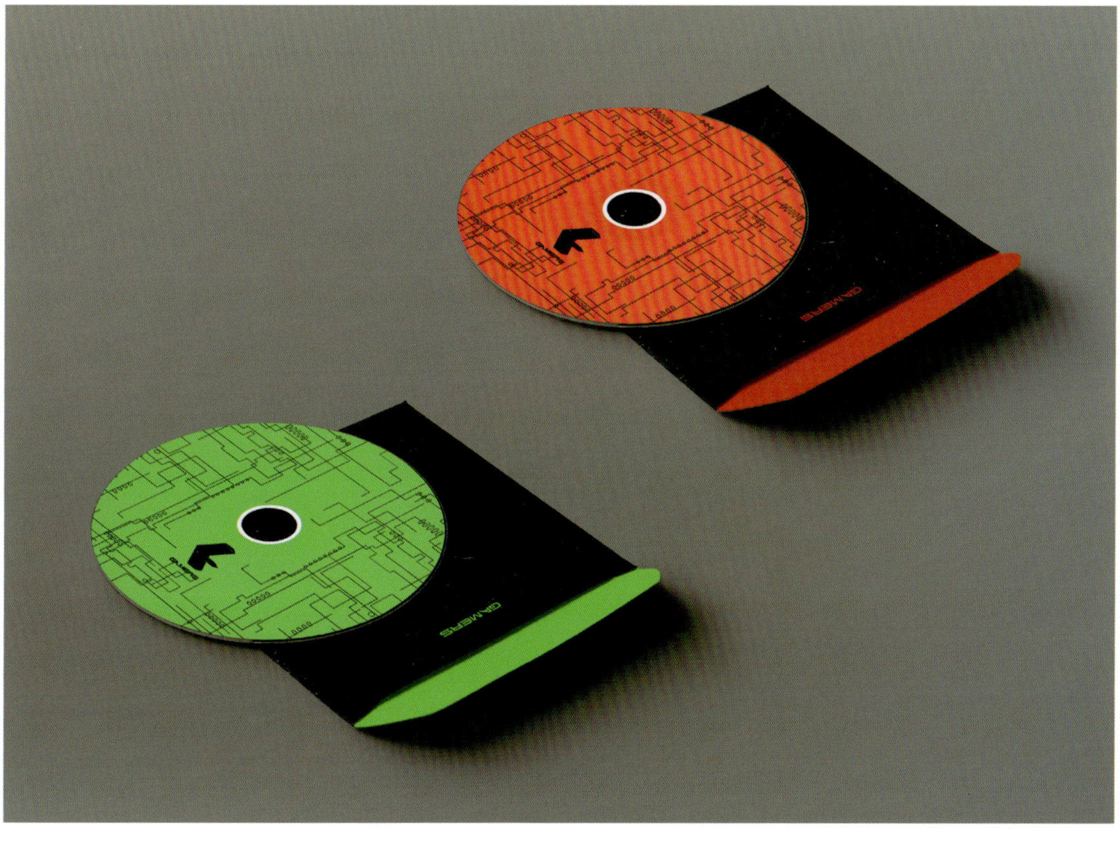

PO⬜SI-
TIVE⬜
SP⬜ACE
积⬜极空间

PO⬜SI-
TIVE⬜
SPAC⬜E
积⬜极空间

Positive Space

In architecture, the external space that is defined with order and function is called positive space. The opposite is negative space. Positive Space is described as small self-organized art organizations in present-day China. The organizations is the hub of the whole art system, linking collages, galleries and museums. They are embedded in different art forms.

Design Agency another design
Design Director Liu Zhao
Art Director Zhan Huode
Designer Liu Zhao, Zhan Huode

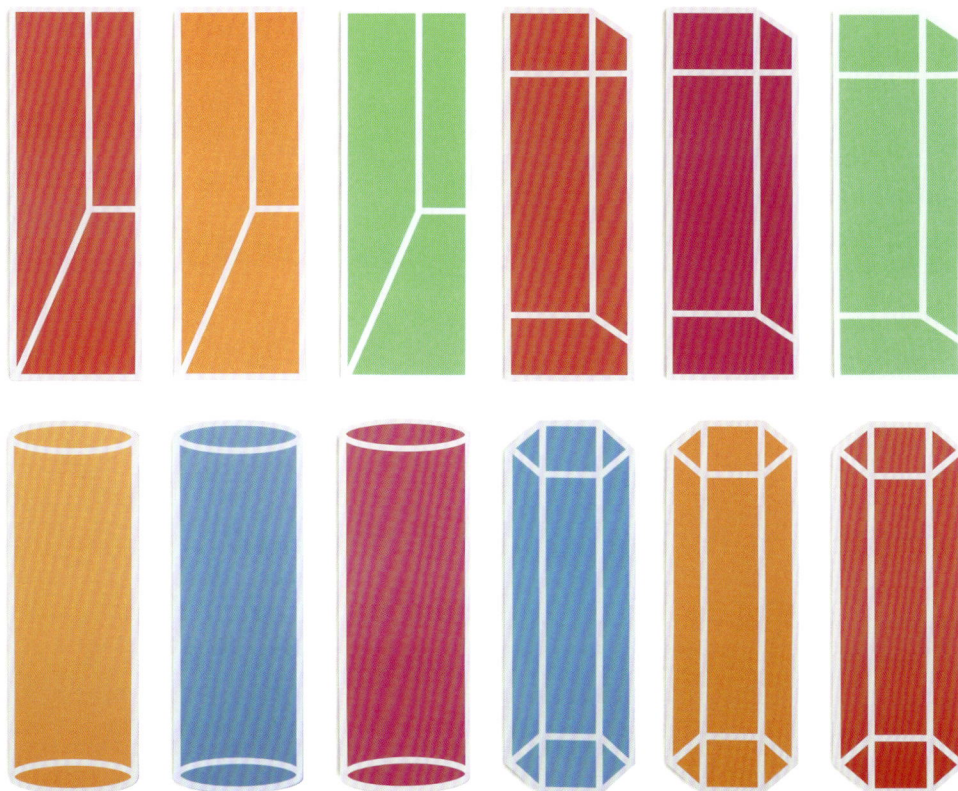

POSI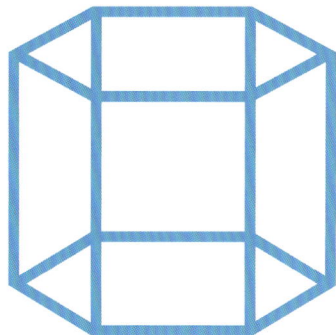-

展览主办：广东时代美术馆 **/ 展览时间：**2014/3/29—5/4 **/ 开幕时间：**2014/3/29

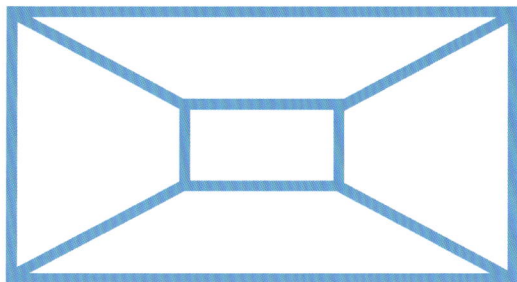TIVE

策展人：鲍栋 **/ 观察员：**蔡影茜、胡斌、李一凡、梁健华、石青

SPAC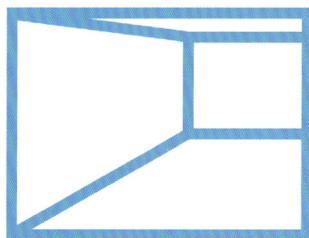E

参展空间：

北村独立工场（成都）、二楼出版机构（北京）、分泌场（北京）、观察社（广州）、黄边站（广州）、箭厂空间（北京）、器·Haus 空间（重庆）、上午空间（上海）、实验工作坊（成都）、腾挪空间（广州）、扬子江论坛（武汉）、杂货铺空间（广州）

积极空间

主办机构： 　　　　**特别鸣谢：** 　　　　**媒体支持：**

≡ 时代美术馆　　时代地产　　雅昌艺术网　　创览生活艺术地图
TIMES MUSEUM　　TIMES PROPERTY　　WWW.ARTRON.NET

广州市白云大道北黄边北路时代玫瑰园三期 广东时代美术馆（地铁 2 号线黄边站 D 出口对面）
免费开放，周一闭馆，节假日除外

2014/3/29-5/4

Transit

Transit is a traveler's kit for contemporary man, concerning their odor and ambitious.

Alejandro Flores adopted spaceman as a concept to interpret its branding story. For four essential products, he designed varied visual identities based on the three dimensional polygons to convey a cosmic atmosphere to customers.

Design Agency
Human. Brand Development
Designer Alejandro Flores

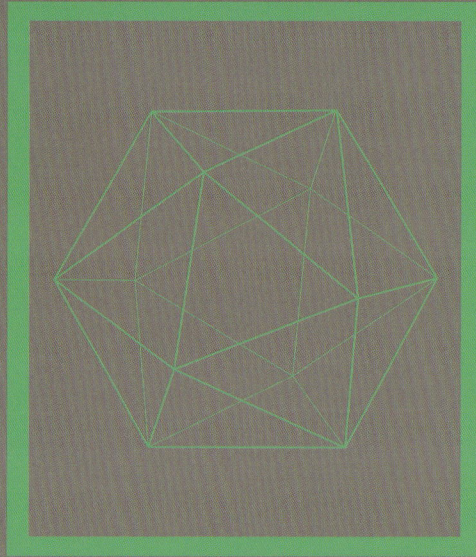

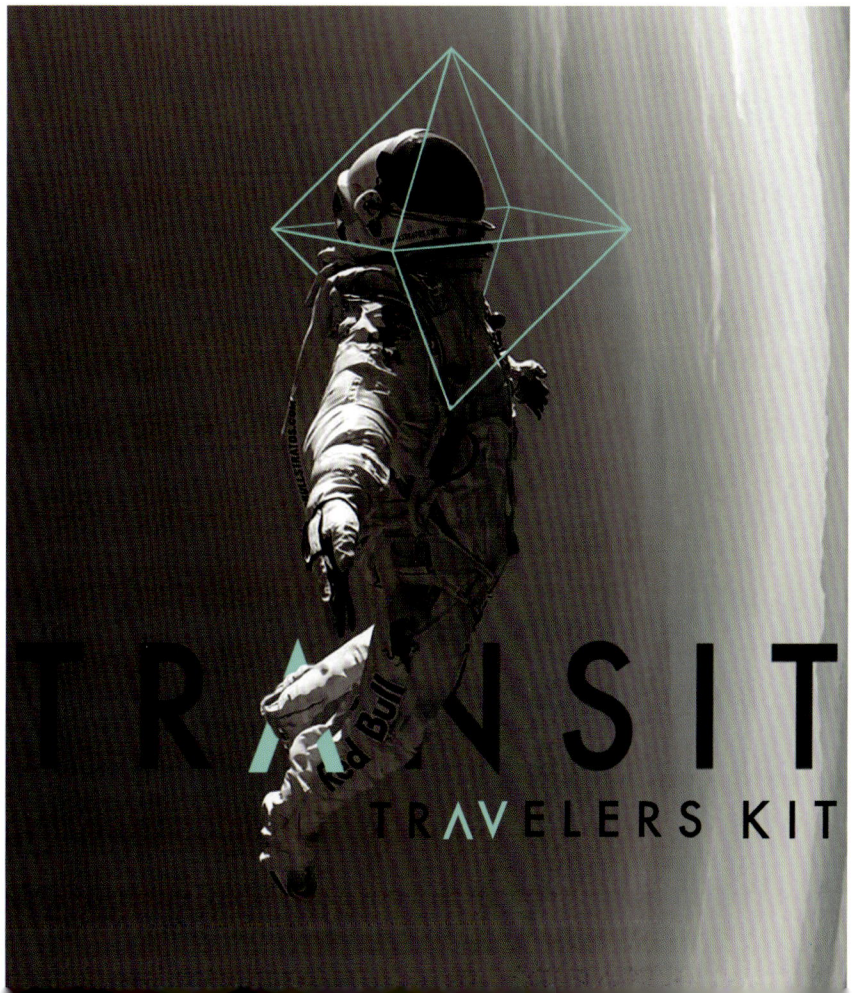

PosLodz!

PosLodz! is a cultural and entertainment association. The name combines the phrase "put some sugar!" with the name of the city where they are based – Lodz. The logo shape is inspired by two sugar cubes, representing culture and entertainment as well as referring to the infinity sign which promotes the continuous growth of art and culture.

Designer Evelina Rosinska

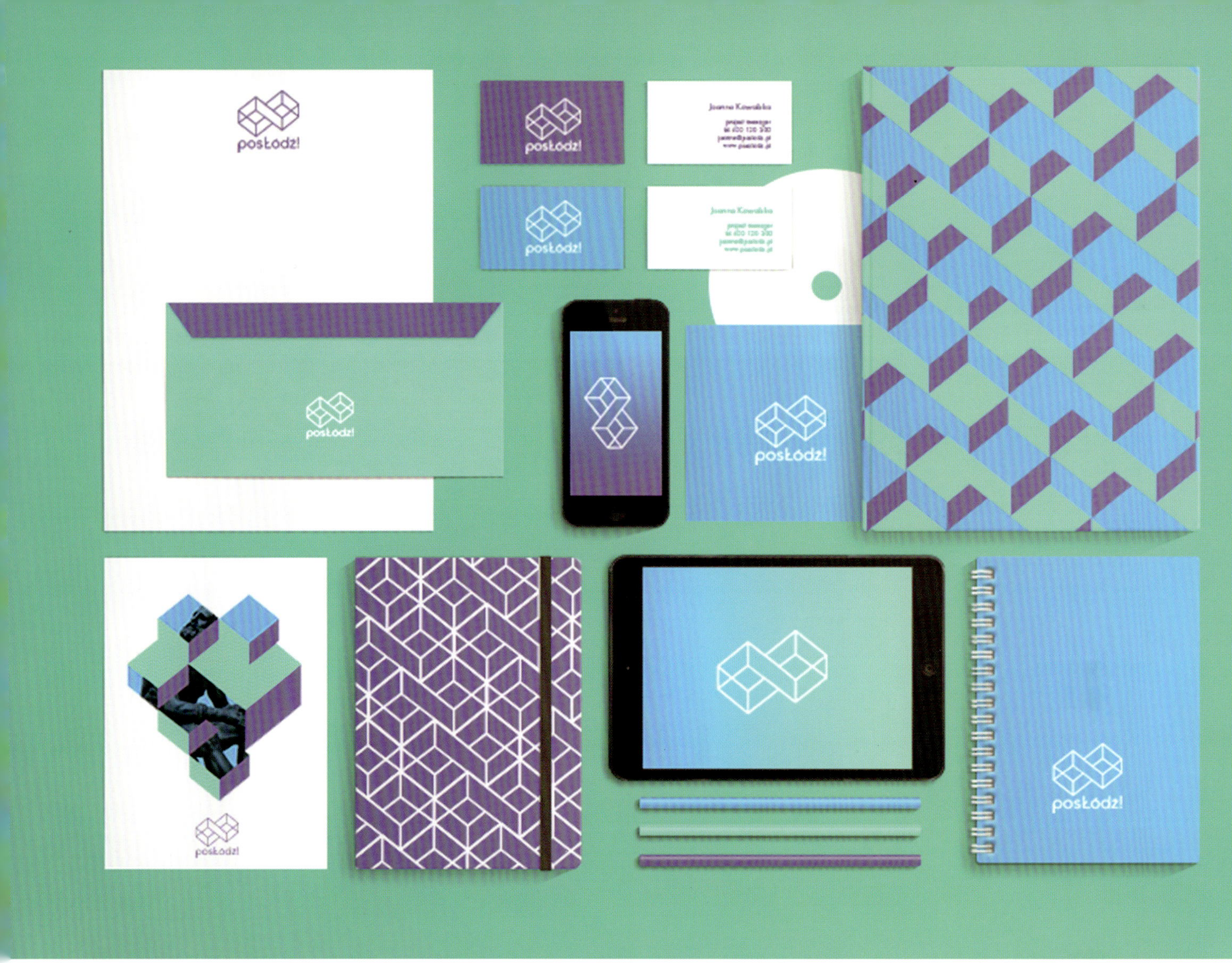
posŁódz!
Joanna Kowalska

posŁódz!
Joanna Kowalska
Adam Nowicki

Romlab

Romlab is an architectural and interior design studio in Oslo led by three energetic women. Bleed were asked to create an identity that is both friendly and dynamic, and redefine their website.

The identity was built upon the name Romlab (room + laboratory) and to resonate with their philosophy of construction and space experience in the shape of cubic. The logotype was derived from the experimentation of two components – rom and lab. The designers kept the most intriguing and legible composition as a logotype, and used the other shapes developed as a foundation for the identity.

The result is flexible yet structured, and easily adapts to any device. It builds up a dynamic and cheerful image without losing the seriousness and professionalism of the company.

Design Agency
Bleed
Designer
Camille Dorival,
Svein Haakon Lia,
Kristoffer Lundberg

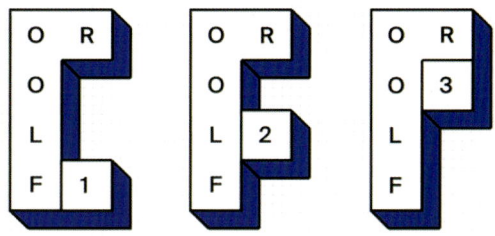

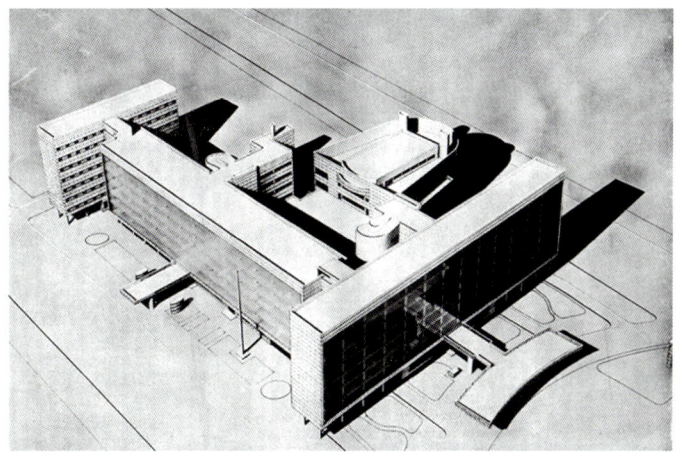

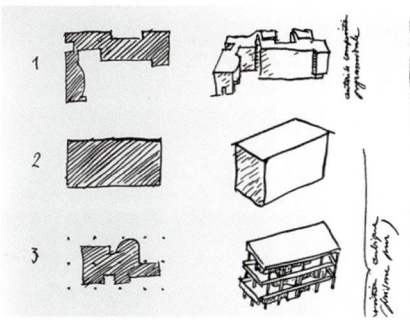

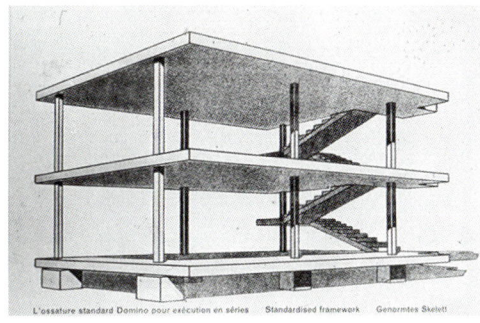

olorisation
shapes

Rom
+Lab

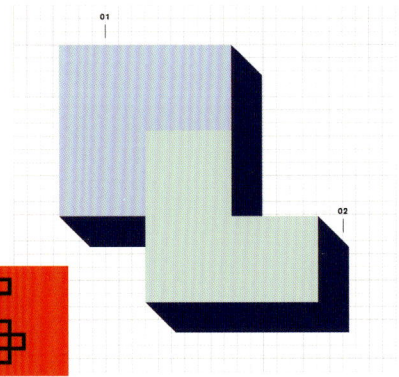

	From bottom left	From top left	From top	From top right	From bottom right	From bottom
Shape 1						
Shape 1						
Shape 2						
Shape 3						
Shape 4						

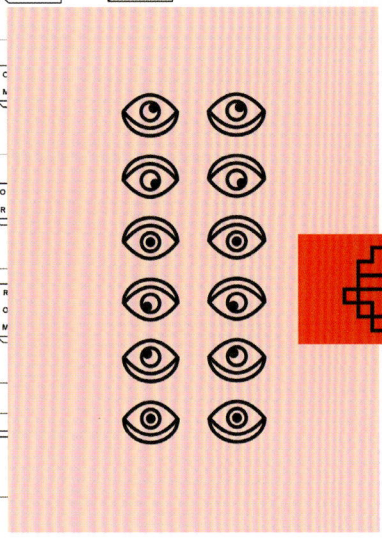

01

02

1. Construction
unc a urna non est congue tempor
sed eu arcu. Mauris congue metus
ipsum, eget feugiat eros connect et.
Vivamus sagittis nisl in justo le tricio,
sed rutrum orci scelerisque.

2. Depth
Integer dictum non tellus et malle
esuada. Nulla sed turpis sapien.
Donec mollis ultricies ante, at for the
est imperdiet neu.

3. Point of view

STATKRAFTS TRONDHEIMSKONTOR HAR FLYTTET INN I DET NYOPPFØRTE BYGGET STÅLGÅRDEN NORD, LITT SYD FORTRONDHEIM SENTRUM. BYGGET BLE TILDELT EIENDOMSPRISEN FOR 2015. ROMLABORATORIET HAR BISTÅTT STATKRAFT ME...

ROMLAB

1.
Architecture

2.
Interior
Design

3.
Based in
Oslo,
Norway

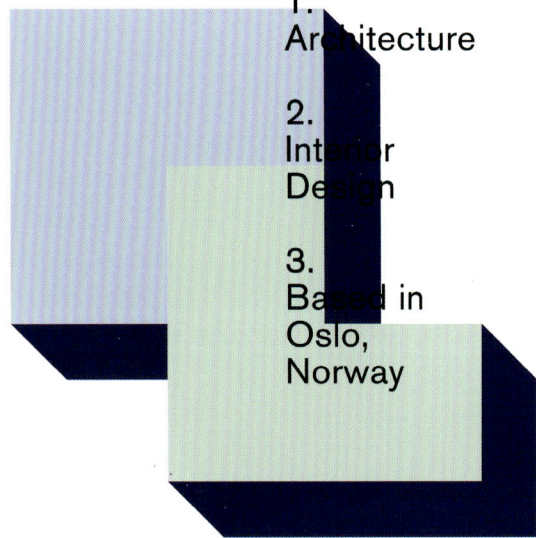

STATKRAFTS TRONDHEIMSKONTOR HAR FLYTTET INN I DET NYOPPFØRTE BYGGET STÅLGÅRDEN NORD, LITT SYD FORTRONDHEIM SENTRUM. BYGGET BLE TILDELT EIENDOMSPRISEN FOR 2015. ROMLABORATORIET HAR BISTÅTT STATKRAFT ME...

ROMLAB

1.
Architecture

2.
Interior
Design

3.
Based in
Oslo,
Norway

STATKRAFTS TRONDHEIMSKONTOR HAR FLYTTET INN I DET NYOPPFØRTE BYGGET STÅLGÅRDEN NORD, LITT SYD FORTRONDHEIM SENTRUM. BYGGET BLE TILDELT EIENDOMSPRISEN FOR 2015. ROMLABORATORIET HAR BISTÅTT STATKRAFT ME...

ROMLAB

1.
ARCHITECTURE

2.
INTERIOR
DESIGN

3.
BASED IN
OSLO,
NORWAY

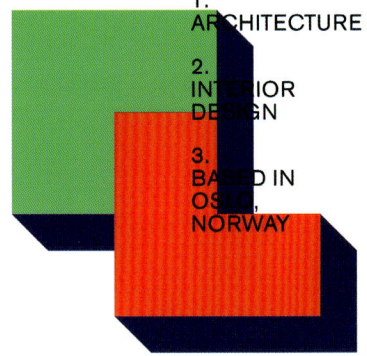

04.
Atelier de Stalingrad

Annet
project

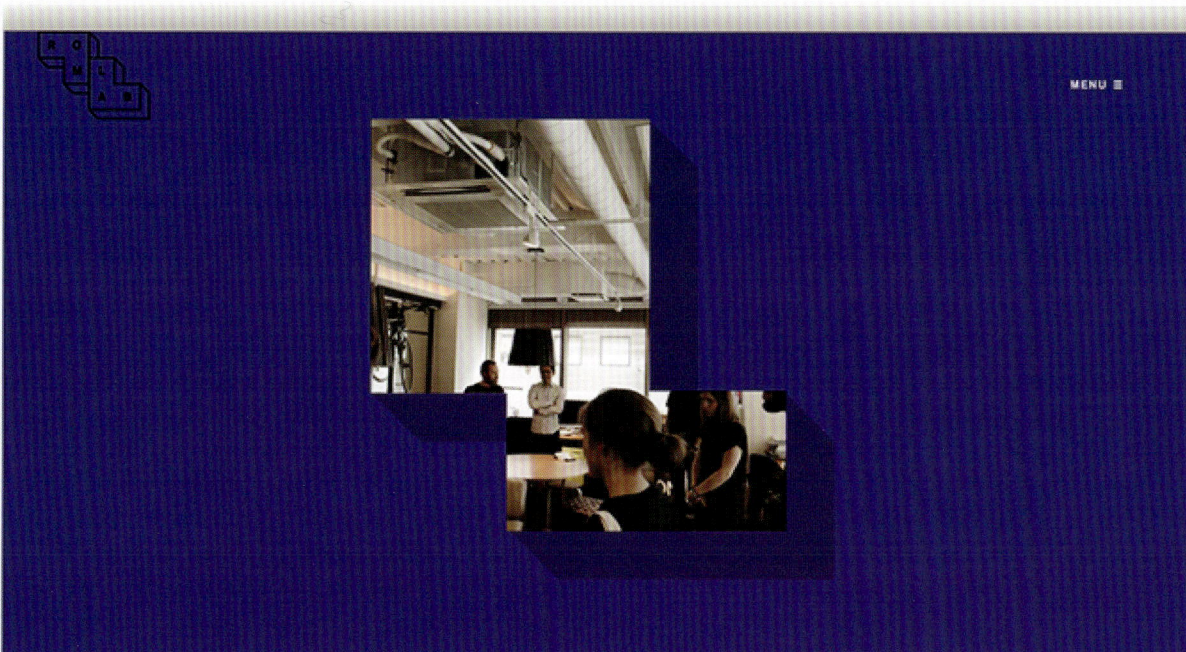

03.
Hotell rehabilitering

Kommersielt
project

02
Statkraft Trondheim

Privat
project

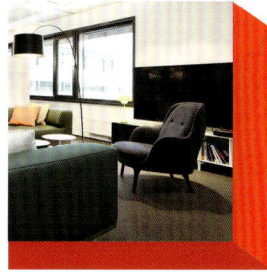

01.
Sverres gate Dorival

Annet
project

R O L
M A B

R O M
L A B

R O L
M A B

R O L
M A B

R O
M L A B

MENU ≡

R O M L A B

MENU ≡

KOMMERSIELT

Statkraft, oppgradering av kontorarealer, Lilleaker

Torshov, Oslo

←

Romlaboratoriet
Latest news, projects and life

KOMMERSIELT · 23 OCT

Tilbygg Heibergsgate

Torgatta, Oslo

KOMMERSIELT · 23 OCT

Statkraft, oppgradering av kontorarealer, Lilleaker

Torshov, Oslo

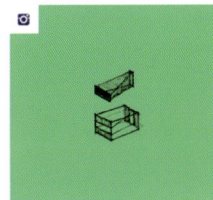

@BLEED: Le Lorem Ipsum est simplement du faux text.
Reference site about #Lorem Ipsum #architecture

23 OCT

@ROMAB: Le Lorem Ipsum est simplement du faux text.
Reference site about #Lorem Ipsum #architecture

23 OCT

KOMMERSIELT · 23 OCT

Sundvolden Hotell nybygg Krokskogen

Torshov, Oslo

KOMMERSIELT · 23 OCT

Ruseløkkveien Restaurantkonsepter

Torshov, Oslo

NEWS

Telenor Fornebu user

@BLEED: Le Lorem Ipsum est simplement du faux text.
Reference site about #Lorem Ipsum #architecture

23 OCT

@BLEED: Le Lorem Ipsum est simplement du faux text.
Reference site about #Lorem Ipsum #architecture

23 OCT

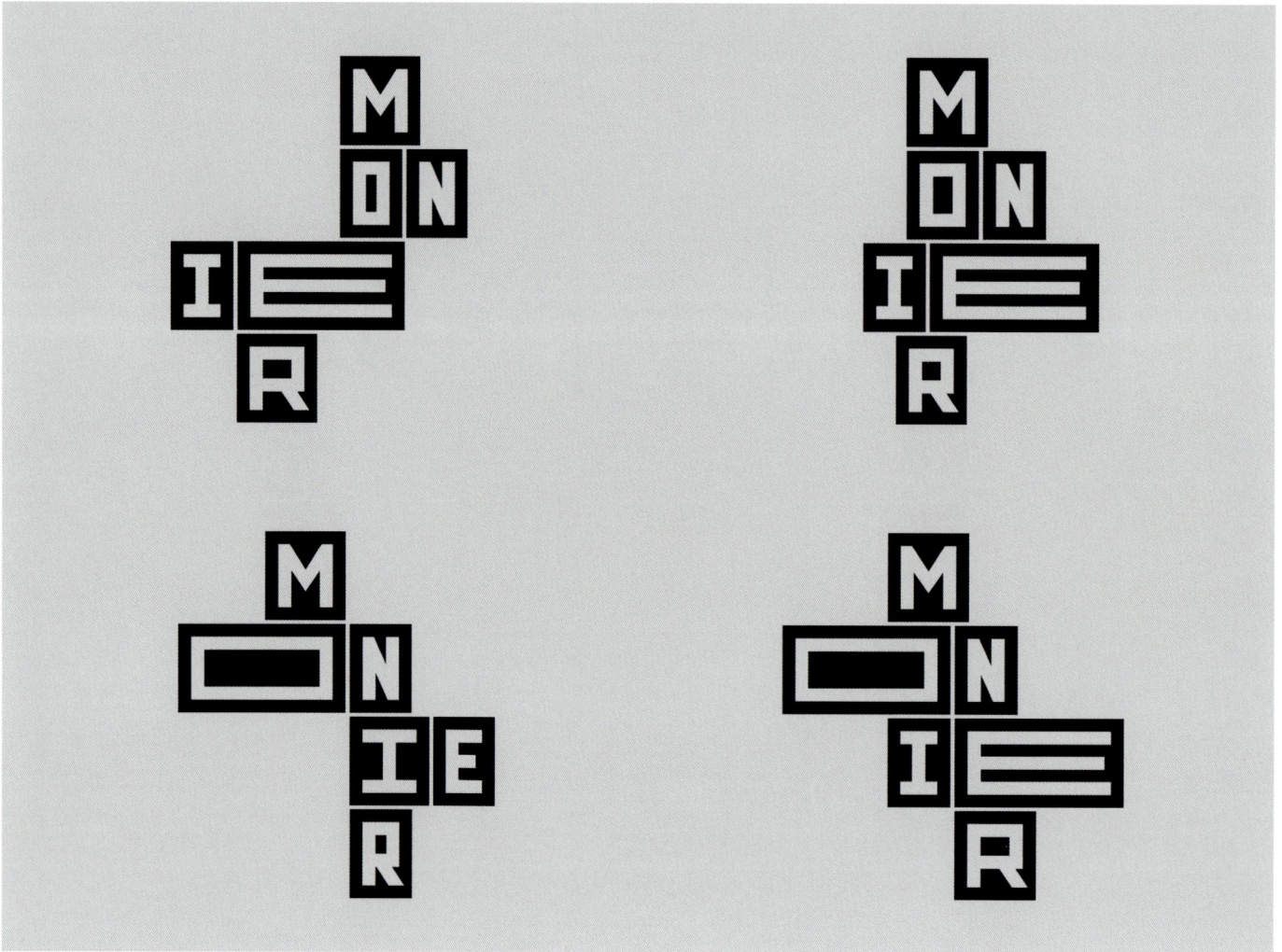

Monier

Monier is a brand new office building owned by Norwegian Property.

The visual identity for Monier was based on the building's architecture which is cubistic and solid. The idea for the logo was derived from the building's three different window shapes, which is an important characteristic of the Monier building.

As for the logotype, Bleed created a custom typeface inspired by the original signage on the construction site. The alphabet was redrawn in three different widths to fit within Monier's three shaped window concept.

Design Agency
Bleed

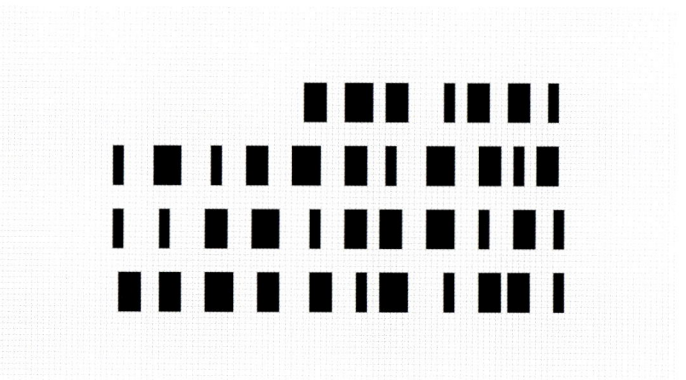

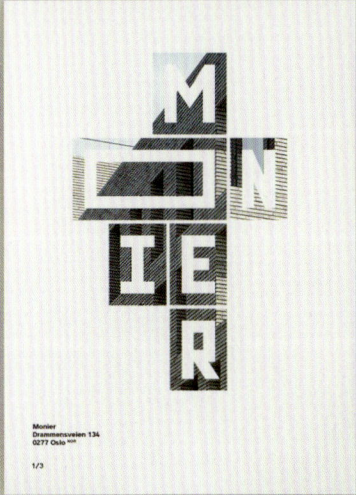

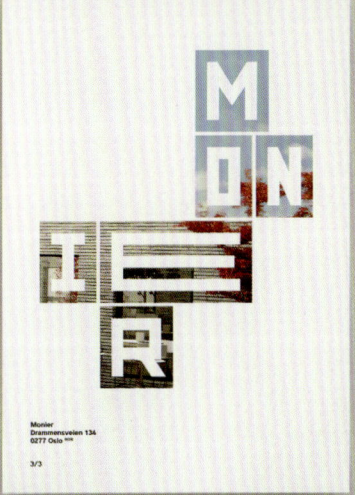

Tomas Saracenos Sundial for Spatial Echoes ▦▦▦▦▦▦▦▦▦

It took about two weeks to assemble Tomás Saracenos' installation "Sundial for Spatial Echoes", located in the main-buildings' atrium at Aker Brygge. Although the assembly took place at night, one could clearly see that the installation grew from day to day and that the atrium was less organized than usual.

Inspired by this, the visual concept for the launch identity was called "Art Under Construction". Origami-paper-statues were created based on the pentagonal shapes of the installations. These were used to tell the same story about the assembly in advertising and invitations.

Design Agency
Bureau Bruneau
Designer
Ludvig Bruneau Rossow
Client
Norwegian Property /
The Kistefos Museum

Senses of Fern – The New Landscape & Environment Art Show

"Senses of Fern" is an exhibition about ferns, held in one of the most representing green house in Taipei. The design was inspired by the curator's statement – a fern in jade. Designers re-built the green house in an abstract form, with the fern placed at the corner. The "green house" has developed in different organic forms just as the natural habitat to enrich the design application.

Design Director Jacky Wong
Designer I Chyi Chang

覺蕨

新創
環境藝術特展

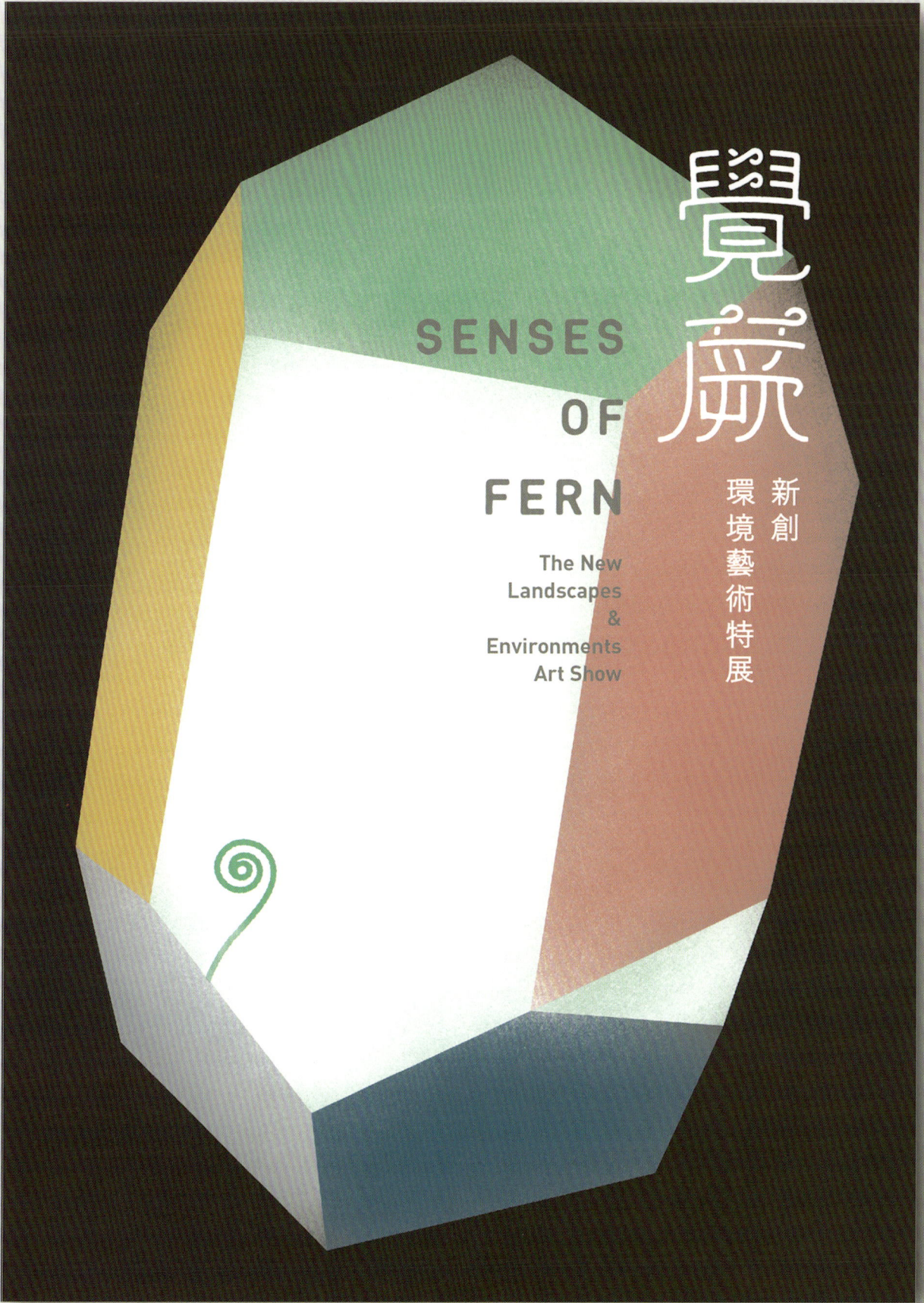

SENSES
OF
FERN

The New
Landscapes
&
Environments
Art Show

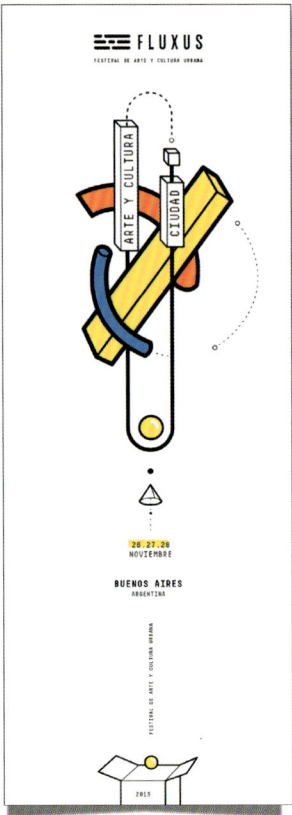

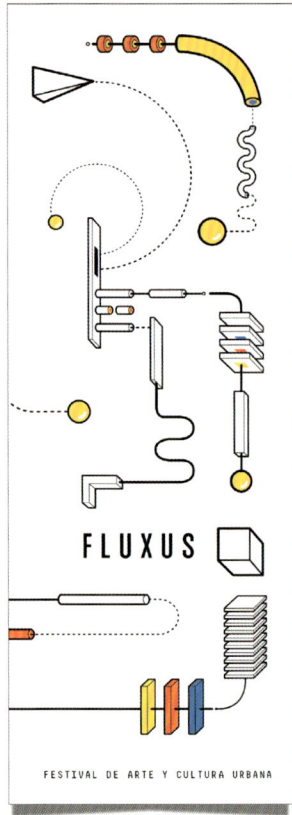

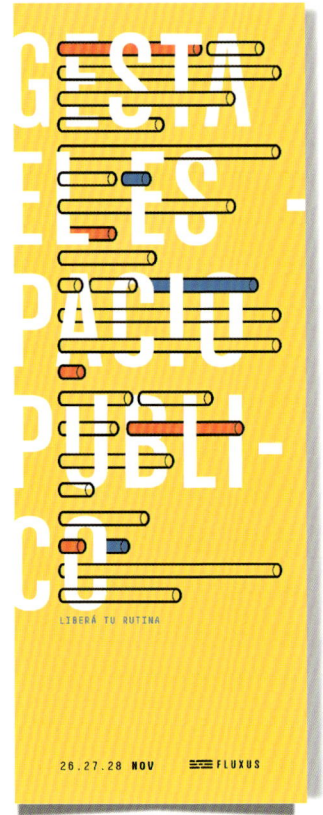

FLUXUS

For Fluxus, a festival of art and urban culture, Nicole Allegri designed a series of posters with colorful abstract motifs, and presented them like assembling blocks.

Designer Nicole Allegri

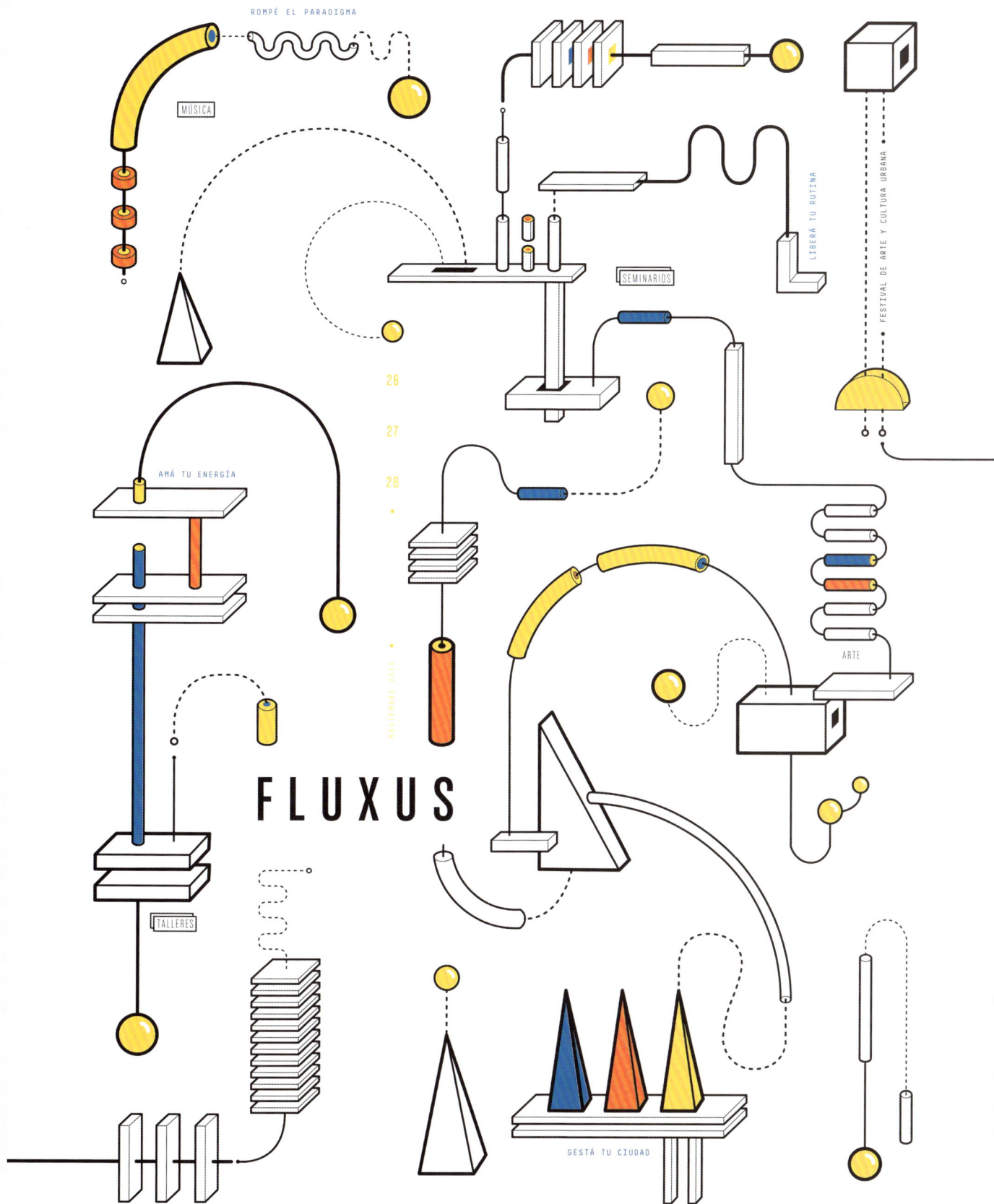

ROMPÉ EL PARADIGMA

MÚSICA

2D or 3D

139

LIBERÁ TU RUTINA

FESTIVAL DE ARTE Y CULTURA URBANA

SEMINARIOS

AMÁ TU ENERGÍA

26
27
28

ARTE

FLUXUS

TALLERES

GESTÁ TU CIUDAD

FRANCESCA FELIDE

ANARIOL BRAM

AKIKO GONDA

HITalk

HITalk is an innovative series of events created to share thoughts and experiences into a creative environment.

FULMINE LAB created a geometric alphabets made of solid and creative figures to reflect the intersection of different minds. The visual identities combine the alphabets and always create different 3D geometric compositions to build new ideas and inspiration forms.

Design Agency
FULMINE LAB
Design Director
Alati Andrea, Simone Mariano
Designer Alati Andrea

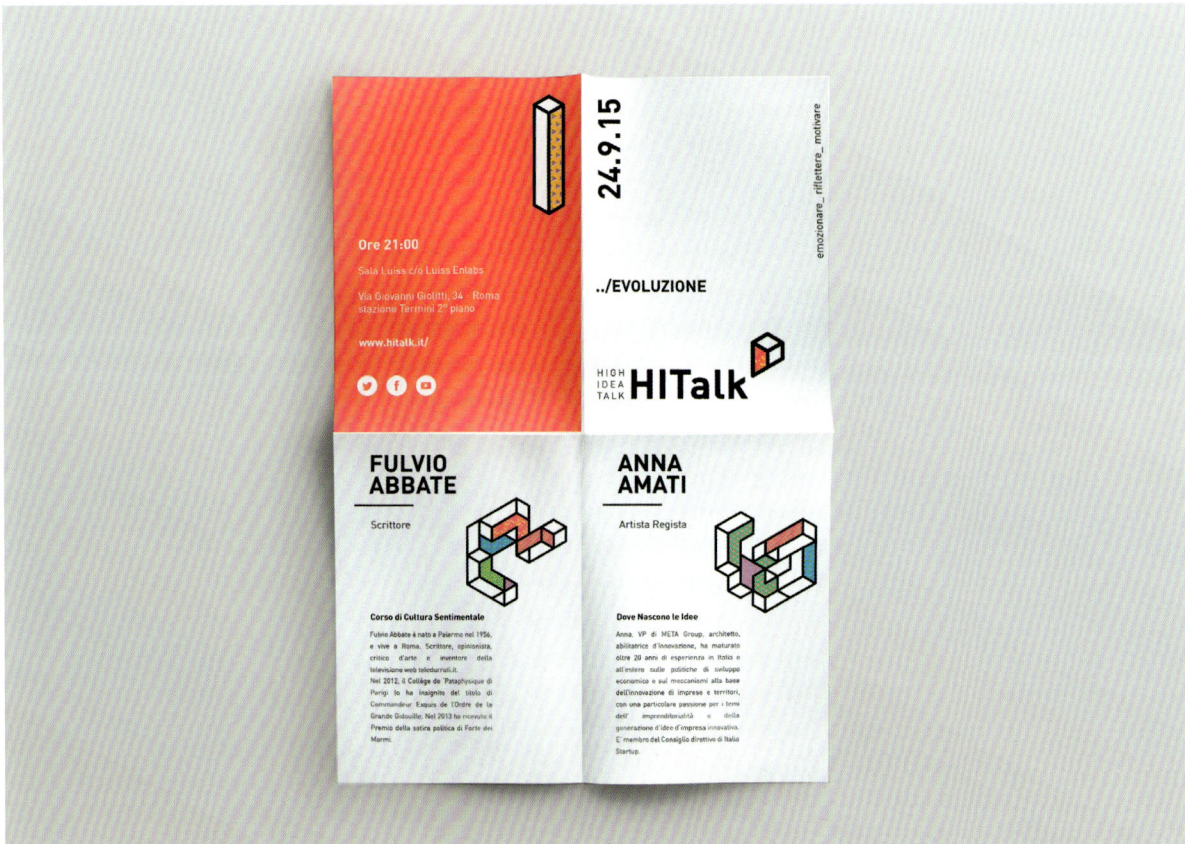

A   B   C   D   E   F   G   H

I   J   K   L   M   N   O   P

Q   R   S   T   U   V   W   X

Y   Z

It was a visual identity for YODEX (Young Designers' Exhibition), which is an annual young talents show in Taiwan. Inspired by chemical experiments, the young designers, like chemical elements, create unexpected surprise when working organically and systematically. Hand drawing was used to enhance the texture of organism. The color scheme also indicates the bright future ahead if they strive with energy and passion.

What's worth mention, this work was designed based on motion graphic so that the flowing lines around the static YODEX leads the visual. Moreover, designing in different dimension also created the sense of space out of the flat graphic.

Design Agency
Bito Studio
Art Director
Keng-Ming Liu
Designer
Chu-Chieh Lee

新一代設計展

YOUNG
DESIGNERS'
EXHIBITION

33nd

-2014-

yodex.com.tw

台北世貿一館
2014.05.17-20
10:00-18:00

優待票 —— $ 150
全票 —— $ 200

經濟部　　　　　12歲以下兒童謝絕入場
經濟部工業局　　售票資訊請上本展網站查詢
台灣創意設計中心　團體預售票4月1日開賣

yodex

UP

This project includes logo design and album cover design for an Indie-Electronic / Indie-Pop artist from Riga, Latvia.

The minimalistic Scandinavian design was inspired by the cold Nordic winter with its white snow, pale moon, and all the stars swallowed by the solid black Nordic sky.

Designer Anne Lise Arnesen

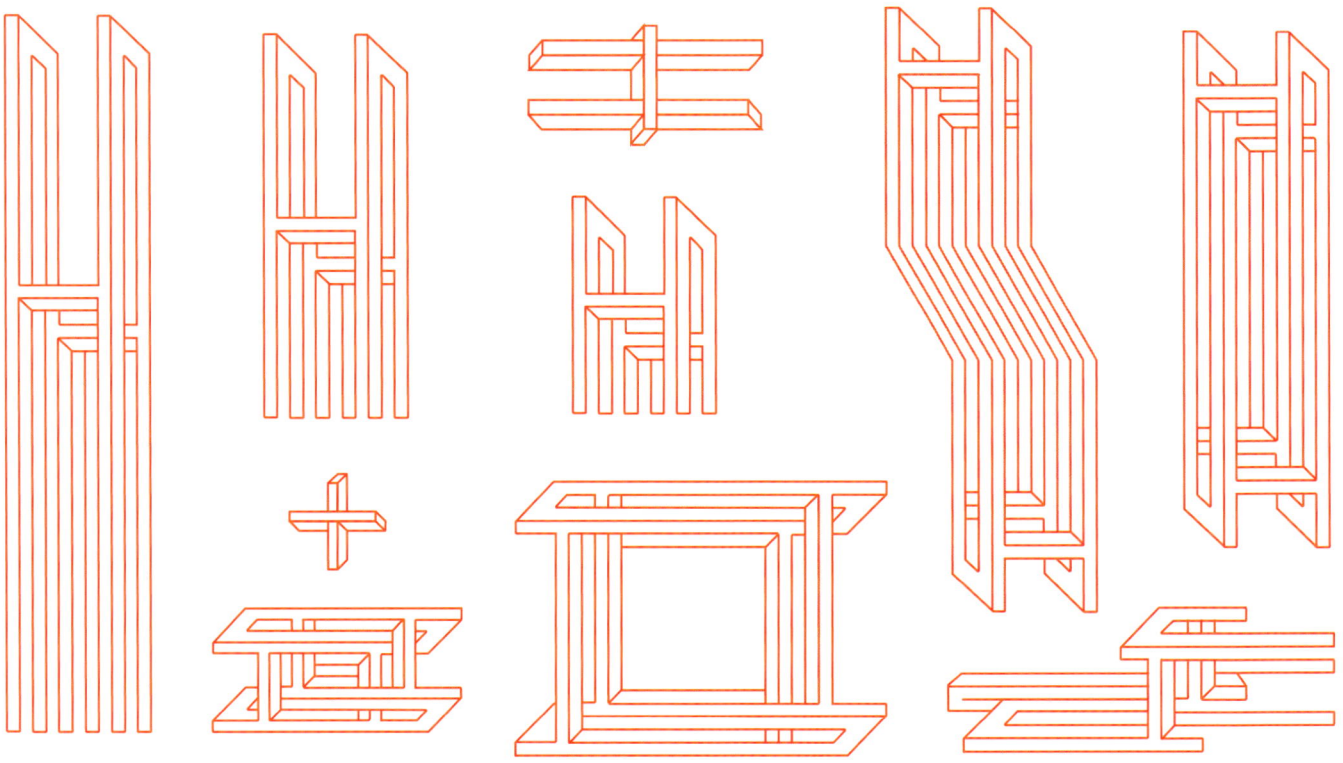

Hook and Line

Hook and Line is a New York based music production collective. Matt Delbridge created a flexible identity system that is based on impossible shapes to represent the disconnection between the often nebulous creative process and the end result. The primary mark is composed of two interlocking H and designed to be warped and distorted while maintaining its geometric impossibility.

Designer Matt Delbridge

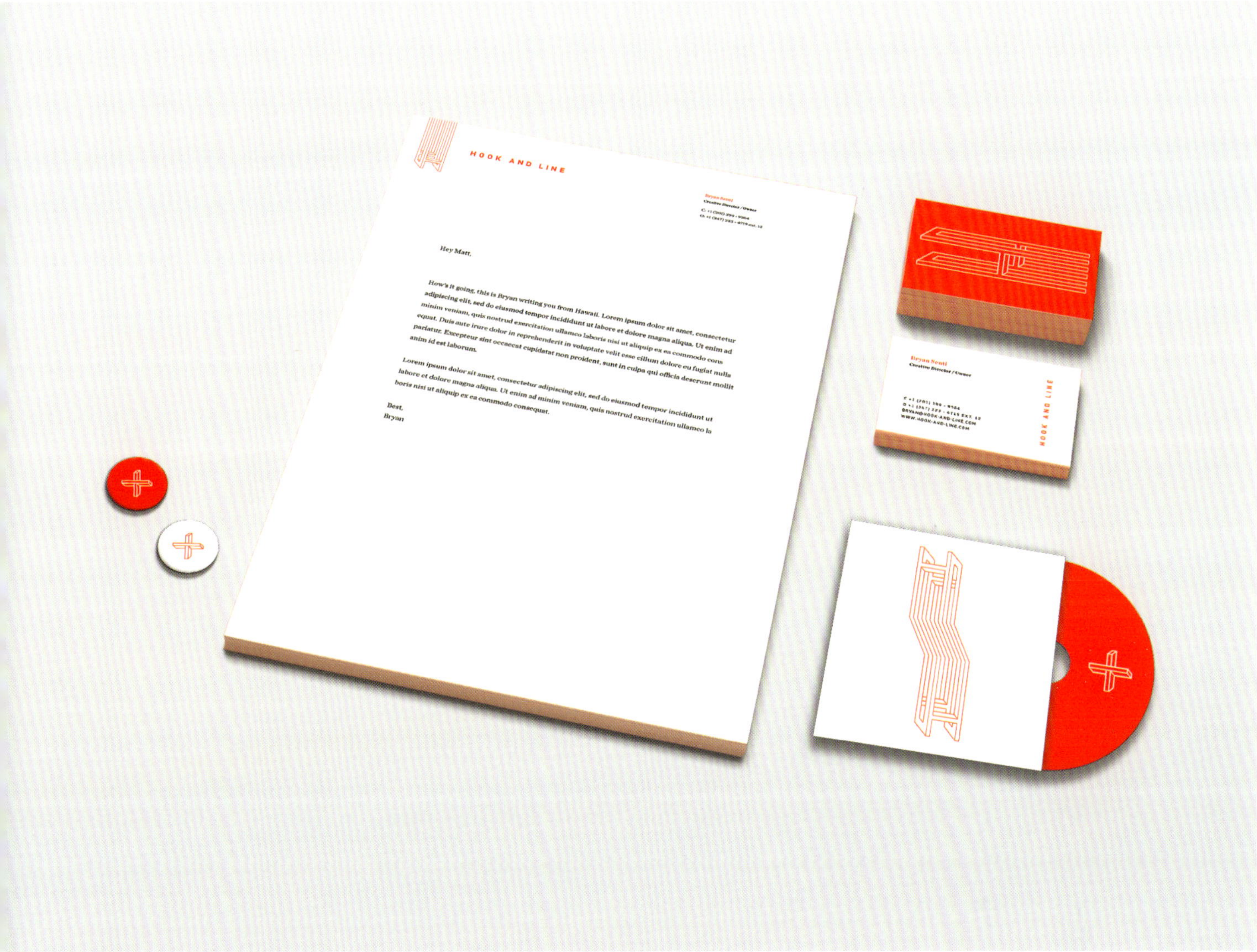
HOOK AND LINE
Hey Matt,
Best,
Bryan

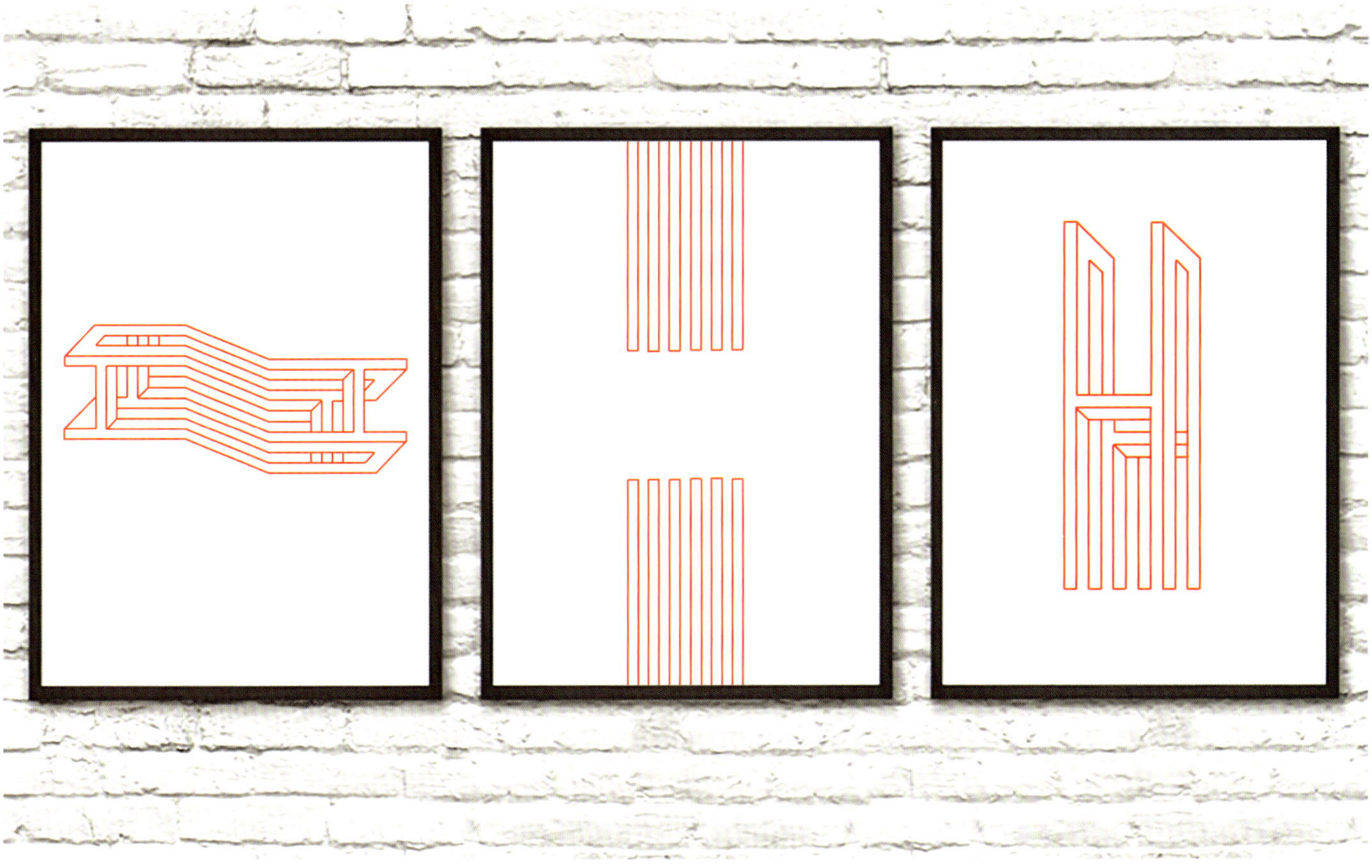

ADCC

The Advertising and Design Club of Canada (ADCC) needed to drive membership. Not only did Blok Design work to add greater, more robust benefits for its members, they also created this provocative piece to communicate the advantages and prestige of belonging to such an august community of like-minded thinkers and creators.

Design Agency Blok Design
Creative Director Vanessa Eckstein, Marta Cutler
Designer Vanessa Eckstein, Patricia Kleeberg, Kevin Boothe
Copywriter Marta Cutler

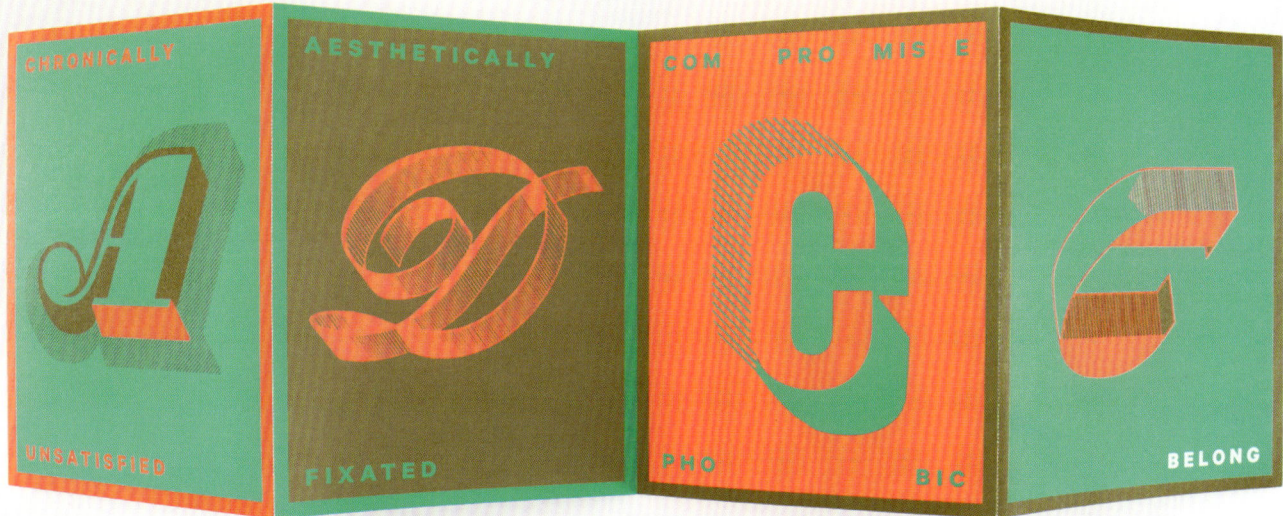

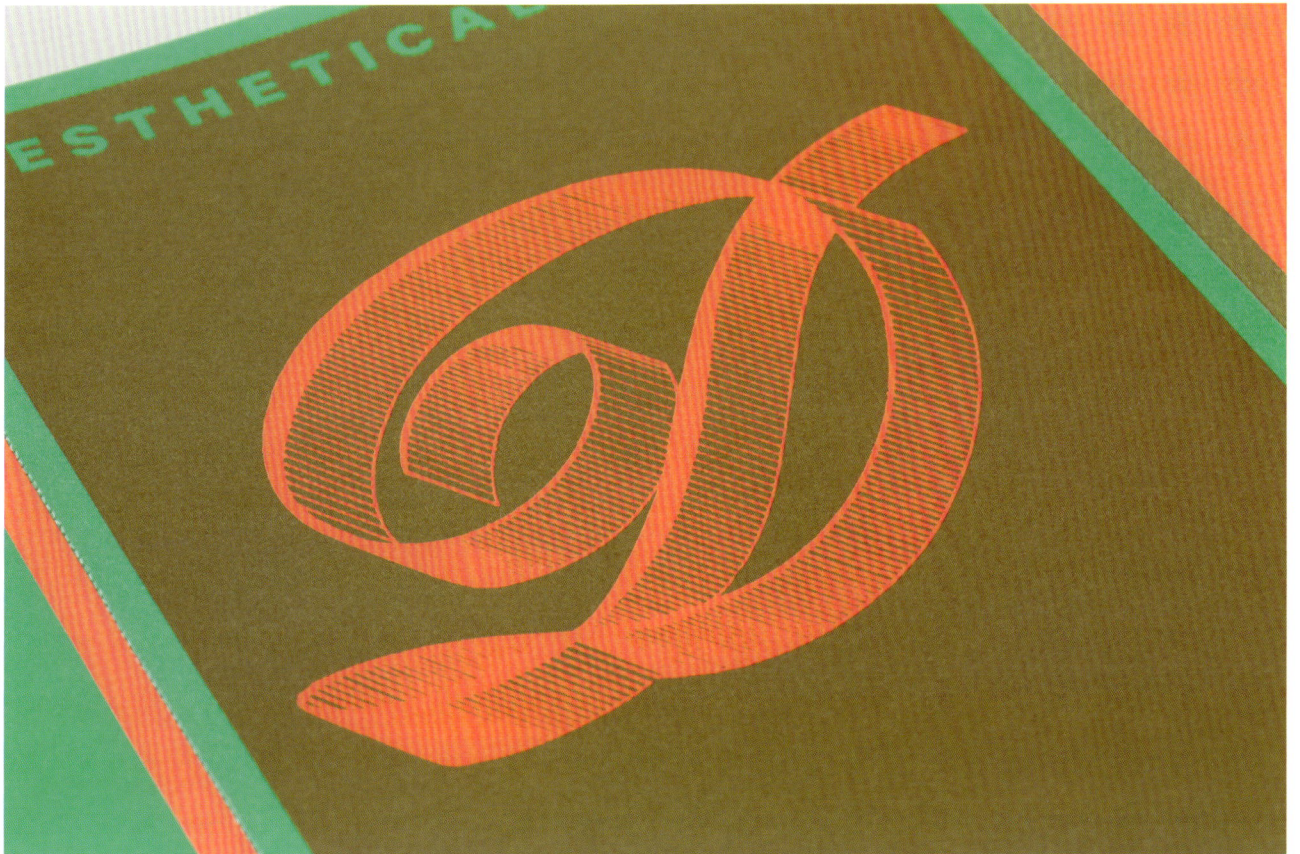

Focus Pocus

Focus Pocus is a campaign for a fictional scientific conference about visual perception, focused on optical illusions about its explanations and causes.

Turboturboturbo used the Penrose-triangle, because it is one of the few optical illusions that can exist in our reality. They observed this triangle from different angles and used these images in the identity. The posters and other stationery items show eight different views of the Penrose-triangle. The design allows the viewer to experience optical illusions, while explaining at the same time how this shape exists in our reality.

Design Agency
Turboturboturbo
Designer
Daan Meulendijks

Arena Cube

The geometric feature of the identity describes the endless possibilities of
the software expanded in different dimensions. The tightly closed shape,
reflecting stability with aplomb, is analogous to the sophisticated and safe
technology provided by this company.

Design Agency NotoriusGrey
Design Director Yorgos Marantos
Art Director & Designer Demetriou Yeorgia

Personal Brand of Christian Dal Mas

The main idea was to take all the letters of designer's name in order to associate each of them to an adjective to describe him. By changing disposition of the letters and playing with colors, the result was a different concept of business cards. This project presents illusion tricks and to show this concept in simple business cards.

Designer
Christian Dal Mas

Nomade Architects

The adaptable visual identity for Nomade Architects articulates around the six letters N-O-M-A-D-E and was built on the principle of the paradoxical perspective.

Design Director
Adrienne Bornstein & Pierre Sponchiado

Chimestry Complex
A l'attention de M. John Smith
45A Club Street.
069422 London

ALBA
ACUÑA CARLOS

NOMADE
ARCHITECTES

Studio 02 Architects

Studio 02 Architects was a visual identity design created for the Architects agency (France). The identity is silkscreen printed with two pantone colors on a blue paper.

Design Director
Adrienne Bornstein, Pierre Sponchiado

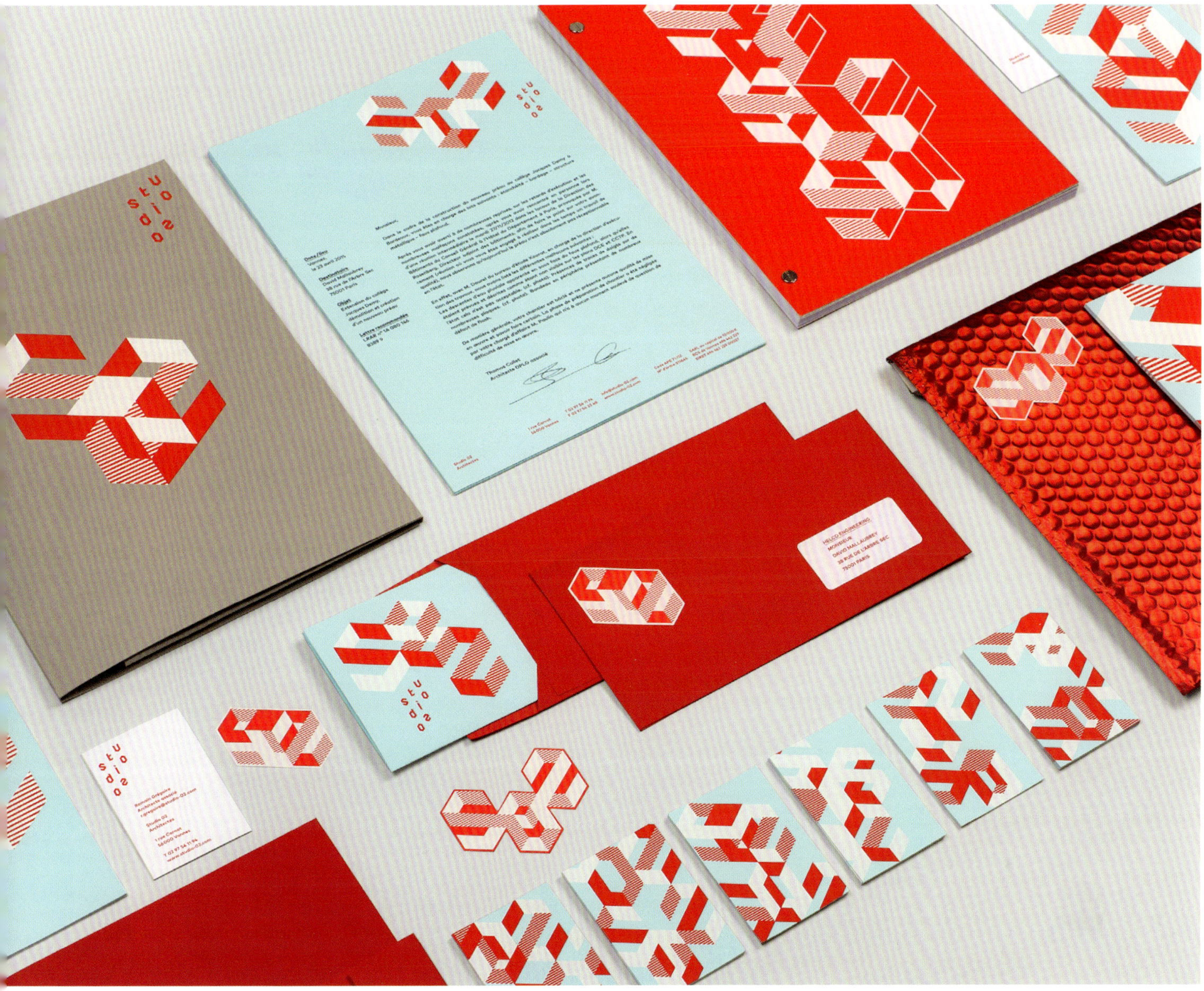

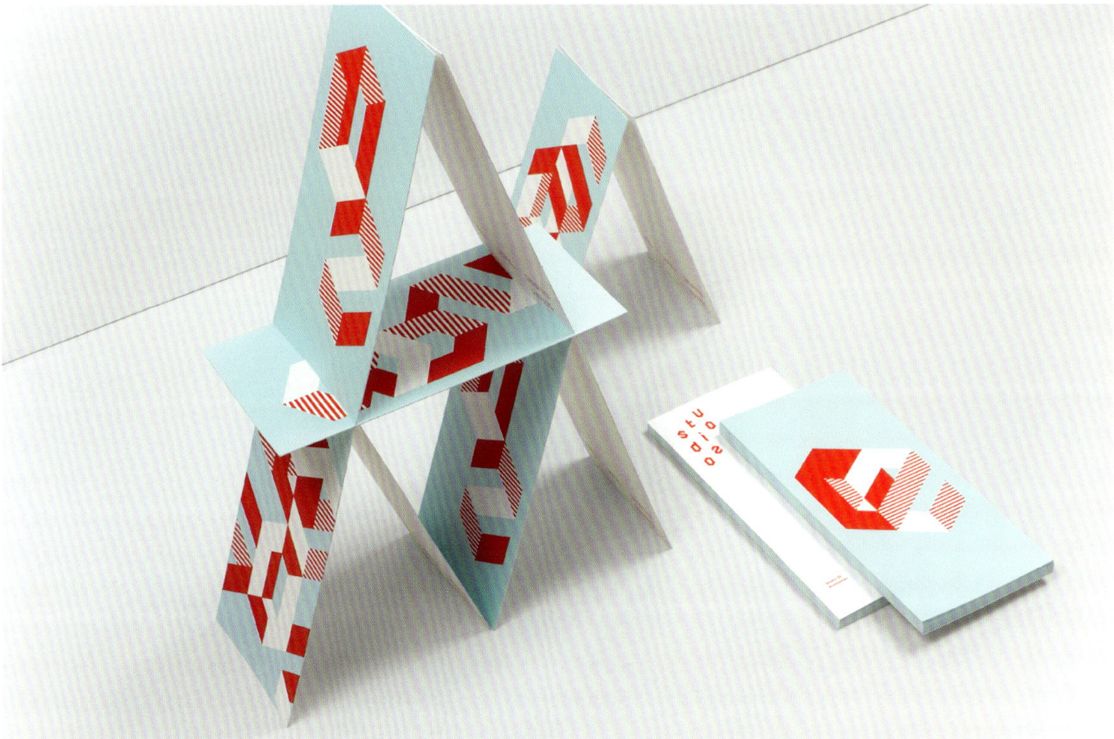

Hays and Ryan Holladay

Hays and Ryan Holladay are brothers and a music duo that evolved into something more diverse with offerings that stretch from sound installations to mobile apps and interactive events. They are exploring somewhere between to showcase them as a band, tech people, and fine artists.

Federico Leggio and Sergi Miral delivered a modern logo, with geometric elements that interact with each other.

Designer
Federico Leggio, Sergi Miral

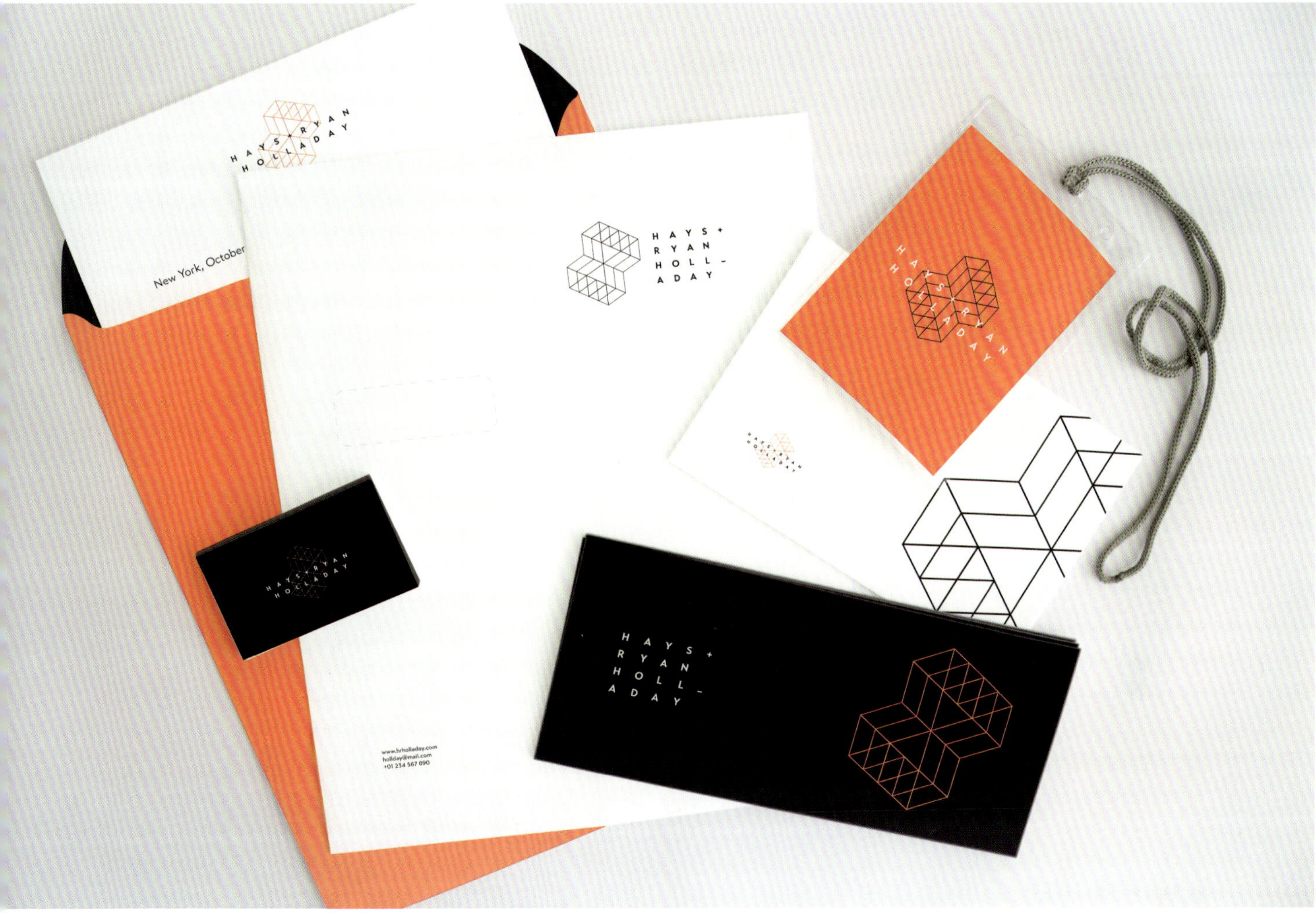
HAYS
RYAN
HOLL-
ADAY
New York, October

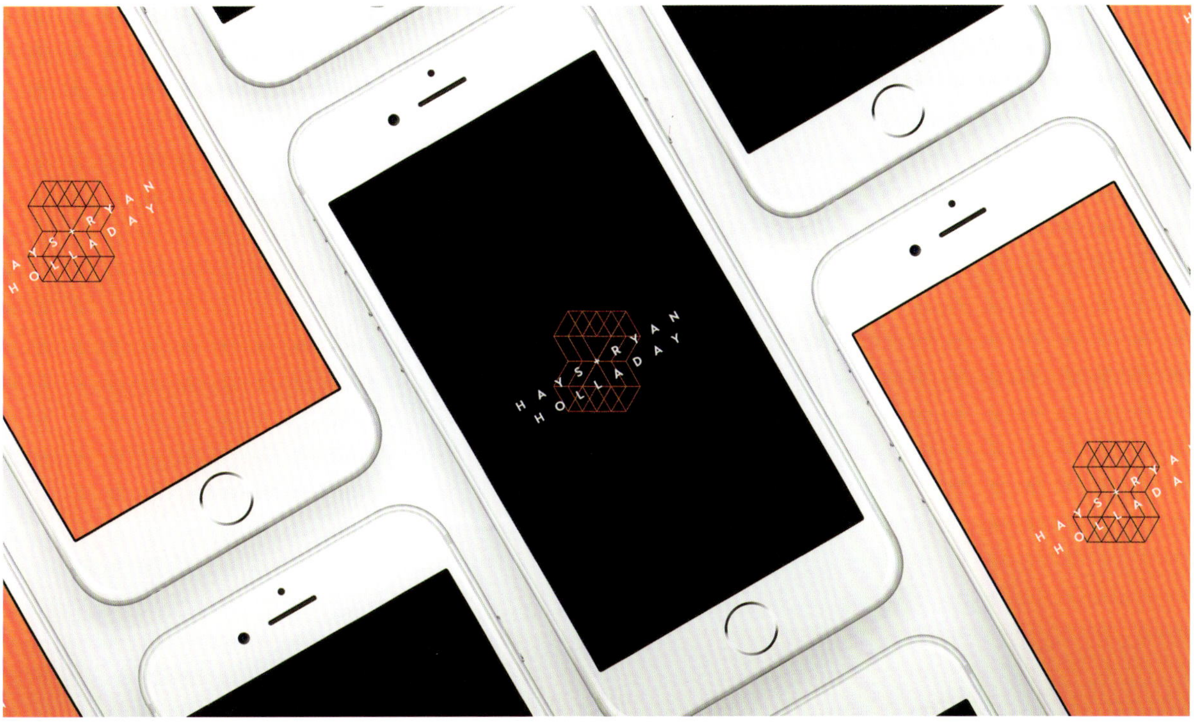
HAYS + RYAN
HOLLADAY

ZigZag

ZigZag is a cultural house for exhibitions, concerts, lectures, and master classes. For a place offering plenty of activities and functions, b.a.-ba created an identity based on a story line that viewer can explore all contents and create a link between them.

Designer b.a.-ba

CITY AS PLAYGROUND
Masterclass
Herzog & de Meuron
Le 25 Février 2015
de 9h à 18h
AMEXICA
Exposition
Adrien Missika
De 12 mars au 25 avril 2015
de 9h à 18h
SWISS BOOKS
Conférence
Aude Lehmann
Les 4 et 6 avril 2015
à 18h45

PROGRAMMATION 2015
ZIGZAG
VOTRE MAISON CULTURELLE
SUR AIX EN PROVENCE

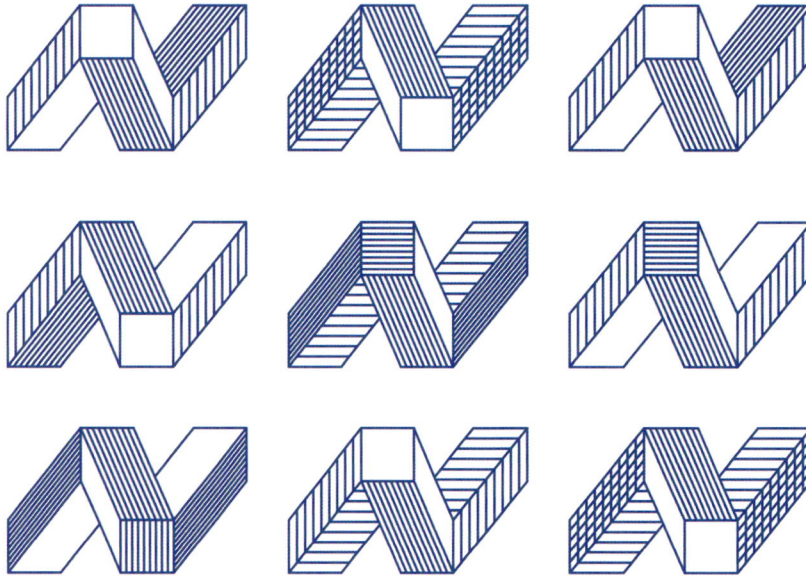

Neus Ortiz

Branding, stationery and corporate materials for a Barcelona based interior and visual merchandising designer Neus Ortiz. The goal was to create a liquid identity, a recognizable, dynamic branding system that can be adapted across different mediums in the same way the designer plays with the three-dimensional space in her every-day job. This is achieved by the use of letter "N" as a container, like a kind of virtual place where anything is possible.

Designer Gerard Marin
Client Neus Ortiz

NEUSORTIZ
INTERIORISTA
Doctor Fleming 4bis
neusortiz@gmail.com
M. 699 296 464
Vilanova i la Geltrú
08800 BCN

NEUSORTIZ
INTERIORISTA

60 DEGREE Identity

60 DEGREE is a design company formed by three partners who collaborate perfectly like a regular triangle with three angles of 60 degrees. 60 DEGREE refers to the angle of balance, harmony, and stableness. Apart from naming, they employed the triangle as the main identifying object and created a dynamic identity which is able to change and yet maintain its consistency.

In addition, the designers extended their design idea in optical illusion, and merged the number 60 with various geometric figures to make 60 DEGREE be able to self-interpret through different facets. The excellent design of unity in diversity makes dynamic identity keep clear recognition and connectivity.

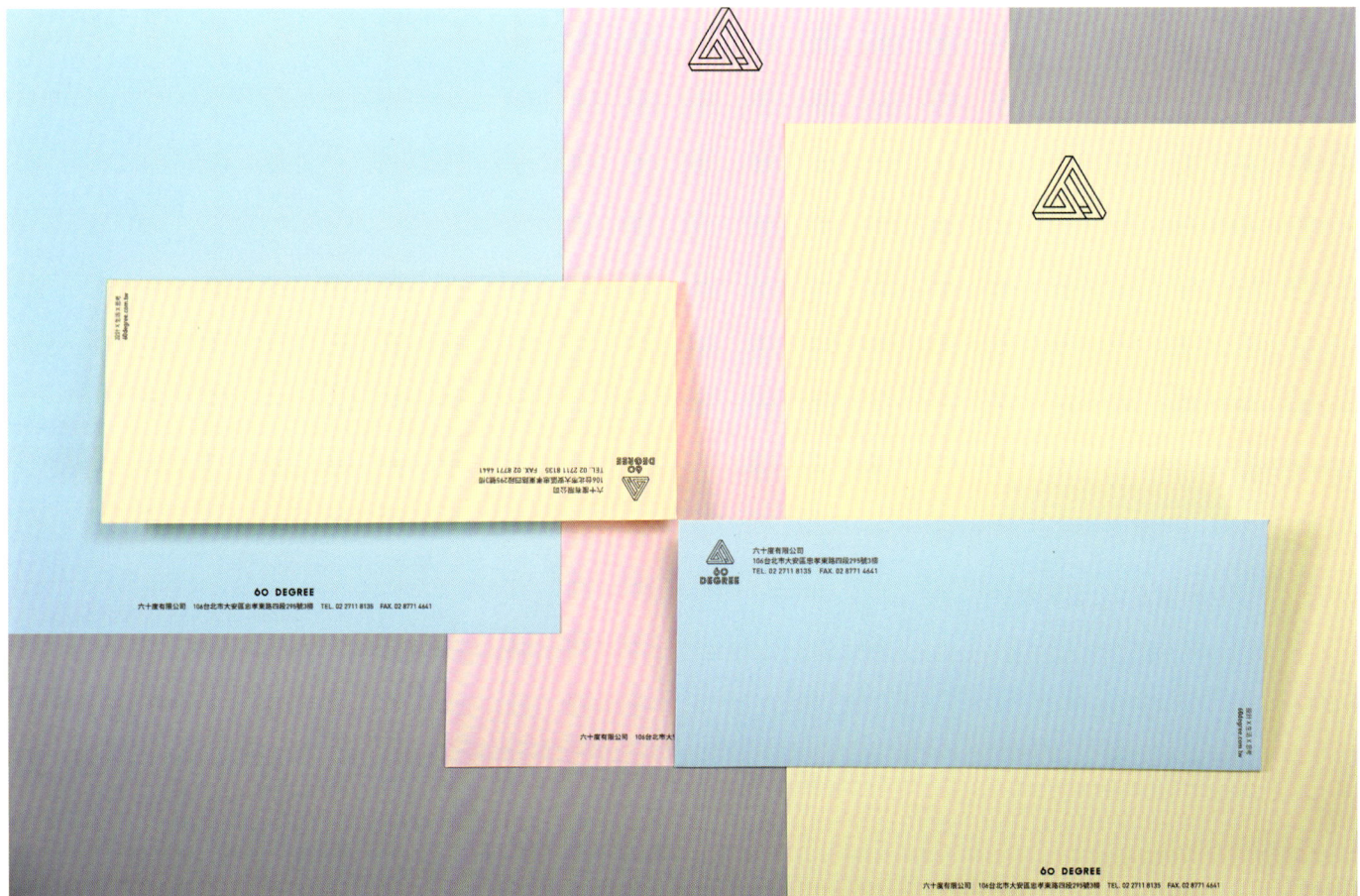

Design Agency 60 DEGREE
Design Director Natalie Liang
Art Director Abingo Wang
Designer Abingo Wang
Photographer Show Leejuan

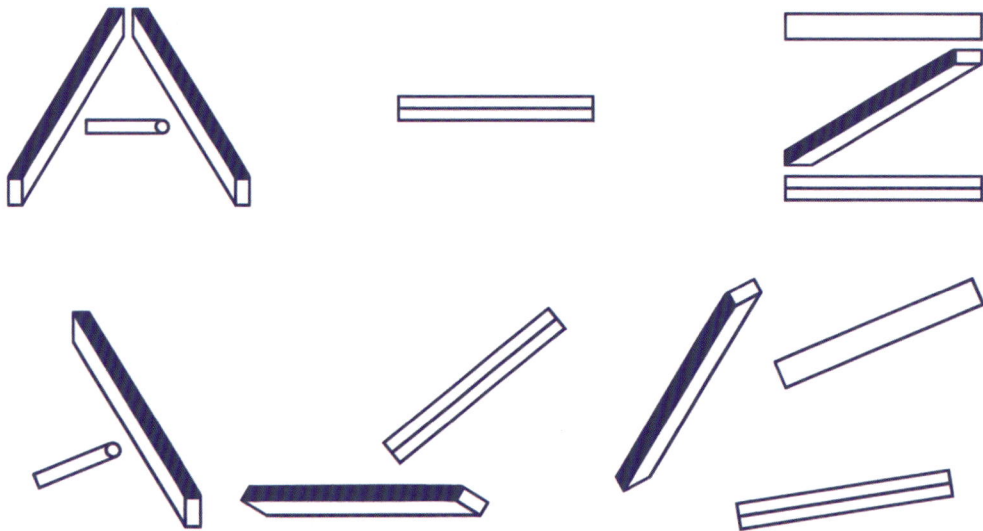

Royal College of Art, Work in Progress Show

"The Work in Progress Show" was an annual event where second year MA students exhibit their mid-term work as an opportunity to try out ideas before the Final Show. Summer Studio and illustrator Maria Ines Gul were selected to design the visual identity for the School of Communication and its three departments: Animation, Information Experience Design and Visual Communication. "Work in progress" is a stage defined by fearlessly questioning and playing with conventions in order to find new "outside the box" creations. The design brief was to illustrate this stage of breaking down and building up in the visual identity.

Design Agency Summer Studio
Design Director
Carolina Dahl, Minna Sakaria
Illustrator Maria Ines Gul

School of Communication
Work in Progress Show 2015
5—8 February 10am—5pm

@RCAevents

Darwin Building
Kensington Gore
London SW7 2EU

Royal College of Art

School of Communication
Work in Progress Show 2015
5—8 February 10am—5pm

@RCAevents

Darwin Building
Kensington Gore
London SW7 2EU

Royal College of Art

Animation is a beautifully eclectic and collaborative practice. In this programme students explore process, design narratives, draw words and conjure sound. Abstraction and narrative, and the imagined, pull and push against each other to

UTOPIA

9%

&3

Utopia

Utopia typeface was designed as part of an overall graphic system and identity for Eventi Letterari – a festival of Literary Events in Monte Verità (literally Hill of Truth). Inspired by the art of M. C. Escher, the typeface was designed based on impossible shapes.

Design Agency RM&CO
Designer Alfio Mazzei

UTOPIE E MAGNIFICHE OSSESSIONI ASCONA 21–24.3 2013

ECOLOGICAL UTOPIAN SOCIETY DESCRIBES NEW WAYS IN WHICH SOCIETY SHOULD RELATE TO NATURE. THEY REACT TO A

PANTONE
102 C

PANTONE
2728 C

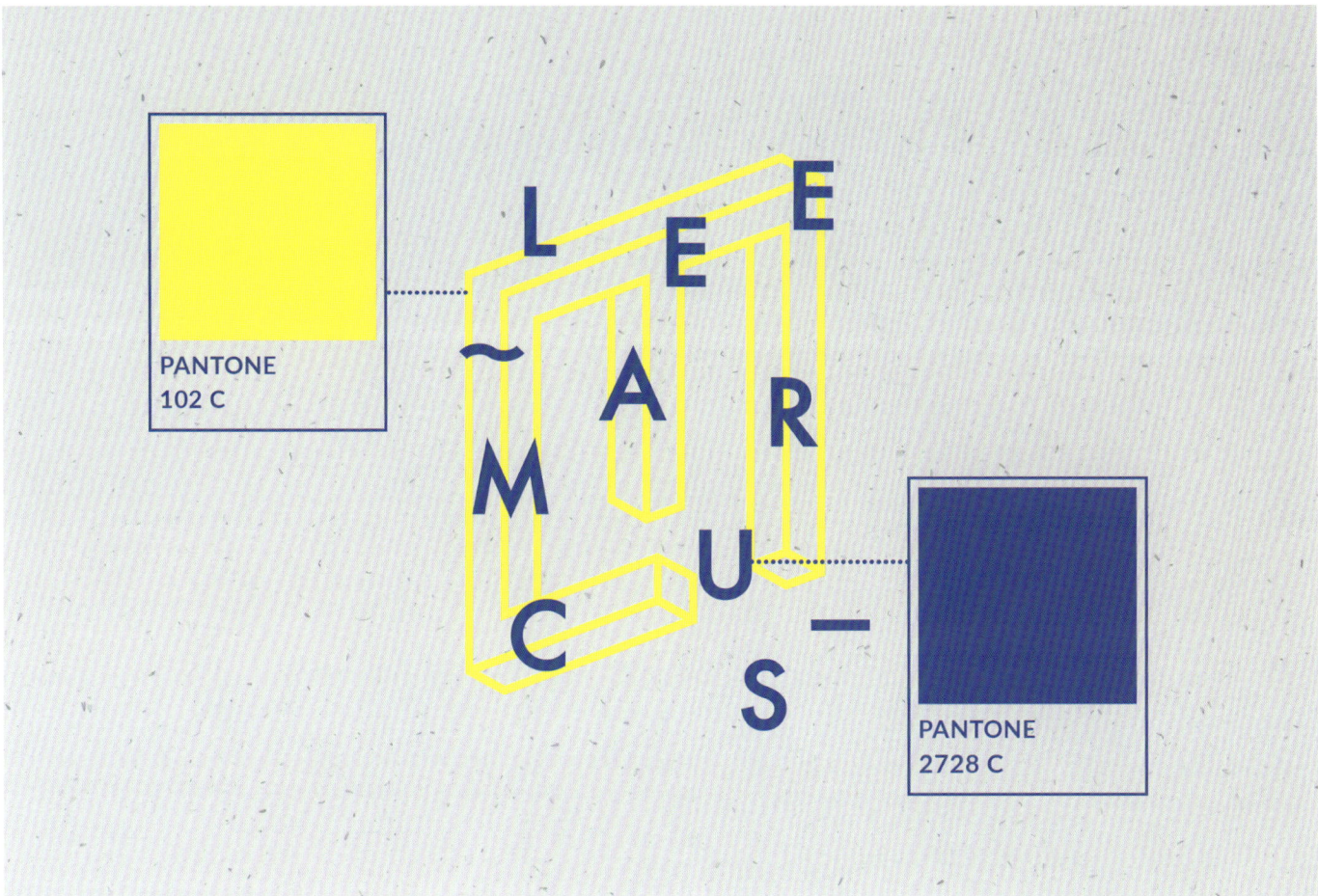

Personal Branding of Lee Marcus

The project brief given was to embark on a self branding assignment with a limited color scheme (2 colors), while still having a strong overall identity that could be repurposed for a multitude of applications. An impossible square served as the basis of the logo form, as its characteristics embody desirable qualities that can seize one's attention.

Designer
Lee Marcus

GRAPHIC DESIGN
& ART DIRECTION

T
+65 9119 6238

M
marc.lyr@gmail.com

W
behance.net/leemarcus

Hidden Secret

This project aimed to find a new way by using typography illusion to raise people's curiosity and promote the shop at the same time. Glyphics is a shop located near Old Street station. They mainly provide the service of signage, lettering and vinyl for walls and windows. Hidden Secret consisted of a series of seven site-specific objects and one window display. The concept aimed to lead people from Old Street station to the window of the shop. The seven locations on the route helped people go in the right direction when they have two choices. Each of the installations used different illusion methods.

Designer Ling-Wen Yen
Photographer Yu Su Lan

Shine Cards

Fur-lined, one of the world's top film production companies, had helped launch Manifest works, which is a job training workshop for the film industry that helps youth emerging from the foster care and criminal justice system. For the holiday season, they wanted to celebrate and honor the first graduating class. "Let It Shine" and its accompanying language capture the organization's vision. The specially designed typography, with its unique finishes and unexpectedly bold color, balances sophistication and modernity with a celebratory spirit.

Design Agency Blok Design
Creative Director
Vanessa Eckstein, Marta Cutler
Designer Vanessa Eckstein,
Monica Herrera
Writer Marta Cutler

Disco Illusions

Poster design for a new Disco, Funk & Soul night starting in Manchester at the Ruby Lounge. The idea was to create something simple but iconic that could easily be adapted and changed for different nights by altering the colors.

Designer Matt Mckinney

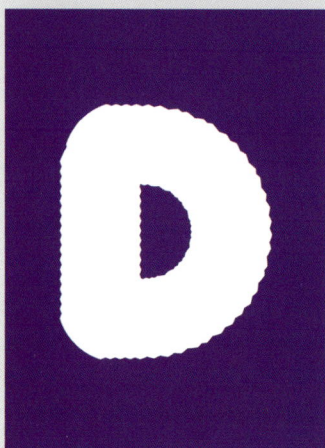

Paradise #20

The Paradise is a house party which takes place in Nantes (France). It was started by Dan Bono and invites, once a year, some of the best DJ's around the world.

Jonathan Gravier has been conceiving the visuals of this event for the last 5 years and is drawing a brand new typography for each edition. For Paradise #20 he created a type that mimicked the mechanical rhythm of house music which was meant to be animated this way. The only colors used for this project were Pantone® red and purple, and the flyer was screen printed on a 0.5 mm thick white Priplak.

Designer
Jonathan Gravier

Stepz

Stepz reached out to Casper Heijkenskjöld for a new logo and a website. The goal was to create a more memorable logo and a website that was easier to navigate and more focused on their vibrant culture. The solution was an identity in motion. A new powerful graphic logo, which become a visual element in itself and show the energy and movement that Stepz consists of, was created. A strong visual presence allowed Stepz to promote them better, and T-shirts with their new logo were sold out within days. The website is kept clean and focused on the content, but still visually striking as it is packed with strong mesmerizing imagery.

Design Agency Glasyr
Designer Casper Heijkenskjöld
Photographer Casper Heijkenskjöld

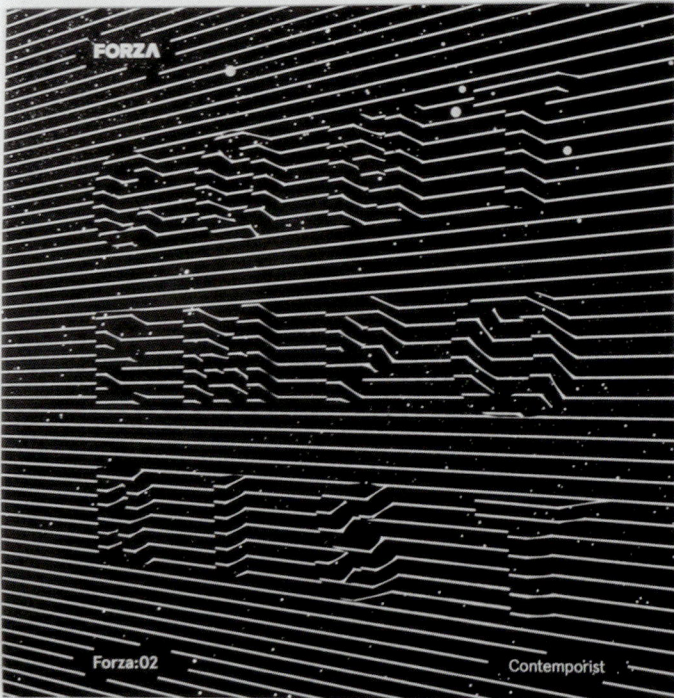

Forza Series

Artwork for a series of releases on techno label Forza, one of the imprint labels on Origami Sounds which focuses more on club based music.

All artwork was based around typography created from geometric forms so as to give them the futuristic look and feel which is representative of the forward thinking and experimental music that is released on the label.

The selection here was from a limited run of special edition screen printed versions speckled with silver foil.

Design Agency ²Fold Studio
Design Director Eddie Cooper
Designer Matt Chatfield
Photographer Chris Van Nigel

Forza:08

Gomorra

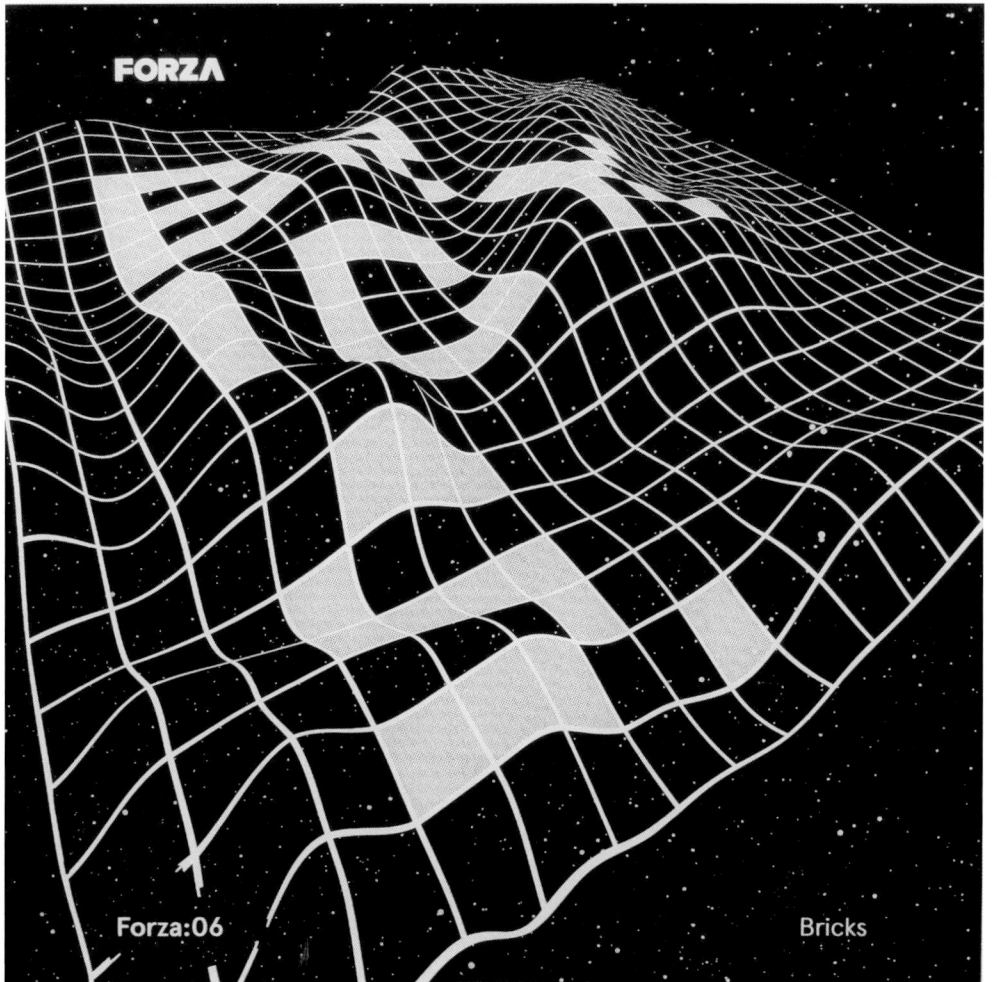

Forza:06

Bricks

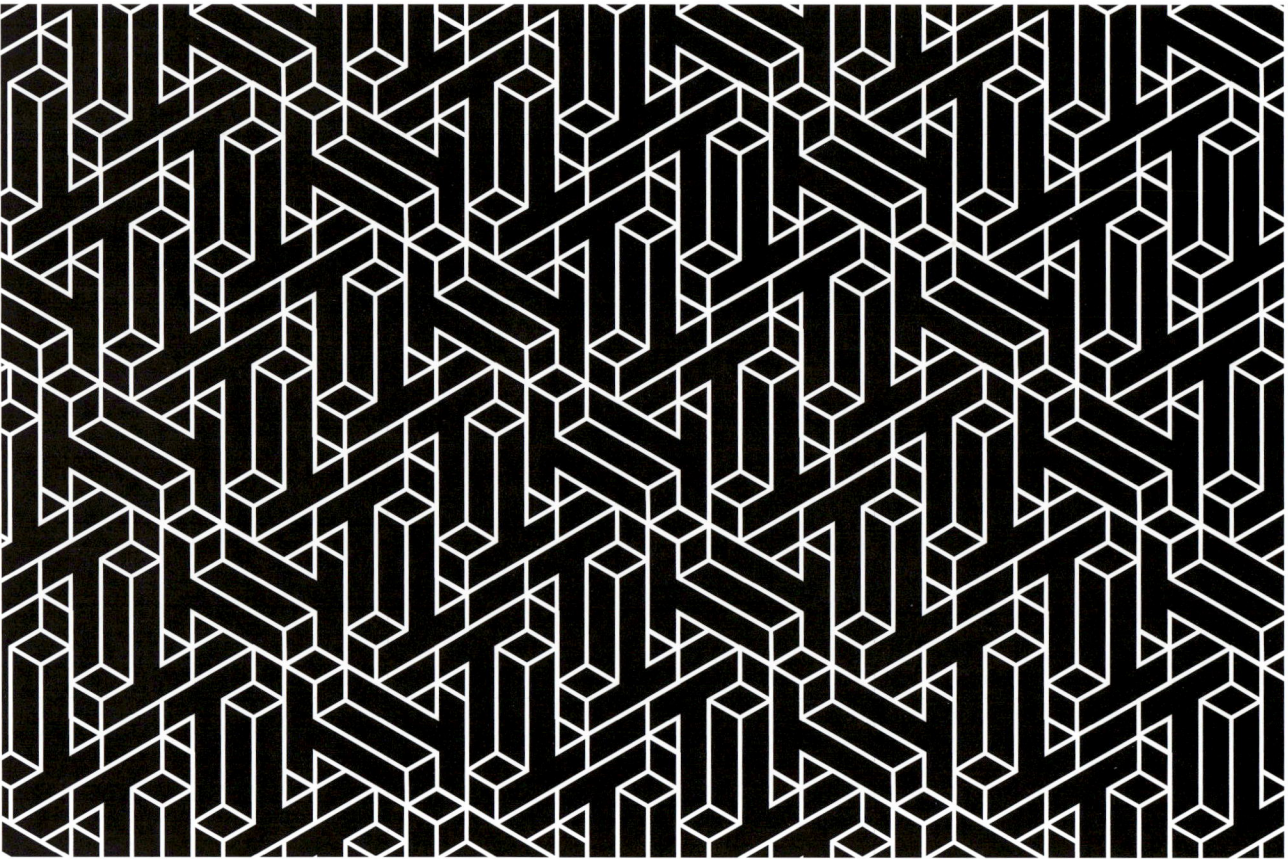

Tatiane Tavares Arquitetura + Construçã

This branding project was designed for an architect whom is known for her ability to multi-task. Her target audiences were mostly investors who valued the way she manage construction deeds. The impossible object is a combination of two letter "T" from her name to resemble a building, and the sophisticated pattern represent, in a unique way, her multitasking qualities.

Design Agency
Toski Graphic Design
Art Director & Designer
Tainá Ribovski

STANDARD:

TRUE NEGATIVE:

STANDARD WITH FILL:

STANDARD INVERTED:

OUTLINE:

OUTLINE INVERTED:

Walkie Talkie

Every generation has its frequency. Logo and visual identity for the Ghent-based content PR outfit Walkie Talkie.

Design Agency
Mirror Mirror

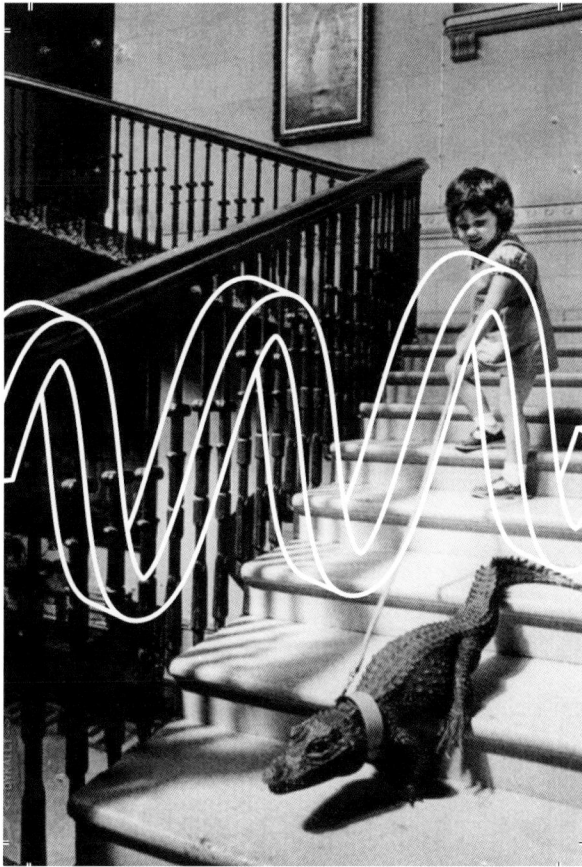

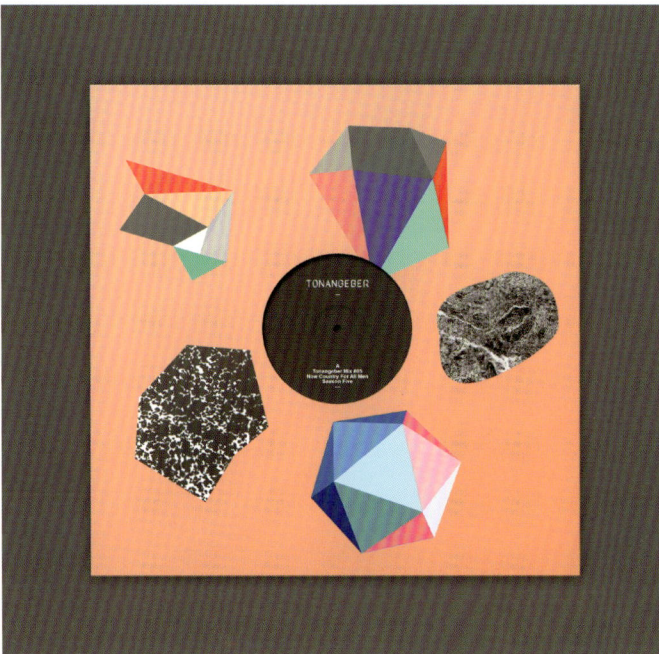

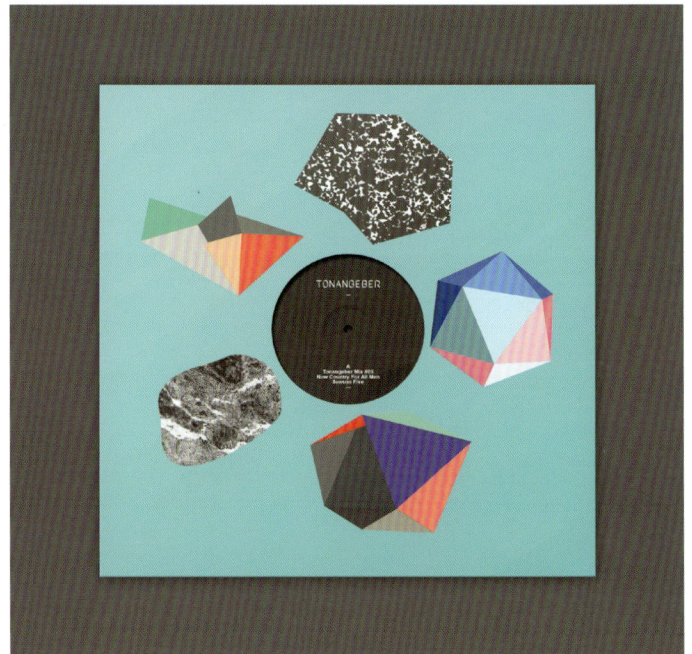

Tonangeber

Tonangeber is a project initiated by Ani and Beda. They make playlists and share them for free on www.tonangeber.ch. TwoPoints.Net was invited to build their website, but ended up designing a flexible visual system which allowed Ani and Beda to design a new cover for each of their playlists. The visual system was implemented in a program, the "supertool", with which Ani and Beda can create their own graphics within the parameters of the visual system.

Design Agency TwoPoints.Net
Web Developer supernodegree
Tool Developer, Video & Audio superhannes
Typeface Designer VLNL Tp Kurier Calligraphic

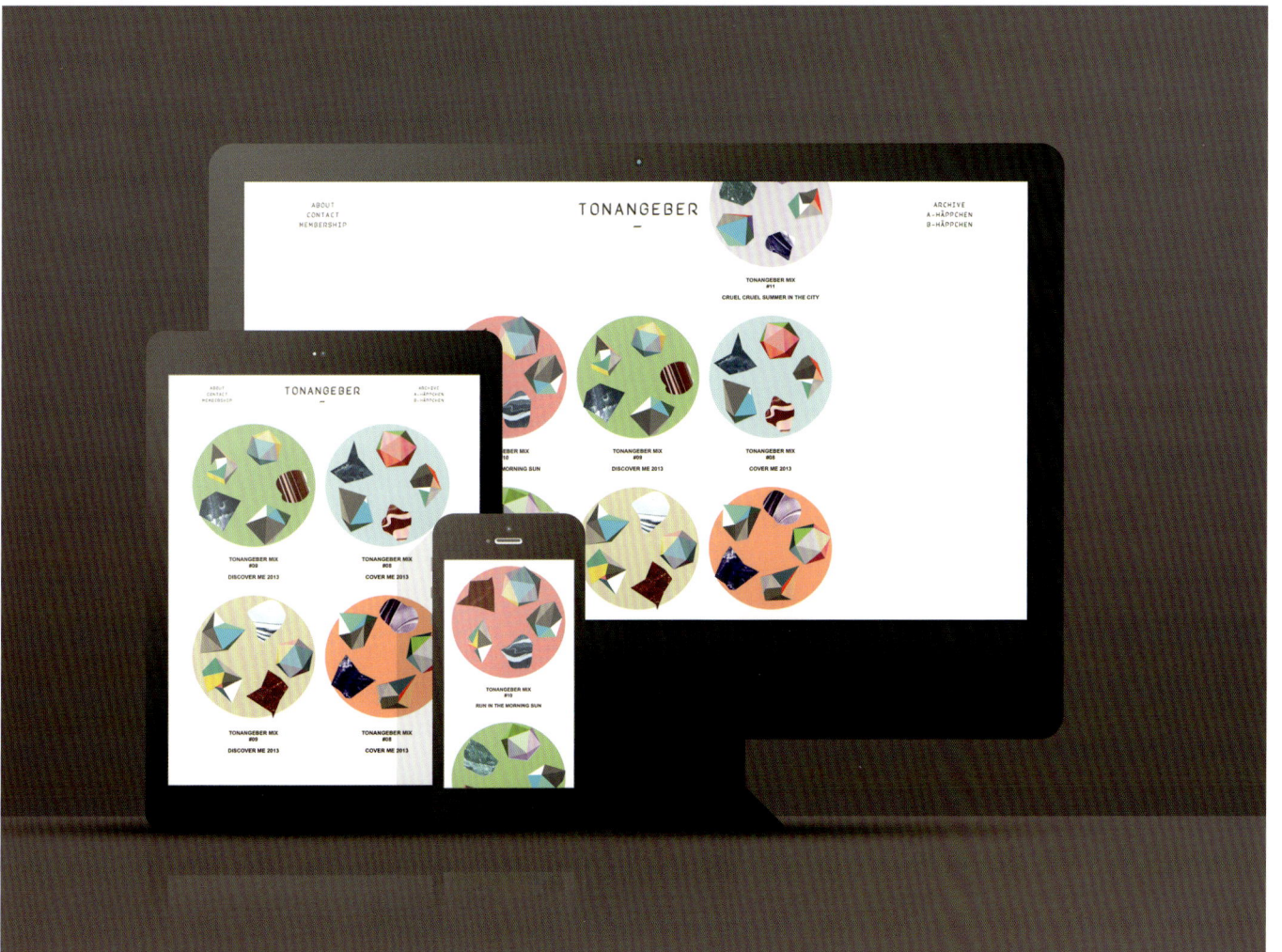

COVER ART
Dubet - Undeviating EP

COVER ART
Caio Stanccione - I Dance You EP

Playperview Records

Record covers design for Playperview Records.

The icon has different interpretations: firstly, it is a representation of the link between the three partners Playperview label. Secondly, it is impossible alignment between the head, the ear, and the heart. Thirdly, it is the icon of "play". Each cover has various meanings depending on the visual identities in order to fit in the specific themes.

Design Agency
Pornographitti Design Explicito

Smile!

Smile! is a big party of electronic music in Londrina, Brazil. Pornographitti was invited to redesign its identity and help it embark for a new journey. A new identity, symbolized the electronic sonic wave, was created and widely applied in invitation cards, T-shirts, and other collaterals.

Design Agency
Pornographitti Design Explicito

SPATIAL EXPERIENCE

Spatial Experience is a matter of perspective. This chapter would be best to describe with one of the works featured: Truth depends on where you see it from. How we recognize objects is mostly attributed to reference. Playing with measurable properties, designers employ multiple methods to create an immersive experience, and invite the audience to encounter their works from the right perspective.

MA Graphic Design Show 2014

This exhibition presented the work of forty-eight full-time and twelve part-time MA graphic design graduates from London College of Communication. Emerging from a challenging research-led site of inquiry, the show invited the visitors to participate in an experience that stood somewhere between an action, a test, a showcase and a conversation.

"A Parallel Approach" is a place of action, not of exhibition. It was an opportunity to associate fragments of research with experimentation and realization; to contemplate aspects that are foreign to one another; to encounter new findings for some that are reminders for others; to activate and interpret; to formulate and consider; to build transitions and justifications; to stop and to think.

Graphic Designer
Dario Gracceva,
Sarah Krebietke

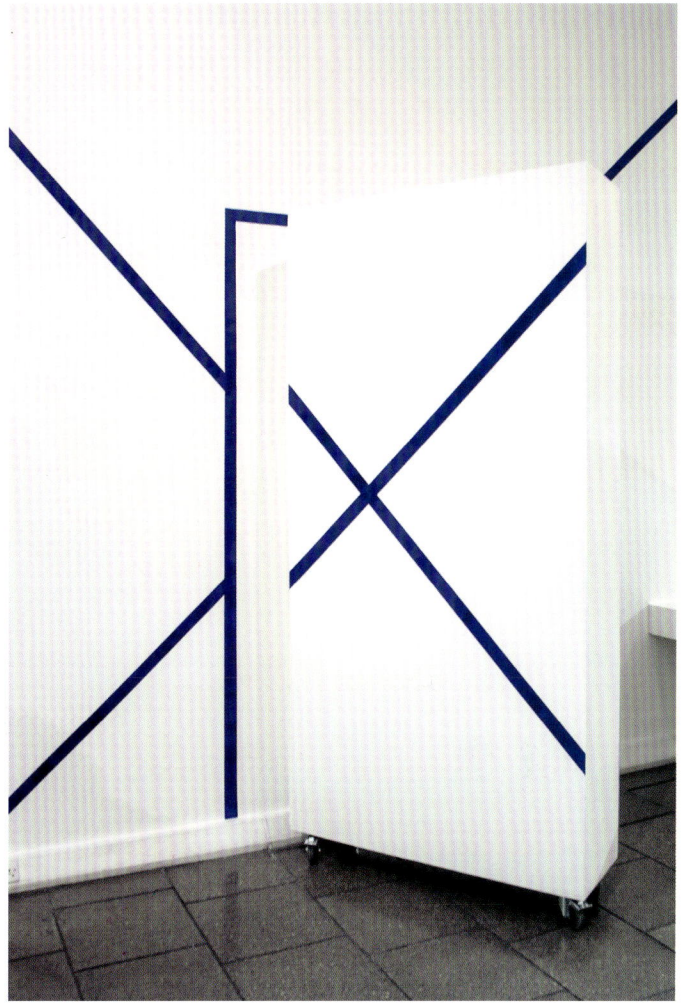

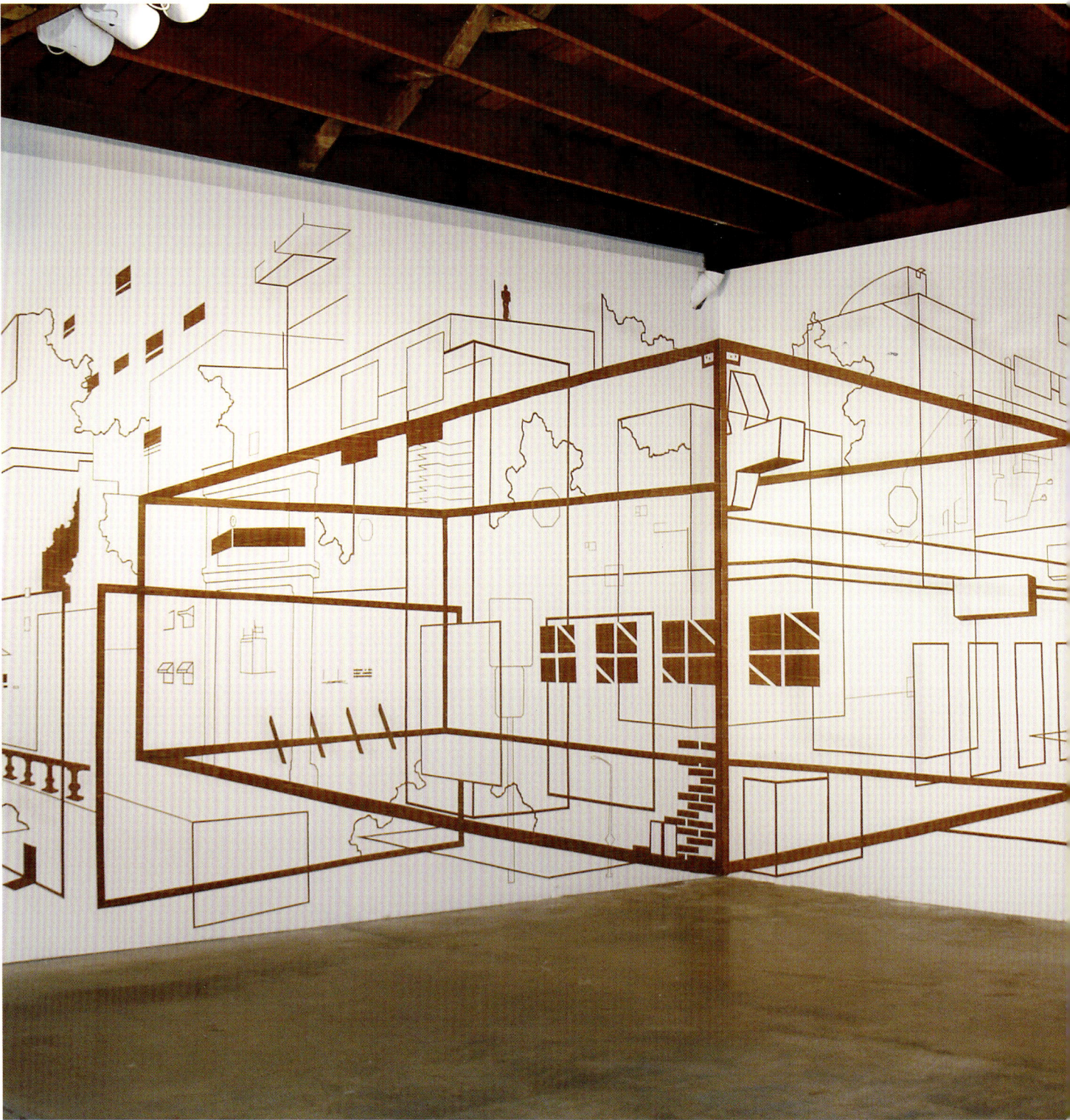

1+1=1

An art installation in Disjecta Contemporary Art Center, Portland OR.

Artist Damien Gilley

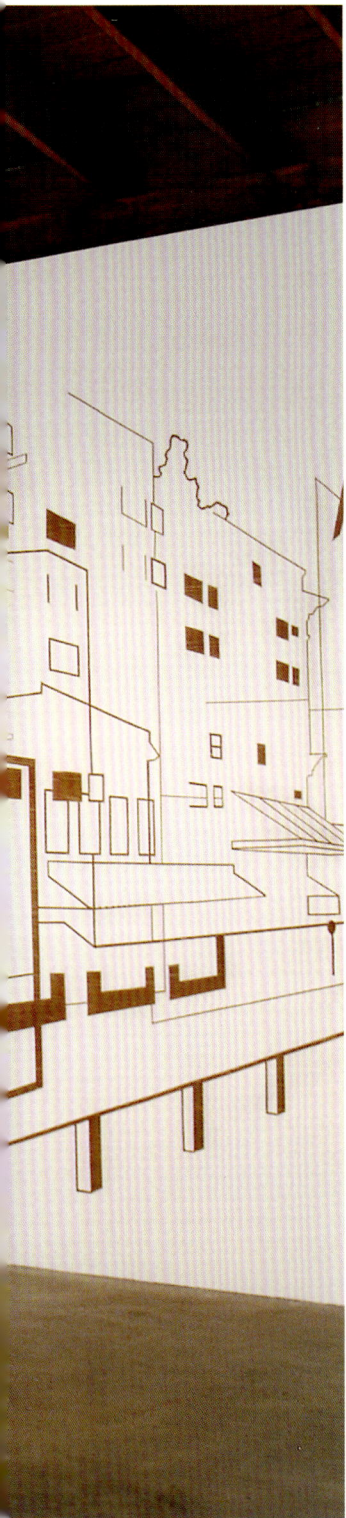

Axis Index

An art installation in Suyama Space, Seattle WA.

Artist Damien Gilley

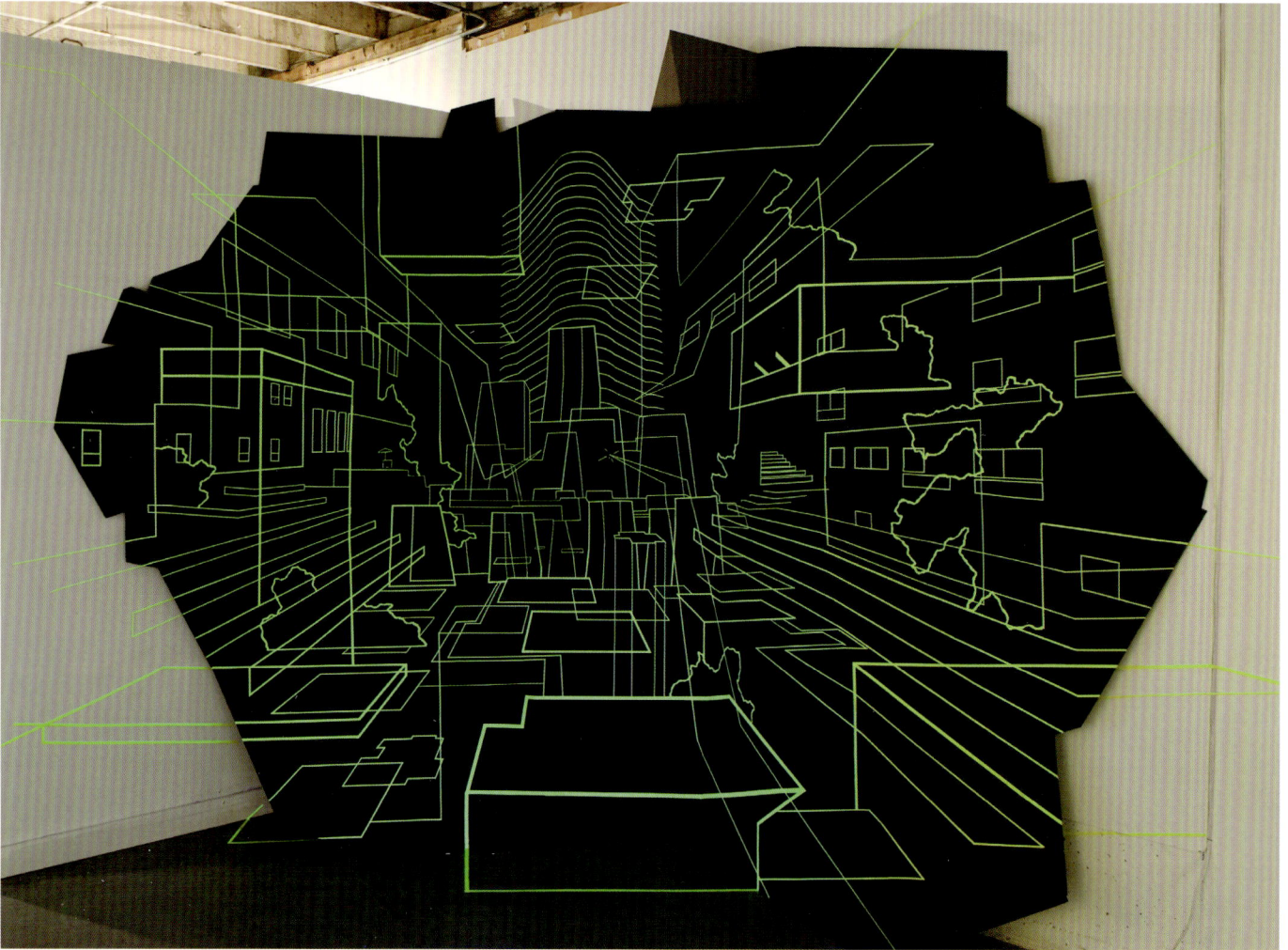

Fortress

An art installation in Worksound Gallery, Portland OR.

Artist Damien Gilley

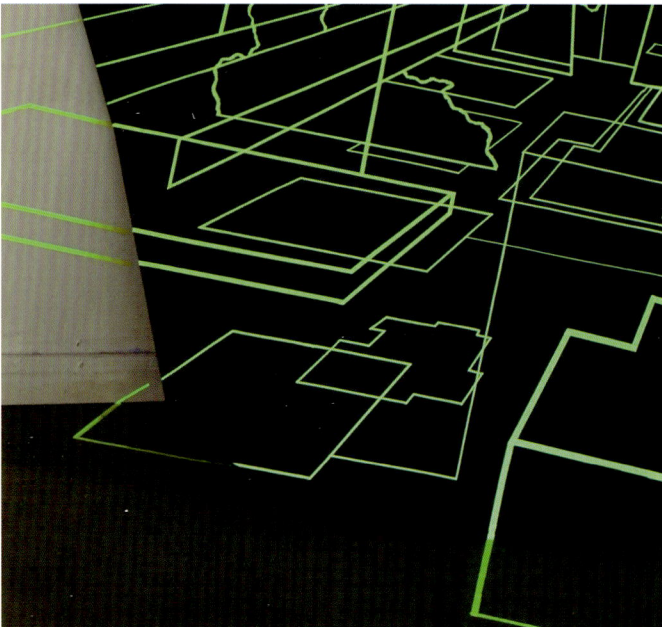

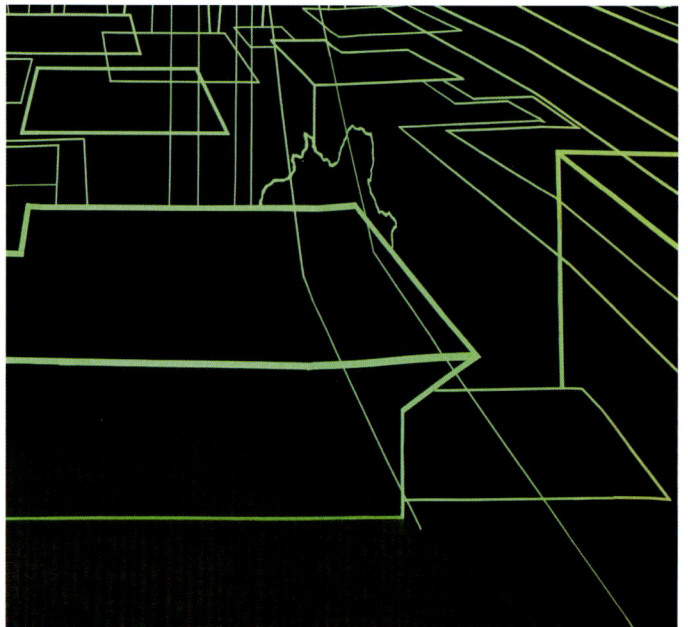

Infinity Room

Infinity Room was an immersive environment project. It was an integral part of his ongoing "Temporary Immersive Environment Experiments" which was a research on audio and visual installations by using the state of immersion.

In this project "infinity" chosen as a concept, Refik used a radical effort to deconstruct the framework of this illusory space and transgress the normal boundaries of the viewing experience. Then it set out to transform the conventional flat cinema projection screen into a three dimensional kinetic and architectonic space of visualization by using contemporary algorithms.

Artist Refik Anadol

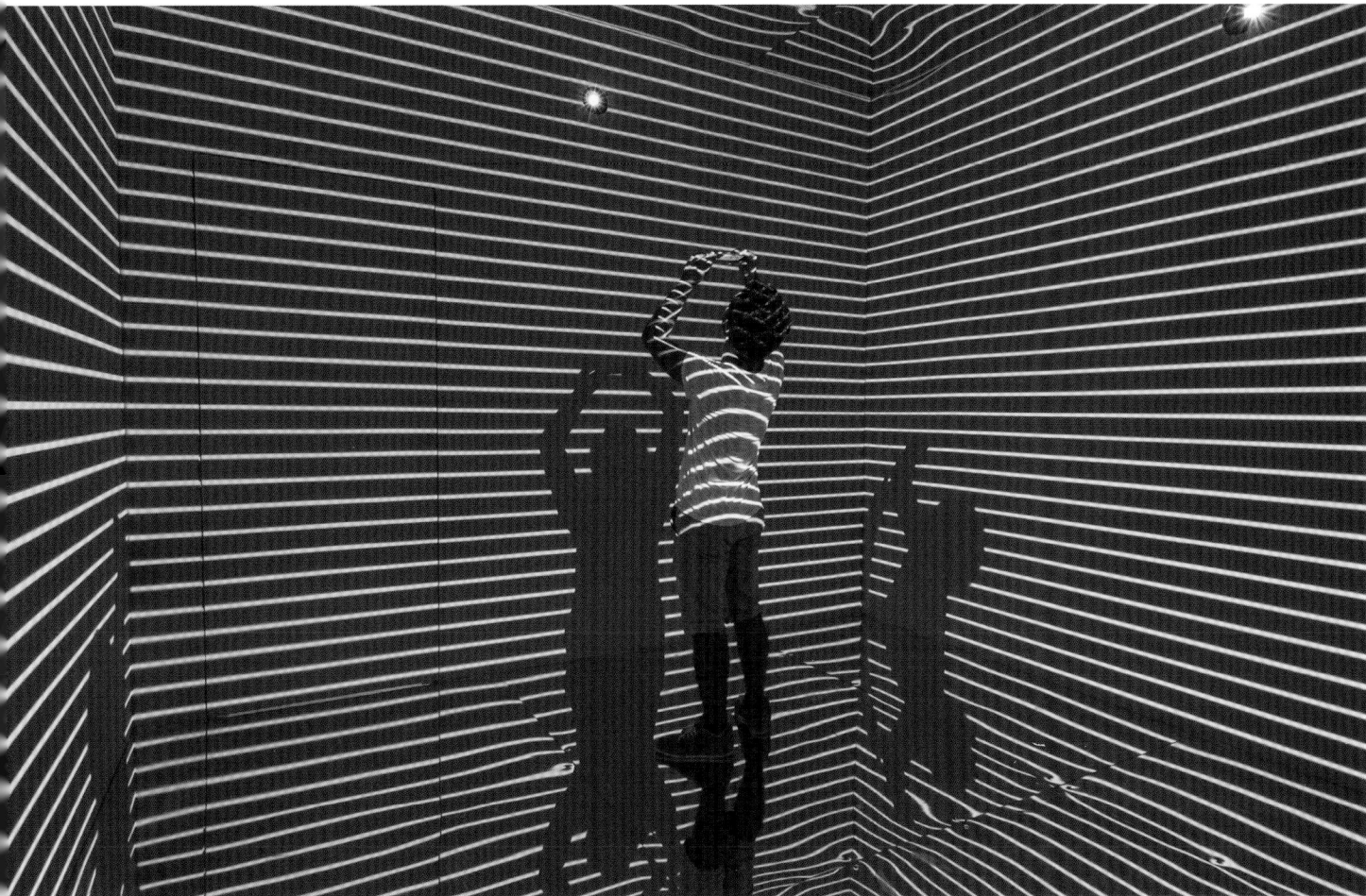

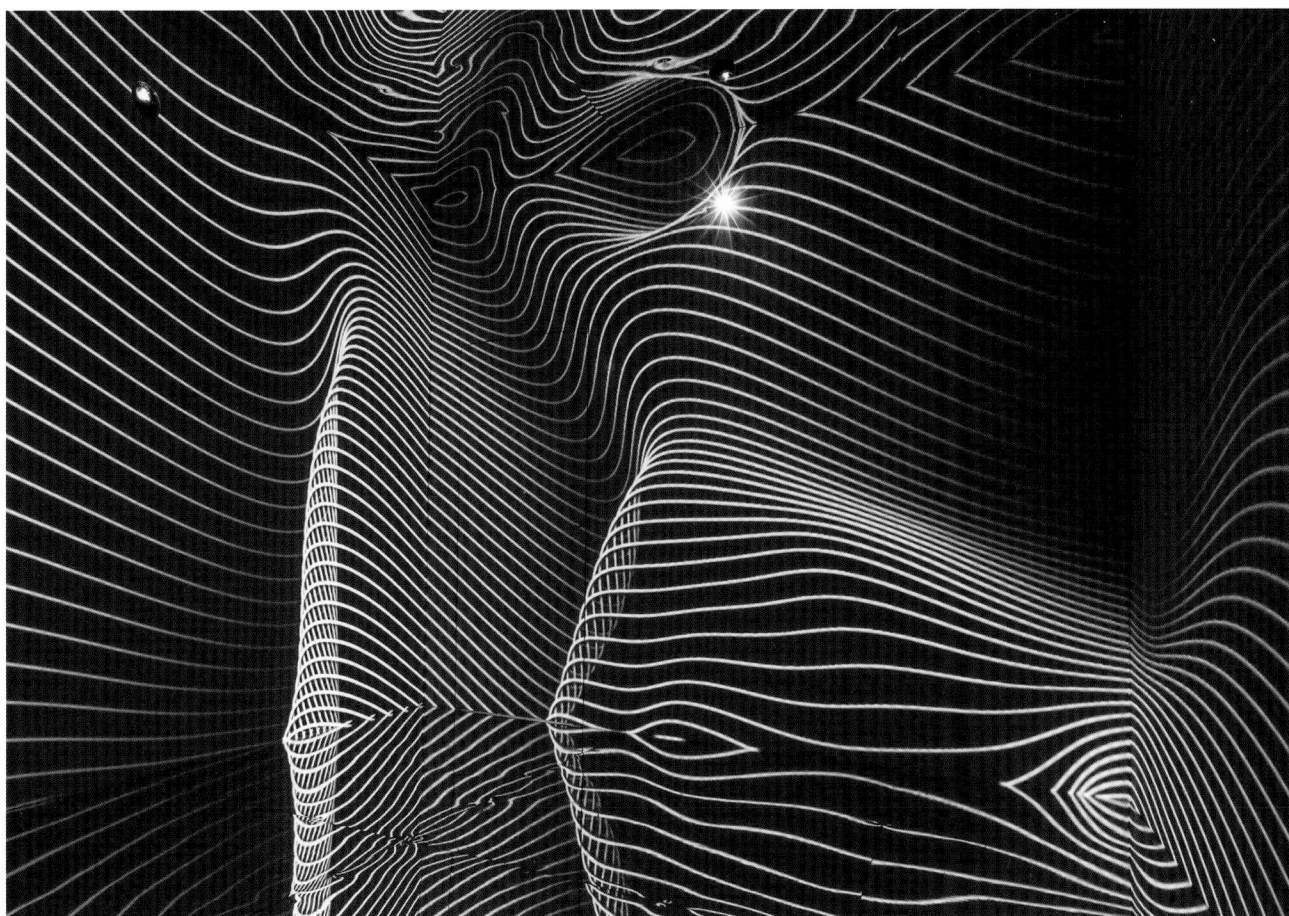

Truth depends on where you see it from ~~~~~~~~~~~~~~~~~~~~~~~~~~~~~~~~~

The exhibition "Truth depends on where you see it from" consisted of three anamorphic installations was set at the Ettore Fico Museum in Torino, a new cultural institution set amidst cutting edge post-industrial architecture.

Truly Design chose to stick to the abstract and geometric shape since they felt it made dialogues beautifully with the works of Florence Henri. They worked with solid and flat geometry, filling it, tearing it apart, switching perspectives, and pushing interaction with the surrounding architecture to the limit.

Design Agency
Truly Design
Art Director
Rems182

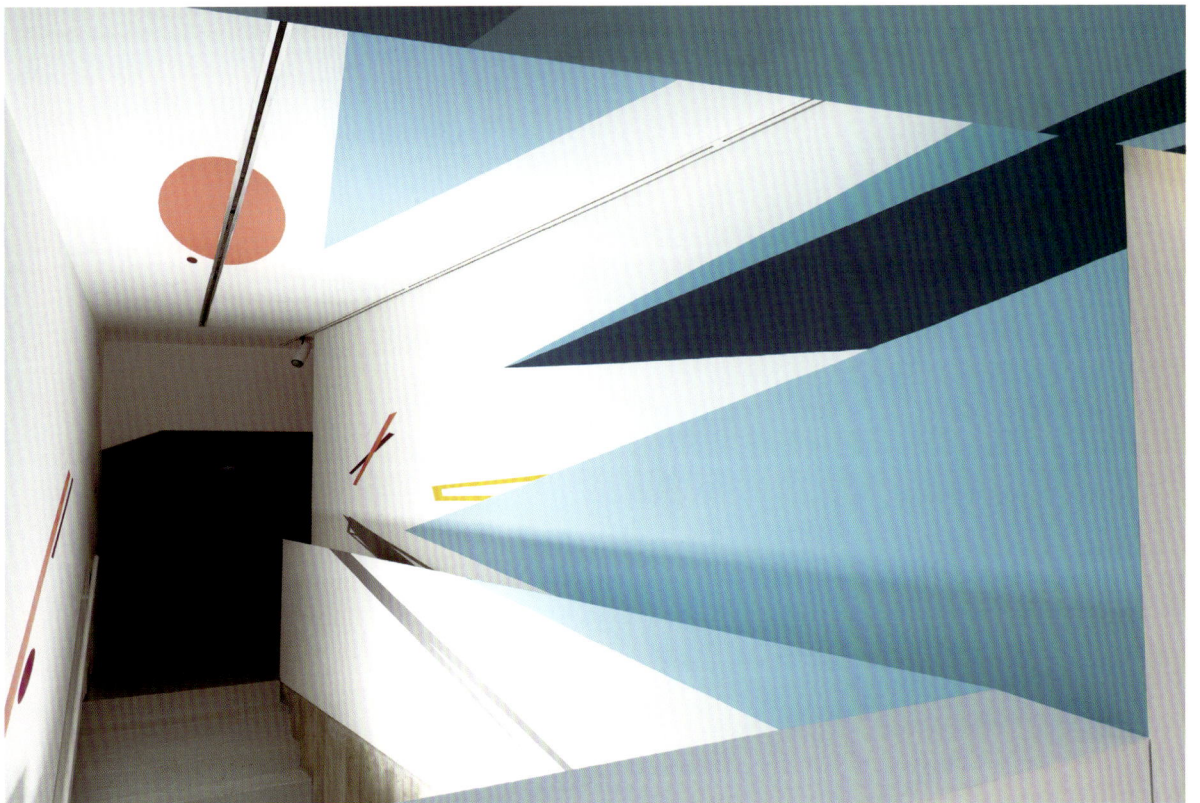

Pegasus

Pegasus was a three-fold creation that equated all the graffiti paintings, as it required the persistent natural decay, removal or covering of the painted surface or destruction of the support which they are painted on. The anamorphic Pegasus, painted at the Fondation EDF in Paris, was the evolution of their destroyed work Medusa. The idea comes from the legend which says that the drops of blood trickled from the beheaded monster gave life to this wonderful winged creature as its natural evolution.

Design Agency
Truly Design
Art Director
Mach505

Callisto and Arcas

The ancient myth of Callisto and Arcade tells the story of a beautiful nymph abducted and seduced by the father of all the gods infatuated of her; the story of how his wife, jealous for his betrayal, transforms the poor nymph into a bear and how, together with the illegitimate son, is transformed into two constellations by Jupiter to save them from the wrath of his wife.

Truly Design turned this story into three anamorphic paintings in one. As the audiences walk from one room to another, they would discover the developments that led to the existence of the two constellations named Ursa Major and Ursa Minor.

Design Agency
Truly Design
Art Director
Mach505

Swell

In this typeface, the height of the letterforms is determined by the frequency of usage of the letter. It highlights the architecture of words and maps the rhythmic ebb and flow of language. The letterforms possess visual qualities reminiscent of the screen and advanced digital modeling programs.

Design Agency Synoptic Office
Design Director, Designer &
Photographer Caspar Lam, YuJune Park

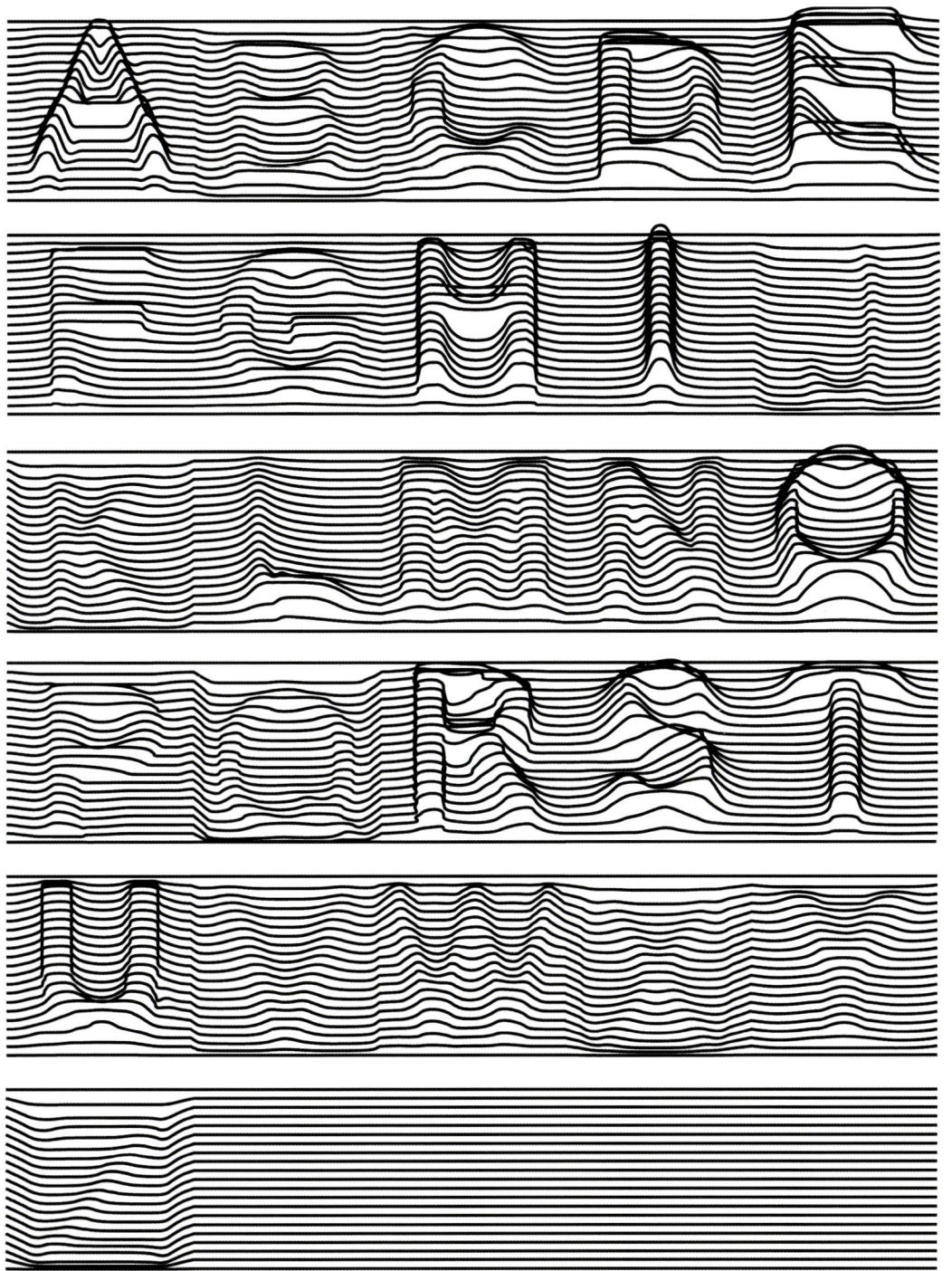

Built Projection

The premise of this project is to bring a peculiar form of representation developed during the sixteenth-century to contemporary communication difficulties through graphic design. Exploring unfolding narratives and uneasy spatial illusions, revealing and concealing information, all of this work was made on-site, with black masking tape, cut by hand and without digital manipulation.

Designer
Alexia Mosby

Chicago Design Museum Installation

Anamorphic typography is a spatial experience in which an arrangement of letters look perfectly set from a single point within a space, while looking distorted from all other points. This particular installation was part of the Chicago Design Museum's Re/View exhibit, which featured work that explored how our vision interprets reality.

Design Agency
Blank is the New Black
Designer
Thomas Quinn

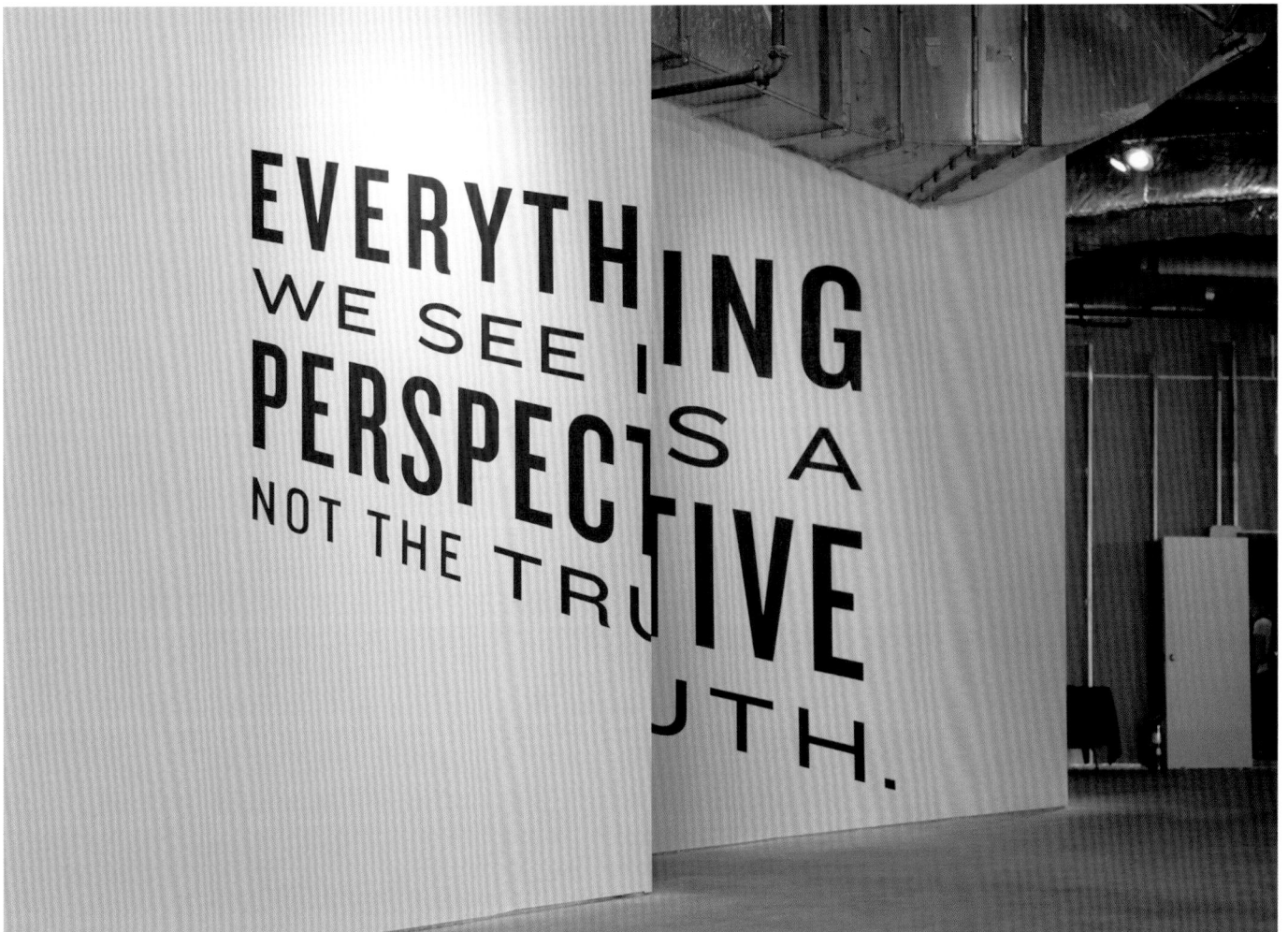

Shift

SHIFT is a typographic installation created for Axisspace, which is a collaborative working space located in Fort Lauderdale Florida.

A fictional office desk in traditional style, including a rotary phone and some other staffs, was created along with a couple of gallons of paint, and some good old hands at work. This work was created to convey the very necessity to SHIFT from the traditional isolated way of working into more open collaborative communal spaces, in which members interact with each other and make part of a working community.

Director David Garcia, Cattia Antezana
Typography Installation Executor
David Garcia, Cattia Antezana, Andrea Perez, Raul Flores
Video Footage Ricardo Ceballos, David Garcia, Cattia Antezana
Video Arcade Fire - No Cars Go

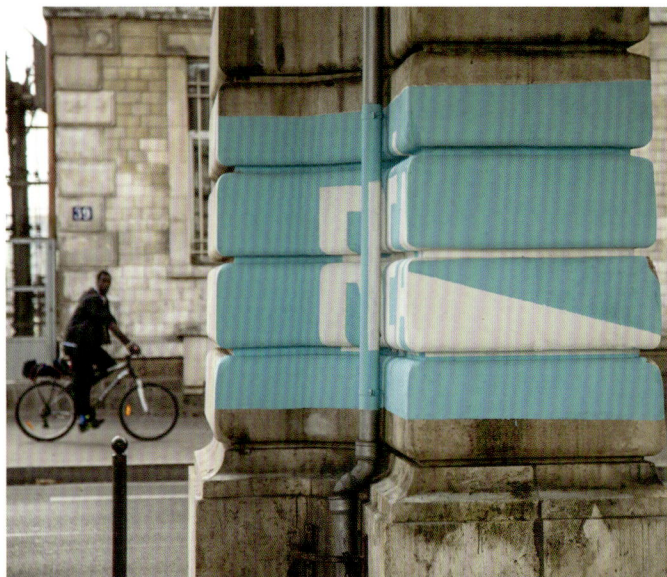

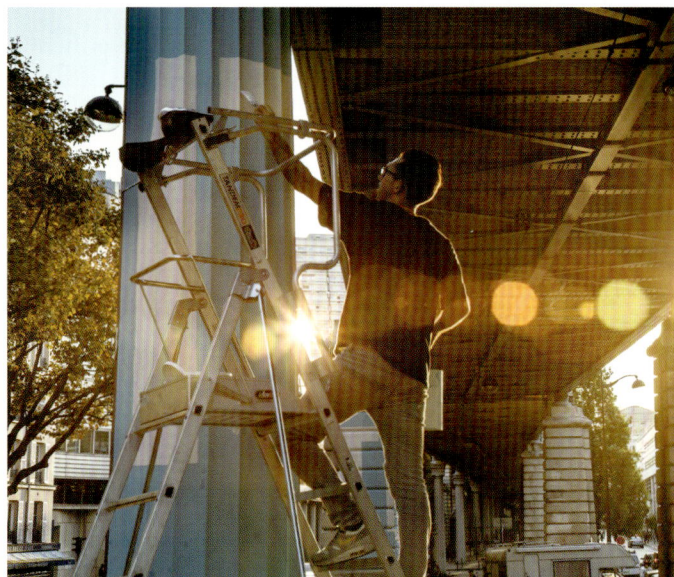

RÉALITÉ

RÉALITÉ was created for "Nuit Blanche", one of the biggest cultural events in Europe took place during the night of 4th, October.

By making an anamorphosis, Boa Mistura used the huge concrete and steel pillars to write the word RÉALITÉ (reality). They played with the meaning of it, and it can only be read from the right spot. They tried to reflect the same reality that some people live under the same bridge, sleeping, or having lunch at the same place. A difficult reality that people usually don't see, but they know it exists.

Design Agency
Boa Mistura
Production
Executor
Eva Albarran and Co
Photographer
Boa Mistura

Mírate a Través de Este Poema de Agua

Boa Mistura proposed a new abstract landscape for St. Bartolomé's square, seeking a contemporary dialogue with the beautiful Gothic church at the top of the square.

The artwork was installed for four days during the "Concéntrico" – Architecture and Design Festival of Logroño. It was created as a forest of triangular prisms based on a grid of hexagons to provide the city new visions.

Design Agency Boa Mistura
Photographer
Pablo G. Mena, Ana Palacios,
KBmayor, Josema Cutillas,
Fátima Ferreira, Boa Mistura

Signaletique journee portes ouvertes Maryse Eloy 〰〰〰〰〰〰〰〰〰〰〰〰〰〰〰

Based on a concept of double reading, Joséphine Thai set up an installation of signage and scenography. Depending on the perspective, the typography transforms into different words. At the entrance of the school, it showed "BIENVENUE" (welcome) when students come to school, while it showed "ABIENTOT" (see you soon) when they leave.

Designer Joséphine Thai

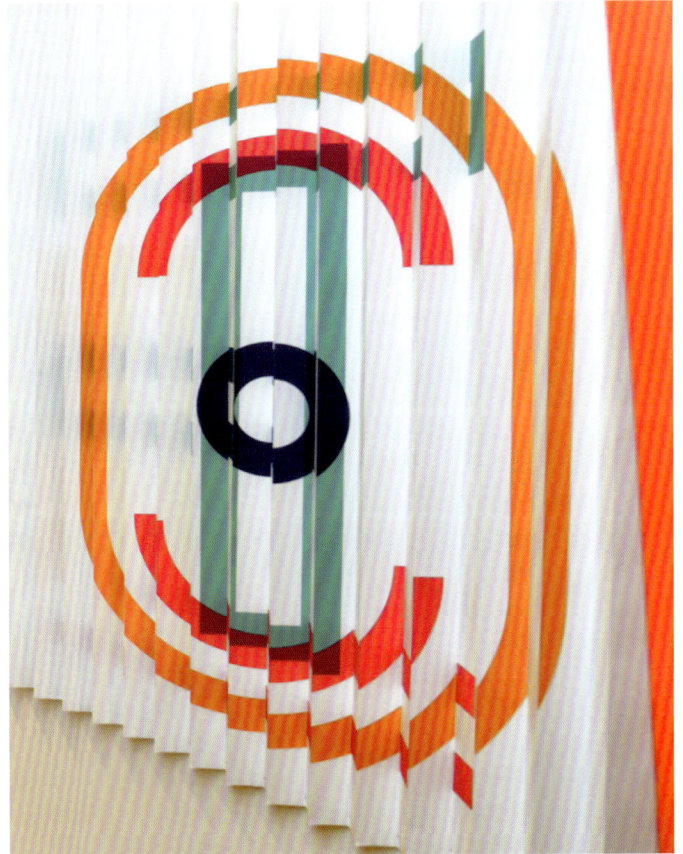

No Cuentes Los Días, Haz Que Los Días Cuenten

Cooperated with the students of the course Boa Mistura gave in the Master of "Efímeras" (Ephemeral) in the ETSAM (Escuela Técnica Superior de Arquitectura de Madrid), the artists looked for a strong motivation for athletes as an encouragement when they trained.

They worked with the quote "Don't count the days, make the days count" of Muhammad Alí, one of the best athletes from all time. Through his forceful voice, he expressed one of the pacifist symbols that claim the rights of the black community and the rejection to the Vietnam War.

They overlapped both phrases making a word game that alters order but retain the origin meaning. The superposition offers them the possibility of working with color to generate a more complex and abstract composition.

Design Agency
Boa Mistura

Magia

In the surroundings of Barranquilla's downtown, Boa Mistura found a tough reality, marked by neglect, trash, and drugs. Even though from this hard reality arises the magic of intense, saturated, and bright colors, Boa Mistura believed that materializing this dialectic magic will generate a new landscape, and a new reality. Therefore, they used a typographic superposition to give birth to a new abstract landscape with abstract color.

Design Agency
Boa Mistura

INDEX

2Fold Studio

2Fold Studio is a graphic design consultancy based in Manchester, UK, founded by Matthew Chatfield and Eddie Cooper.

2Fold embraces a unique and contemporary design style, and offers concept driven ideas. As a studio, they love working on projects within the cultural and musical sector as they are allowed to experiment the outcomes which always lead to indeed interesting and innovative design work.

They produce a diverse range of work across multiple disciplines including identity, print design, and web design.

www.2foldstudio.co.uk

485 Design

Based in the North Island of New Zealand, 485 Design is a multi-awarded company with a talented team of designers and creative thinkers that love to push boundaries. They love well-thought through design that makes clients' business more remarkable and disruptive.

www.485design.co.nz

60 Degree

Co-founded by three partners, 60 Degree pursues the ideal of a more wonderful life. They interpret various challenges in life and work through diverse perspectives and designs, and collaborate closely with their clients to bring amazing works in perfect touch.

The execution of each of their project is strategically optimized through design, from status exploration, core brand appeals, to brand creativity development. They plan core-penetrating tools to combine strategy and design with better precision, in order to meet every customer's need.

Wholeheartedly living and feeling, they incorporate their own experiences in observing and savoring the possibilities in life, and contemplating its essence. Being open-minded and the strength from friends and partners, they strive to shape a better life and fill it with happiness. Through 60 Degree's understanding with brand and design, they intend to convey positive energy to entire human race and the world.

www.60degree.com.tw

A Green Hill

A Green Hill is a Hong Kong based graphic studio. They believe that good work must be both creative and effective, and it is what they pursue. To strike a perfect balance between both sides, the work will be solid and 3-dimensional.

As the market becomes increasingly competitive, resources are always limited, and the industry is becoming tougher, A Green Hill embraces challenge with passion, patience, open minds, they continue to learn from everyday work and lives.

aghhongkong.com

Adobe Design

The Adobe Design Group is a global design organization responsible for the user experience of most of Adobe's products. They create smart, sophisticated applications for a wide variety of devices, from desktop computers to laptops to mobile phones and beyond. They're a hundred-plus architects, academics, sculptors, DJs, writers, designers, and engineers. They come from all over the world; their expertise ranges from interaction and visual design to research, information architecture, and programming.

behance.net/AdobeDesign

Adrienne Bornstein

Adrienne Bornstein is a graphic designer based in Paris. She is always searching for new expressions, new supports, new manufacturing techniques, in order to produce a modern and rigorous graphic design.

www.adriennebornstein.com

Alati Andrea

Andrea is an art director with a ten years experience in several fields of creative communication. He has worked with international companies and startups. His approach to design world is radically and powered by deep study of the product. Be ready to push any idea, he is a also a web lover, digital media chef, and color master carpenter.

www.behance.net/fulminelab

Alexia Mosby

Alexia Mosby is a graphic designer specializing in branding and design strategy. She works on multi-platform brand campaigns, with an emphasis on large scale brand installations. Her clients include Converse, Reebok, RISD, Budweiser, Foot Locker, the Howard Hughes Corporation, as well as numerous start up companies. Alexia studied graphic design at Rhode Island School of Design, and lives and works in New York City.

cargocollective.com/alexiamosby

Andrew Carter

Andrew Carter is a freelance graphic designer from Malta. He loves everything with graphic design, especially typography.

www.carterandrew.com

Angel J Gonzales Echegaray

Angel J Gonzales Echegaray is a graphic designer originally from the city of Lima in Peru. He graduated from the San Ignacio de Loyola Institute. With a focus on brand identity, he worked as a freelance designer. He is passionate about different arts such as architecture, illustration, and photography from which he draws inspiration. His design objective is to find an effective and appropriate solution for clients without losing the sense of aesthetics and sophistication.

www.behance.net/angel_ge88f69c

Anna Kulachek

Anna Kulachek is a Moscow-based graphic designer from Ukraine. With an internship at the Fabrica Benetton communication centre, She is currently an art director at Strelka Institute of Media, Architecture and Desig in Moscow, and a teacher at HSE Art and Design School.

kulachek.com

Anna Lindner

Anna Lindner is a graphic designer and illustrator from Sweden, currently based in Utrecht, The Netherlands. She is obsessed with bright colors, geometry, the 80's, tropical plants and interiors. With a strong passion for branding, styling, print and packaging, she creates playful and innovative solutions to build engaging experiences.

www.annalindner.com

Anne Lise Arnesen

Anne Lise Arnesen is a Scandinavian designer and still life photographer base in Bergen, Norway. Graduated in 2012 from Solent Southampton University with an Bachelor of Arts in Graphic Design, she is currently working as an inhouse graphic designer at the Scandinavian eyewear brand KAIBOSH.

https://www.behance.net/ANLI
P143

another design

another design is a transmedia visual design team with members from various professions of graphic design, multimedia design, product design, and photography. The multidisciplinary integration encourages them to challenge the traditional way of thinking, expand the boundary of design language, and explore the diversity of design in different fields. Specializing in design strategies crossing culture and business, the team devotes to providing professional services and innovative strategies for its clients by seeking the balance between cultural and commercial programs.

www.another-lab.com
P122 – 123

Atelier BangBang

Atelier BangBang was born in February 2012 during the final studies project of Simon Laliberté, a graduated student in Graphic Design at University of Quebec at Montreal, UQAM. Atelier BangBang is not only a screen-printing workshop for paper and fabrics, but also a multidisciplinary studio of design. The workshop is intended to be a reference at Montreal in the field of screen printing and graphic design. He aspires to work with a diverse clientele and provide quality personalized service.

atelierbangbang.ca
P080 – 081

Atipus

Atipus is a graphic communication studio founded in Barcelona in 1998. They are a team of expert professionals, trained in various disciplines with a focus on corporate identity, art direction, packaging design, and web services. Their aim is to communicate through good graphic work, conceptually and simply.

www.atipus.com
P066 – 067

Aurélien Hervé, Chloé Méot, Tian Bai & Yili Sun

These four designers are currently graphic design students based in Nantes, France.

www.behance.net/aurelienherve
chloemeot.com
neco-designstudio.com
Behance.net/yili_sun
P088 – 089

b.a.-ba

b.a.-ba is a graphic design studio founded in 2014 by Benoit Hody and Aloïs Ancenay. They share an open approach to graphic design, responding to cultural, institutional, industrial, and personal projects. Their two distinct characters allow them to approach each project with two complementary points of view in order to provide an appropriate answer. They always treat projects as a real partnership with their client which result in the form and its support are the most suitable for each project. Whether digital or print projects, they bring special attention to typography and media.

www.b-a-ba.works
P158 – 159

Blank is the New Black

Blank is the New Black is a small creative studio located in Chicago, Illinois USA founded by Thomas Quinn in 2011. While their main expertise is in web and print design, they make a point of branching out and working outside their comfort zone on a variety of projects from typeface design to artistic installations.

www.blankisthenewblack.com
P218 – 219

Bleed

Bleed design studio creates identity and experience through concept development, art direction, graphic design and service design. Their works represents a mix of cultures and disciplines to challenge today's conventions around art, visual language, interaction, media and identity.

www.bleed.com
P128 – 131; P132 – 133

Blok Design

Blok is an award-winning design studio that works across media and disciplines, collaborating with leading thinkers and creators, companies and brands from around the world, taking on projects that blend cultural awareness, art and humanity to advance society and business alike.

Clients hail from Argentina to Canada and have included top global brands such as Nike, Pepsi, the Miami Art Museum, ING, José Cuervo and Nestlé. The studio also initiates and produces independent curatorial and publishing projects, with a vision to expand their understanding of the world around them.

Blok's work is the recipient of numerous international awards and is frequently published in leading books, periodicals and blogs worldwide. Their work has been exhibited from Japan to Germany, most recently at Museo Tamayo, Mexico City, and the Bienal Iberamericanna de Diseño, Spain, and is represented in the permanent collection of the Library of Congress in Washington.

blokdesign.com
P146 – 147; P172

Boa Mistura

Founded in late 2001, Madrid, Spain, Boa Mistura is a multidisciplinary team with roots in graffiti art. They develop their work mainly in public space across the globe.

Though their studio located in Madrid, they spend the day from here to there, living among paint buckets, computers, and ping-pong matches. They are obsessed with their work, and regard it as a tool to transform the street and create bonds between people. They feel a responsibility with the city and time they are living in.

www.boamistura.com
P222 – 223; P224 – 225; P230 – 231; P232

Bureau Bruneau

Bureau Bruneau is a design studio in Oslo, Norway, run by graphic designer Ludvig Bruneau Rossow.

www.bureaubruneau.com
P134 – 135

byHAUS

byHAUS is a design studio founded by Philippe Archontakis and Martin Laliberté, two accredited graphic designers based in Montreal. The studio specializes in creating distinctive identities that drive success. They believe that graphic design can be a powerful driver of success for any project or organization, and simple messages are strong messages. Core ideas should be very clearly expressed. This is really the essence of minimalism.

www.byhaus.ca
P012 – 013; P118 – 119

Drew Watts

Drew Watts is currently a designer and art director located in Omaha Nebraska. With his creating heavily rooted in strong conceptual ideas, Drew has experience working in multiple disciplines ranging from identity and branding to interactive and environmental design. His clients range from fortune 500 companies to small local businesses.

drewwatts.com
P032 – 033

Emilia Ferraresso

Emilia Ferraresso is a graphic designer born in the city of Neuquén, Patagonia Argentina. In 2009 she moved to Buenos Aires, where she currently lives, and studied graphic design at the University of Buenos Aires. In 2013, she started working in the design team for the Club Cultural Matienzo, a space dedicated to Buenos Aires' emergent culture events. Graduated in 2014, She worked as a freelancer in different projects thereafter.

www.behance.net/EmiFerra
P108 – 109

Evelina Rosinska

Graduated with a MA in Design from the Academy of Fine Arts in Lodz, Poland, Evelina Rosinska is a graphic designer from Poland and currently based in London. Her speicalty and main interests are branding and the creation of visual identities, along with web design and development on cms platforms.

www.behance.net/evelinaro
P126 – 127

Federico Leggio & Sergi Miral

Federico Leggio is a Sicilian, while Sergi Miral is a Catalan. Though they come from different backgrounds, they work as a team and cover a wide range of full projects including brand identity, graphic design, web and app design and development.

Federicoleggio.it
sergimiral.com
P156 – 157

Gerard Marin

Gerard Marin is a graphic designer based in Vilanova i la Geltrú, Barcelona. The focus of his work is developing visual identities and surprising design solutions to solve clients' communication problems.

He is currently working at Toormix studio, also combined with his freelance work for a full range of clients.

www.gerardmarin.com
P160 – 161

Gold & Wirtschaftswunder

Gold & Wirtschaftswunder is a Stuttgart-based design agency since 2005. The studio name recalls Germany's "economic miracle." Their design projects include international and German clients, with a main focus on corporate design, branding, and spatial communication. In addition to their professional work they regularly hold lectures in different universities and design classes.

www.gww-design.de
P090 – 091

Gustav Karlsson Thors

Gustav Karlsson Thors is a Stockholm-based freelance graphic designer, specializing in branding and packaging.

www.gustavkarlsson.com
P034 – 035

Hiromi Maeo

Bearing the pursuit for timeless design with grasp of essence in mind, Hiromi Maeo has been involved in CI and VI for company branding, art direction, etc. Past few years his works has been featured in various design related to web and publications around the world. In September 2015, he has been appointed as the first Japanese mentor by internationally recognized association, ico-D mentorship program 2015.

www.behance.net/enhanced_hiromimaeo
P100 – 101

Human. Brand Development

Humans shape their planet. Design shape humans. Design is their legacy. Taking this as the principle, they firmly believe in the power of design onto society. Consequently, they believe that every project is part of their legacy to human kind.

They contribute to brands positioning and value by creating captivating applications thoroughly made by a design process based on client and consumer needs. By Human, for Humans.

byhuman.mx
P124 – 125

I Chyi Chang

I Chyi Chang is an independent graphic designer based in Taipei. She tends to use soft pastel colors and self-created textures as a vital element for visual design as well as an illustrator.

ichyi.com
P136 – 137

Infinito Consultores

Infinito Consultores is a branding agency founded in 2005 in Lima, Peru. From packaging to small film festivals, Infinite is versatile enough to take any kind of client, big or small. Listening to the client's need and discovering insights guide them to a different way of resolving a graphic is one of core values.

infinito.pe
P038 – 039; P056 – 057

INSTID

INSTID runs place and corporate branding programs and advises on identity and communication matters.

www.instid.org
P052 – 053

IS Creative Studio

Founded by Richars Meza, IS Creative Studio is an international branding firm with offices in Lima, Madrid and Tokyo. IS Creative has gained a global vision through their 20 years experience working in New York, Tokyo, Madrid and Lima with clients from various industries. The passion for their work and their international customers has made them natural cool hunters. They have vision, intuition and sensitivity to collect demographic information for new markets and consumer trends. To differentiate, observe and analyze these trends, they understand what the new benchmarks of creating successful strategies are. Their work process is based on extensive research, working as a team with their clients on strategic plans, questioning established truths, generating new ways, transforming perceptions and maximizing the value proposition. They create memorable brand experiences that go beyond the product, giving almost revolutionary and unique solutions that create loyalty beyond reason.

www.iscreativestudio.com
P078 – 079

Jonathan Gravier

Jonathan Gravier is a French graphic designer. He lives and performs in Nantes where he created JoG-Factory in 2012. He mainly works out on graphic design, typography, and multimedia. He is also the artistic director in the Fly Designers agency.

For each project he pays a very special attention to typography: "The anatomy of typography makes stronger the meaning of the words and ideas."

jog-factory.com
P174 – 175

Joséphine Thai

Joséphine Thai is a freelance graphic designer based in France.

cargocollective.com/josephinethai
P226 – 229

Lee Marcus

Lee Marcus is a Singapore based graphic designer.

www.behance.net/leemarcus
P168 – 169

Ling-Wen Yen

Ling-Wen Yen was born in Taipei, Taiwan. She graduated from MA Graphic Design at London College of Communication in 2014. Now she works as a freelance graphic designer and illustrator in London. In her work, she mainly focuses on identity, branding and illustration. Vintage market and nature are her best inspirations.

www.behance.net/yenlingwen
P170 – 171

Marina Goñi

Located in Getxo, Spain, Marina Goñi is a graphic design studio, specializing in brand creation and management. They focus on the identification of each business singularity in order to boost it and make it clear and recognizable to the public. They help the rise of new brands and their reposition to make them grow.

www.marinagoni.com
P048 – 049

Marina Willer / Pentagram

Marina is a partner at Pentagram – the world's largest independent design consultancy. She is a graphic designer, art director and filmmaker whose clients include Tate, Serpentine Galleries, Oi (Brazil's largest Telecom provider), MTV and Richard Rogers. She is a member of the AGI (Alliance Graphique Interrnationale) and has been nominated for the Design's Museum Design of the Year award for her identity for the Serpentine Galleries.

www.pentagram.com
P096 – 097

Matt Delbridge

Matt Delbridge is a designer originally from the Bay Area. He currently works at Google Creative Lab and as an adjunct professor in the design department at the School of Visual Arts and a lecturer at Cornell Tech. Matt has worked for clients such as Nike, Apple, Hermes, Facebook, and the City of New York. His work has been recognized by AIGA and appeared in numerous publications. He received a BFA with destination from the California College of the Arts in 2011.

www.mattdelbridge.com
P144 – 145

Matt Mckinney

Matt Mckinney was trained as an interior designer and had spent 11 years in interior design for a variety of international retail clients. Afterwards, he worked as a designer and an art director for his own clothing label Origin68. He has a good understanding of both graphic and spatial design, which give him confident in all disciplines of design.

cargocollective.commattmckinney
P173

Menta Picante

Menta Picante is a branding design studio based in Guadalajara, México. Their clients come from varied industries in México as well in United States and Panamá.

They focus in developing great brands by collecting right information and defining those values and distinguishing elements with graphic communications. Their works are distinguished and widely acknowledged.

www.mentapicante.mx
P028 – 029

Mind Design

Mind Design is a London-based independent graphic design studio founded by Holger Jacobs in 1999 after graduating from the Royal College of Art. The studio specializes in the development of visual identities and has worked for a wide range of clients in different sectors.

www.minddesign.co.uk
P046 – 047

Mirror Mirror

Mirror Mirror is a multi-disciplinary visual communication studio based in Antwerp. They create communicative brand identity through clever concepts and striking graphic design.

www.mirrormirror.be
P030 – 031; P182 – 183

Murmure

Based in Caen and Paris, Murmure is a French creative communications agency specializing in designing strong visual identities. Led by two art directors Julien Alirol Ressencourt and Paul, the agency produces singular creative projects embraced both aesthetic and adapted to customers' problems. They respond to the client's aims and objectives, guiding and advising in order to provide them with original, creative and aesthetic projects that they are proud of.

murmure.me
P040 – 041; P042 – 043; P062 – 063

Nicole Allegri

Nicole Allegri is a graphic designer based in Buenos Aires.

www.behance.net/nicoleallegri
P138 – 139

NotoriusGrey

NotoriusGrey is a creative partnership based in Greece and in Cyprus. The studio produces and forms visual identities, both digital and print, by utilizing all mediums to express and to design a brand.

www.notoriusgrey.com
P149

Pornographitti Design Explicito

Pornographitti Design Explicito is a graphic studio based in Brazil. They dedicate to creating impressive communication design with bold visual elements and expressions.

pornographitti.xxx

Refik Anadol

Refik Anadol is a media artist and director born in Istanbul, Turkey in 1985. Currently lives and works in Los Angeles, California. He is a lecturer in UCLA's Department of Design Media Arts.

He is working in the fields of site-specific public art with parametric data sculpture approach and live audio/visual performance with immersive installation approach, particularly his works explore the space among digital and physical entities by creating a hybrid relationship between architecture and media arts. He holds a master of fine arts degree from University of California, Los Angeles in Media Arts, master of fine arts degree from Istanbul Bilgi University in Visual Communication Design as well as bachelors of arts degree with summa cum laude in Photography and Video. Co-founder and Creative director at Antilop.

www.refikanadol.com

RM&CO

RM&CO, founded in 2013 by Pete Rossi (ADC YG 9) and Alfio Mazzei, is an independent, award winning, multi-disciplinary graphic design, visual communication and branding consultancy with studios based in the UK and Switzerland. RM&CO have been awarded and recognized by ADC, D&AD and Graphis.

They are firm believers in pushing boundaries, but their meticulous approach, based on research and development allows them to serve their client's purpose with passion, detail, dedication and love to find the right and relevant solutions to a wide variety of projects and commissions.

rossimazzei.com

Sciencewerk®

Sciencewerk® is a creative studio conjoining art, design, and technology. They always believe that good design intersect between art and science where process, collaboration, experimentation, exploration are critical. At Sciencewerk®, they help people to develop visual communication and design language for their business or product through various media applications from identity, typography, graphic, print, illustration, interactive, installation, exhibition, to art. Their designers have been featured in D&AD, Crowbar, Computer Arts, Asia Pacific Design, IDN, 360 Design, Underconsideration, The Jakarta Post, Behance, among others.

sciencewerk.net

Shine Visual Lab

Shine Visual Lab is a brand and visual communications studio. It is a platform for creatives from various disciplines to come together and channel their passion into crafting integrated solutions that fulfill strategic communication goals.

At the heart of Shine is the spirit of exploration. They strive to uncover the intangible essence of brands and translate them into distinctive and effective communications, executed with finesse and punctuated with an element of surprise that is uniquely Shine.

They believe their enthusiasm to explore new ideas and push creative boundaries serves as the driving force to produce works that would help their clients shine in their industries.

shinevisuallab.com

Stahl R

Stahl R, a Berlin based internationally recognized design studio, was founded in 2012 by Tobias Röttger and Susanne Stahl. It offers unique design solutions for a broad range of clients from both commercial and cultural fields, and provides a diverse range of design disciplines: from visual identities, publication design, environmental design, editorial and art direction, to time-based media and digital projects. Driven by both research and concept, Stahl R believes in a project-specific approach that leads to thoughtful, intelligent and innovative work. The studio is a dynamic system in scope and scale, strengthened by a network of talented creatives from all disciplines.

www.stahl-r.com

Studio fnt

Studio fnt is a Seoul based graphic design studio that works on prints, identities, interactive and digital media, and more. It collects fragmented and straying thoughts, and then organizes, and transforms them into relevant forms.

www.studiofnt.com

StudioMakgill

StudioMakgill is a Brighton-based design studio, founded in 2007 by Hamish Makgill. Their design is guided by one overarching philosophy: to make beautifully simple work. Their focus is on the creation of brand identities that work as well in print as they do on screen. They work for a range of clients within a variety of sectors, and they are as comfortable creating an identity for a range of cosmetics as they are a look and feel for a successful tapas restaurant in north London. They are passionate about good design and revel in the detail of a project. They look to inspire their clients whilst having a lasting effect on their business.

www.studiomakgill.com

Summer Studio

Summer Studio is a graphic design agency founded in 2014 by Carolina Dahl and Minna Sakaria, when they study at the Royal College of Art in London. Their concept-driven designs are often manifested in typography with character and narrative. They believe individual traits combined with consistent communication leads to successful typography and graphic design solutions, creating something they refer to as "characteristic type."

summerstudio.co.uk

Synoptic Office

Synoptic Office is a multidisciplinary design studio operating in the space between graphic, interaction, spatial and product design. The studio's work has been exhibited internationally and has been recognized by Fast Company Design, iDn, Neshan, Etapes, It's Nice That, and the Muckenthaler Gallery.

Synoptic Office was selected to participate in BIO23, the 23rd Biennial of Design at the Museum of Architecture and Design in Ljubljana, Slovenia and has exhibited at the Ningbo Museum of Art in China.

synopticoffice.com

ACKNOWLEDGEMENTS

We would like to thank all of the designers involved for granting us permission to publish their works, as well as all of the photographers who have generously allowed us to use their images. We are also very grateful to many other people whose names do not appear in the credits but who made specific contributions and provided support. Without these people, we would not have been able to share these beautiful works with readers around the world. Our editorial team includes editor Javier Zheng and book designers Yunshu Liu, Yingqiao Chen, to whom we are truly grateful.

Tainá Ribovski

Tainá Ribovski is a designer and art director freelancing in Brazil. When she first got knowledge about the design field, she knew it was her career to be. Graduated in Graphic Design, she focuses on identities, the most fascinating branch in her opinion. For her, companies are not the only goal. Every person, living being, group, object, party or event, has its own complexion and personality, so therefore, can be translated in a visual identity. All nuances and details are fuel and inspiration for creating strategic brands and projecting businesses for life.

www.toski.com.br
P180 – 181

Toormix

Toormix is a design studio based in Barcelona working to help clients boost their business through design. Founded in 2000 by Oriol Armengou and Ferran Mitjans, Toormix is an experienced team that works in close collaboration with local and international clients with a clear focus on innovation and brand development. They are consultants for ideas that help companies gain value, be more visible, and achieve greater success with design.

toormix.com
P050 – 051

Truly Design

Mauro149, Rems182, Mach505, and Ninja1, who are all graffiti and graphic design enthusiasts, met in the late 90's amid abandoned places and suburbs, where they first experimented with street art. A passion and friendship culminated in a common project started in 2003 under the name Truly Design Urban Artists.

Commitment to constant research for new forms of visual language enable the collective to progress technically and experimentally, leading to showcasing work at collective and personal exhibitions in foundations, museums, and private galleries across the globe. The four artists' characteristics converge throughout the years in a project which identifies them amid the international street art panorama: the use of anamorphic painting applied to urban art, which generates visionary 3D images resulting from an optical illusion created from perspective and architecture, as yet one of Truly Design's most distinctive elements.

truly-design.com
P204 – 207; P208 – 209; P210 – 213

Turboturboturbo

Turboturboturbo is a graphic design studio in Eindhoven with a passion in branding and identity and all visual communications for print and web. With an aim to bring bright ideas and convincing design, they focus on embodying every new assignment with powerful solutions for clients with spunk.

www.turboturboturbo.com
P148

TwoPoints.Net

TwoPoints.Net, a design studio specializing in flexible systems for visual identities and editorial projects, are based in Hamburg, Berlin and Barcelona, and work with clients everywhere.

TwoPoints.Net emerged in 2000 at the Royal Academy of Arts in The Hague (NL). The name refers to the colon that marks the transition between the speaker and his message. Despite being a small office, they oversee large-scale projects that involves excellent professionals from diverse fields; a network that changes according to each project.

www.twopoints.net
P102 – 103; P184 – 185

Valentin Noguès

After graduating from Maryse Eloy School of Arts in Paris, Valentin Noguès moved to London to work as a graphic designer. His work is mainly focused on type and creating a coherent system. He currently works across several projects between Paris and London.

cargocollective.com/valentinnogues
P026 – 027

WAAITT

WAAITT (They are all in this together) is a multidisciplinary design studio in Copenhagen. They specialize in graphic design and art direction for photo, video, and audio. The studio was established by school friends Anders Rimhoff, Jess Jensen, and Dennis Müller in 2011. WAAITT produces visual identities, websites, campaigns, editorial design, films, motion graphics, and music for a variety of clients working in a broad range of different fields.

www.waaitt.dk
P086 – 087

WeLoveNoise

WeLoveNoise is an alias of Luke Finch, and an online creative outlet of his professional projects, private commissions, and design experiments.

Luke is a creative director and designer, who approaches design by fusing design and technology to create captivating and thoughtful experiences across multiple forms of communication – digital, analogue and environmental for brands such as Pepsi, Playstation, Google, BBC and AT&T.

www.welovenoise.com
P054 – 055; P076 – 077